Prepare for the Great Tribulation and the Era of Peace

Prepare for the Great Tribulation and the Era of Peace

Volume I:
July 1993 – June 1994

by John Leary

Queenship
PUBLISHING COMPANY
P.O Box 42028 Santa Barbara, CA 93140-2028
(800)647-9882 Fax: (805) 569-3274

The publisher recognizes and accepts that the final authority regarding these apparitions and messages rests with the Holy See of Rome, to whose judgement we willingly submit.

– The Publisher

Cover art by Josyp Terelya

©1996 Queenship Publishing

Library of Congress Number # 95-73237

Published by:
Queenship Publishing
P.O. Box 42028
Santa Barbara, CA 93140-2028

Printed in the United States of America

ISBN: 1-882972-69-4

Acknowledgments

It is in a spirit of deep gratitude that I would like to acknowledge first the Holy Trinity: Father, Jesus, and the Holy Spirit, the Blessed Virgin Mary and the many saints and angels who have made this book possible.

My wife, Carol, has been an invaluable partner. Her complete support of faith and prayers has allowed us to work as a team. This was especially true in the many hours of indexing and proofing of the manuscript. All of our family has been a source of care and support.

I am greatly indebted to Josyp Terelya for his very gracious offer to provide the art work for this publication. He has spent three months of work and prayer to provide us with a selection of many original pictures. He wanted very much to enhance the visions and messages with these beautiful and provocative works. You will experience some of them throughout these volumes.

A very special thank you goes to my spiritual director, Fr. Leo J. Klem, C.S.B. No matter what hour I called him, he was always there with his confident wisdom, guidance and discernment. His love, humility, deep faith and trust are a true inspiration.

My appreciation also goes to the Father John V. Rosse, my good pastor at Holy Name of Jesus Church. He has been open, loving and supportive from the very beginning.

There are many friends and relatives whose interest, love and prayerful support have been a real gift from God. Our own Wednesday, Monday and First Saturday prayer groups deserve a special thank you for their loyalty and faithfulness.

Finally, I would like to thank Bob and Claire Schaefer of Queenship Publishing and their spiritual director, Fr. Luke Zimmer for providing the opportunity to bring this message of preparation, love and warnings to you the people of God.

John Leary, Jr.
January 1996

Dedication

To the Most Holy Trinity

God

The Father, Son and Holy Spirit

The Source of

All

Life, Love and Wisdom

Publisher's Foreword

John has, with some exceptions, been having visions twice a day since they began in July, 1993. The first vision of the day usually takes place during morning Mass immediately after he receives the Eucharist. If the name of the church is not mentioned, it is a local Rochester, NY, church. When out of town, the church name is included in the text. The second vision occurs in the evening either at Perpetual Adoration or at the prayer group that is held at John's home.

Various names appear in the text. Most of the time the names appear only once or twice. Their identity is not important to the message and their reason for being in the text is evident. First names have been used when requested by the individual. The name Maria E. which occurs quite often is the visionary Maria Esperanza Bianchini of Betania, Venezuela.

We are grateful to Josep Terelya for the cover art as well as the art throughout the book. Josyp is a well-known visionary and also the author of *Witness* and most recently *In the Kingdom of the Spirit.*

This volume covers visions from July, 1993 through the end of June, 1994. Volume II, which is now being produced, contains visions from July, 1994 through June, 1995 and will be released in early spring of 1996. We expect to release Volume III in early summer, 1996.

The Publisher
January, 1996

Foreword

It was in July of 1993 that Almighty God, especially through Jesus, His Eternal Word, entered the life of John Leary in a most remarkable way. John is 53 years old and works as a chemist at Eastman Kodak Co., Rochester, New York. He lives in a modest house in the suburbs of Rochester with Carol, his wife of 30 years, and Catherine, his youngest daughter. His other two daughters, Jeanette and Donna, are married and have homes of their own. John has been going to daily Mass since he was 17 and has been conducting a weekly prayer group in his own home for 22 years. For a long time he has been saying 15 decades of the Rosary each day.

In April of 1993 he and his wife made a pilgrimage to Our Lady's shrine in Medjugorje, Yugoslavia. While there, he felt a special attraction to Jesus in the Blessed Sacrament. There he became aware that the Lord Jesus was asking him to change his way of life and to make Him his first priority. A month later in his home, Our Lord spoke to him and asked if he would give over his will to Him to bring about a very special mission. Without knowing clearly to what he was consenting, John, strong in faith and trust, agreed to all the Lord would ask.

On July 21, 1993 the Lord gave him an inkling of what would be involved in this new calling. He was returning home from Toronto in Canada where he had listened to a talk of Maria Esperanza (a visionary from Betania, Venezuela) and had visited Josyp Terelya. While in bed he had a mysterious interior vision of a newspaper headline that spelled "DISASTER." Thus began a series of daily and often twice daily interior visions along with messages, mostly from Jesus. Other messages were from God the Father, the Holy Spirit, the Blessed Virgin Mary, his guardian angel and many of the saints, especially St. Therese of Lisieux. These messages he recorded on his word processor. In the beginning they were quite short but they became more extensive as the weeks passed by. At the time of this writing he is still receiving visions and messages.

These daily spiritual experiences, which occur most often immediately following Communion, consist of a brief vision which becomes the basis of the message that follows. They range widely on a great variety of subjects, but one might group them under the following categories: warnings, teachings and love messages. Occasionally, there are personal confirmations of some special requests that he made to the Lord.

The interior visions contain an amazing number of different pictures, some quite startling, which hardly repeat themselves. In regard to the explicit messages that are inspired by each vision, they contain deep insights into the kind of relationship God wishes to establish with His human creatures. There also is an awareness of how much He loves us and yearns for our response. As a great saint once wrote: "Love is repaid only by love." On the other hand God is not a fool to be treated lightly. In fact, did not Jesus once say something about not casting pearls before the swine? Thus there are certain warnings addressed to those who shrug God off as if He did not exist or is not important in human life.

Along with such warnings, we become more conscious of the reality of Satan and the forces of evil "...which wander through the world seeking the ruin of souls." We used to recite this at the end of each low Mass. In His love and concern for us, Our Lord keeps constantly pointing out how frail we humans are in the face of such evil angelic powers. God is speaking of the necessity of daily prayer, of personal penance, and of turning away from atheistic and material enticements which are so much a part of our modern environment.

Perhaps the most controversial parts of the messages are those which deal with what we commonly call Apocalyptic. Unusual as these may be, in my judgment, they are not basically any different than what we find in the last book of the New Testament or in some of the writings of St. Paul. After a careful and prayerful reading of the hundreds of pages in this book, I have not found anything contrary to the authentic teaching authority of the Roman Catholic Church.

The 16th Century Spanish mystic, St. John of the Cross, gives us sound guidelines for discerning the authenticity of this sort of phenomenon involving visions, locutions, etc. According to him, there are three possible sources: the devil, some kind of self-imposed hypnosis or God. I have been John's spiritual confidant for over two years. I have tested him in various spiritual ways and I am most confident that all he has put into these messages is neither of the devil nor of some kind of mental illness. Rather, they are from the God who, in His love for us, wishes to reveal His own Divine mind and heart. He has used John for this. I know that John is quite ready to abide by any decision of proper ecclesiastical authority on what he has written in this book

Rev. Leo J. Klem, C.S.B.
January 4, 1996
Rochester, New York

Visions and Messages of John Leary:

Wednesday, July 21, 1993:(1:30 a.m.)
Right before going to sleep, after my night prayers, I had a picture of the word *"Disaster"* as if on a newspaper page.

Friday, July 23, 1993:
In church, after meditation after Communion, I had an image of *"Hol"* as part of the HOLLYWOOD sign in Los Angeles, California.

Sunday, July 25, 1993:
In church during meditation after Communion, I had an image of darkness-like black clouds with a slight sliver of light at the top. A thought process word of *"Darkness"* came later in explanation. During Mass I had a few whiffs of the odor of musk that I smelled previously at the base of the Crucifixion in Jerusalem. I also sensed some tingling at the fourth and fifth Sorrowful Mysteries of the Rosary.

Tuesday, July 27, 1993:
In my room at home after praying the Rosary and my consecration prayers, I had an image of the Pope's robes spread out in black. The word *"Death"* came shortly after.

Wednesday, July 28, 1993:
After our prayer group prayed the fifteen decade Rosary, I saw planes flying into the air with the word *"War."* This referred to a new war of some proportion in the Mid-East area.

Thursday, July 29, 1993:

(No Image) After and during Communion, I saw the word *"Demons."* I sensed there will be an increasing presence of demons both visibly and invisibly.

During the day, an answer to the question of what good will come of these visions was that they are *"Warnings."* They are coming rapidly because time is short before events will start to happen.

Friday, July 30, 1993:

After Communion, I saw a huge crevasse on the Western seaboard of the U.S. With the word *"Earthquake."* I was taken-back by how tremendously large this appeared. It went from Northern Oregon to San Diego, California.

During the day, I had a strong desire to pray more before the Blessed Sacrament and spend less time on my computer.

Saturday, July 31, 1993:

After Communion, I saw a dove which appeared flying. The word *"Holy Ghost"* came to me and later a feeling of *"Peace."*

Later, before the Blessed Sacrament, I asked for confirmation of these visions. I noticed one of the stained-glass windows was a picture of the Holy Ghost—more than just a coincidence that I had that vision in the morning. They had Nocturnal Service—it made up for when I missed mine due to a wedding conflict.

Sunday, August 1, 1993:

After Communion, I saw a small circle—at first I was not sure what it meant. Later, it was made clearer that it was some volcanic activity since there was an orange crater. I was looking right down on top of it. I did not know where it was occurring.

Note: I asked the Lord if the visions could be a little bit clearer so I could distinguish what they were. From here on the images became very clear in brilliant colors.

Monday, August 2, 1993:

After Communion, I saw a huge crater with steep walls. The rocks were very vivid in color, primarily orange. I do not know exactly what caused it or how old it was.

Later, at the Adoration Chapel, I had a vision of many white crosses in a field like a cemetery.

Tuesday, August 3, 1993:

After Communion, I saw a golden pyramid with rays of light spreading out from it. There appeared to be something at the top of the apex. It was like the symbol on the back of the one dollar bill.

Later, at the Adoration Chapel, I had a vision of Christ alive— hanging on the cross. I felt the sins of the world were crucifying Him again.

Wednesday, August 4, 1993:

After Communion, I saw trees and houses being carried away by high waters of a flood. The words of *"Damage"* and *"Destruction"* came. I felt the destruction on the Mississippi will worsen over time.

Later after the fifteen decade Rosary at the prayer group, I saw a beautiful blue sky with tongues of fire coming down to the earth like at Pentecost.

Thursday, August 5, 1993:

After Communion, I saw a great darkness with a point-source of light coming down showing a spotlight image on the ground. I felt this could be Christ as the light in the darkness trying to give us hope in the coming trials.

Later, after Communion, I saw an ethereal image of Our Lady standing on the left side of an altar with wood behind. At first it was like a brilliant light coming from her heart area and gradually I could see white lines of her robes but I could not see her face—it was too brilliant.

Friday, August 6, 1993:

After Communion, (Feast of the Transfiguration), I saw a hill with trees and the Lord in dazzling white robes above the earth with so much brightness I could barely see His shape. Then the scene changed to a quick glimpse of heaven with Christ on His throne and myriads of angels and saints around Him in splendor. These visions were so breathtaking I had a hard time holding my composure. "Praise Jesus," "Thank you Jesus" was all that I could think of.

Saturday, August 7, 1993:

After Communion, I saw a man dressed in black on a funeral bier. At first, I could not see his face. Next, I saw a vision from the direction of his feet. It was the Pope's white vestments with gold trim again on a funeral bier. No mistake about his death—no date was given. Afterward, saying the Rosary I said the "Descent of the Holy Spirit" decade which seemed to give me a confirmation.

Later at St. Cecilia's Holy Hour during quiet time I saw a crucifix with a gold corpus. The thought message "Jesus on the cross is crying." Then other crucifixes appeared and again came the same message of Jesus crying. He was crying over the sins of many who were rejecting Him.

Sunday, August 8, 1993:

After Communion, I saw several monstrances with the Blessed Sacrament exposed. Finally, I saw one monstrance with two angels—one on either side kneeling and praising Jesus in the Blessed Sacrament. A thought word came *"Eucharist."* I had asked for a message word this time. I have a feeling the Lord wants me to be closer to the Blessed Sacrament—one hour a day when possible. Also, it was to encourage the displaying of the Blessed Sacrament for the faithful to lead others back to Christ.

Later, at the Adoration Chapel, I saw a huge flash in one vision followed by a vision of huge clouds of smoke rising from that area of the blast. The word *"Bomb"* came with it. It was big enough to appear like an atomic weapon. No dates or location were given.

Monday, August 9, 1993:

After Communion, I saw a picture of a dove shedding rays of light on the world and the thought message came *"Holy Ghost."* This felt like the Holy Spirit spreading His graces over all of us.

Later, at Holy Hour, I saw a monstrance of the Blessed Sacrament followed by another vision of a purple circle (or Host). I asked for a message of explanation and the thought word *"Passion"* came to me. This was confirmed seeing another stained-glass window that was purple with a dove and Holy Eucharist Host in it. Right after this vision, we did the Chaplet of Divine Mercy.

Tuesday, August 10, 1993:

In church, I had a sense of imminent death and *"Blood."* Again I saw an image of Pope John Paul II at a distance. I was drawn to all the red colors around—wine, vestments (St. Lawrence, martyr), red on tapestry, red flowers. After Communion, I had a very close-up view of Pope John Paul II's face wincing in pain and afterward I saw a brief vision of some very sinister eyes—like a demon.

Later, at the Adoration Chapel, I saw a man that had dark long hair with fairly tan skin on his arm. A thought message came *"Anti-Christ."* Initially, I could not see his face. Then another vision appeared of greenish glowing eyes that had rays coming out. I got the feeling not to look into his eyes or you might get hypnotized.

Wednesday, August 11, 1993:

After Communion, I saw a person standing alone (looked like a man) and he was surrounded by bright orange flames. The thought word came *"Flames."* I asked for where this was if on earth and the answer was *"Yes."* Later, Lydia, my mother-in-law, saw a setting sun with a man in flames as well—very vivid description the night before—maybe confirmation.

Later, after the prayer group at our home, I asked for a message for our group—if it be God's will. I received several images of Our Lady—one at a distance, one very close-up, and one coming a little distance away. The most powerful one was a very vivid picture of part of a Rosary being held by Our Lady but I did not see her face. The word *"Rosary"* came which was a way of telling us thank you for all the prayers being said for her intentions.

Thursday, August 12, 1993:

After Communion, I saw a huge box standing still in the middle of a stream or river. Then I had an image of a main street in an old western town—I have seen some in Colorado. I asked for a thought message of explanation and the word *"Cabrini"* gradually crossed in front of me and I immediately associated the springs at the Cabrini Shrine with this stream. Also, in the first reading Joshua had the Ark of the Covenant stand in the River Jordan to stop the waters for the people to cross on dry land.

Later, at the Adoration Chapel, I saw dollar signs floating around and then I saw a sense of "Black" as in like a "Black day on Wall Street." This was followed by a quick glimpse of Wall Street itself. The word *"Bankruptcy"* was written in very bold big letters before me.

Friday, August 13, 1993:

After Communion, I saw Pope John Paul II raising the Host at the Consecration of the Mass and the next scene I saw him rising upwards towards heaven.

Later, at the Adoration Chapel, I saw from a considerable distance away the start of an explosion with a flash. Then I saw another vision where it mushroomed out into a huge cloud of smoke. The word *"Atomic"* was displayed in blocked letters at an angle where the last letters were the largest. Several more images of bomb clouds appeared. Later, for ten seconds the lights and fans went dark and silent and then came on again in the Chapel.

Notes: I was encouraged to be a prayer warrior for Jesus.

Saturday, August 14, 1993:

At night about 1:40 a.m. My wife, Carol and I both smelled whiffs of roses (not Carol's perfume) about five times during the night.

After Communion, I saw a man in position with a rifle aimed to the front where there was a big crowd. I saw this picture at least three times from different positions. The thought word came to me *"Shooting."* When I was wondering at the significance, I had a brief picture of John Paul II.

Later, at the Adoration Chapel, (2:15-3:15), I saw a vision of a small hill with Christ on the cross. Next to Him and strung out down the hill as far as I could see were other crosses with bodies on them but I could not recognize anyone. A thought message came *"Martyrs."* Note: This was the feast day of Maximilian Kolbe, martyr.

Sunday, August 15, 1993: (Feast of the Assumption)

During the Mass, as the Host was consecrated and every time it was lifted, I could see some small image of Mary with the Host. After Communion, I had an image of Mary dressed in blue kneeling and holding up a cross with Jesus on it (I saw a corpus but not living colors). The words were: *"To Jesus through Mary."* Then I saw another scene where there was a bright sun and Our Lady dressed in white standing in the sun. The thought words came: *"Clothed in the sun."* There was a beautiful feeling of her visitation and tears.

Later, at Holy Hour, for Consecration to Mary, during Exposition of the Blessed Sacrament, I had first a scene which showed the Statue of Our Lady of Fatima. Afterward, I saw another scene of a huge red Host with red rays stretching out.

Monday, August 16, 1993:
After Communion, I saw a huge boat very much like Noah's ark. It first was displayed from the side looking down then the scene quickly zoomed down to the bottom of the bow looking up at the tremendous size of the ark. The thought words came *"As in the days of Noah."* This was followed by a scene of what looked like the DARKNESS to come. Again this scene was followed by a raining-down of fire from above as a purification of the earth. I felt this would be a time like Noah's day when men and women had fallen away from God and God has come to purify the earth with fire instead of a flood.

Later, at the Adoration Chapel, I was struck by a brilliant light so bright I looked around the room and did not see the source. It was from like a spotlight. Then I saw several spotlights coming to the ground in a pitch darkness. I received the message: *"God's people will be protected."*

Tuesday, August 17, 1993:
After Communion, I saw a black man in a light and the words came: *"Don't have prejudice."* This seemed to have a general meaning.

Later, at the Adoration Chapel, I at first saw what looked like an Oriental rug with stars on it. Then the words came: *"Dome of the rock."* This referred to the Temple in Jerusalem. Then I saw a majestic vision of the New Jerusalem with brilliant golden walls gleaming. My attention was then drawn to a picture of the Golden Gate and the words came: *"Christ will enter the golden gate soon."*

Wednesday, August 18, 1993:

In church, I had a beautiful image of Our Lady standing with her arms outstretched. I asked for a message, but it was hard to concentrate since the Mass abruptly ended and the lights were turned out. A word started to come but I could only see *"Here—."* Then it came more clearly later—*"Heresy."* I felt Our Lady wanted us to pray for the protection against the many heresies of our day.

Later, at the prayer group, at our home, I saw Christ on the cross crucified and the thought words were: *"Come, follow Me."* This had the feeling that we are to take up our crosses and suffer through the coming times with Christ leading us.

Thursday, August 19, 1993:

After Communion, I saw a picture of Europe with ten flags belonging to the financial group (Maastricht Treaty) of Europe which: *"The beast will lead."*

Later, at the Adoration Chapel, I saw at first a beautiful glowing gold cloud with a vague image in it. Then I had the sense that this message was coming from God the Father. In the next scene there was a red picture of a "Burning bush." This was followed by a scene of the Ten Commandments' Tablets again with brilliant rays coming out. I then asked if there was a message for me and the words came: *"Your life is everlasting."*

Friday, August 20, 1993:

After Communion, I had a beautiful scene of Jesus as the "Infant of Prague." He was glorious and I had a beautiful sense of visiting Him at Communion time—a real unity with Him. I asked if He had a message for me and the words came: *"Pray for sinners."* This feeling of helping souls back to God continues to appear as my mission with these visions.

Later, at the Adoration Chapel, at Midnight, I saw at first molten rock from an underwater volcano making new land and received the word *"Rebirth."* Then I had another vision of the globe of the earth with one side very dark and the upper right corner ablaze with light and the words received were: *"The new earth."* I had the feeling this would be like the time of the Garden of Eden before the fall.

Saturday, August 21, 1993: (Feast of St. Pius X)

After Communion, I saw several big thick crosses which seemed to represent cathedral churches and the message came: *"Pray for the protection of the Church."*

Later, at 5:00 Anticipation Mass, after Communion, I saw an American flag with no stars and the message came: *"Disunity."* There were no stars because people and states were not getting along. Then I saw a strong wind come and blow the flag apart. I felt this meant there would be many problems and chaos for the country in the future.

Later, at Nocturnal, I saw at first many bright white rings with planets circling the sun—a picture of the solar system. Then I saw a white object get bigger and bigger and finally I could see a comet headed for the earth. The word *comet* came to me for emphasis of what I saw. Then I had a scene of the earth and all at once I could see a trail of flames shooting up from the earth. The thought word *"Fire"* came to me. It was as if the comet skimmed across the surface igniting a fire in its trail. This vision was so heavy, again I was taken back.

Sunday, August 22, 1993:

At Marmora, Canada at the tenth Station I saw Our Lady dressed in brown (Mt. Carmel) and she showed me an empty cross. Our Lady was asking us to strip ourselves of worldly affections as pride and cares of this world and take up our crosses and bear them. I smelled roses at the 11th Station five times—Mary was present.

Monday, August 23, 1993: (Feast of Rose of Lima)

After Communion, I saw an image of St. Joseph standing on the altar holding a staff and a white lilly flower. A thought message came: *"Freedom for the poor."*

Later, at the Adoration Chapel, at first I saw a bright trail. Then I saw a scene of a sun or ball of fire moving toward us straight on. The words came: *"Punishment and chastisement."*

Tuesday, August 24, 1993:

After Communion, I saw a book with what looked like an angel writing in names. This was the *"Book of Life."* Also, a message came: *"Pray and avoid the beast."*

Later, at the Adoration Chapel, I had some strong attempts by the devil to invade my vision space. Afterward, I had a beautiful scene of Our Lady in the sky dressed in blue and beside her a cross with a brilliant light emanating from the middle. The thought words *"Permanent Sign"* came.

Wednesday, August 25, 1993:

During Mass I had a strong sense I was getting a message about some destruction on the U.S. Eastern coast. After Communion, I saw a car riding along on a highway when suddenly I saw a huge wall of water come and bury the car. I had the thought words *"Tidal wave."* Later, I saw a picture of the east coast, but I could not determine where along the coast.

Later, at the prayer group, at our home, about the time of the "Agony in the Garden" decade, I saw some pillars and later I had a vision of inside the Church of Gethsemene. Then I had a quick vision looking down on Christ praying. After the Rosary was over and we had quiet time, I saw a saint (St. Louis' feast day) praying. Then I saw a lot of people kneeling and praying. The thought message came: *"Won't you pray one hour with Me?"* I felt the Lord is asking us to pray one hour a day when possible.

Thursday, August 26, 1993:

During the Mass I saw a picture of a large-faced clock at 7:30. After Communion, I saw a dark scene with one large bright cloud where it looked like Jesus coming on a cloud which moved towards me. The thought words came *"Watch with Me."* (Note: The Gospel was of Christ warning that the Master will return when the servants least expect it.)

Later, at the Adoration Chapel, I saw a nun and it came to me that it was St. Teresa of Avila. The next scene I saw her at the bottom of a stairway looking up to the Infant Jesus. The words came: *"My Jesus in me and me in Jesus."* The feeling was that our will should be one with the Divine Will.

Friday, August 27, 1993:

After Communion, I saw a priest offering Mass with a cross in front of the altar. I was seeing this for a fair amount of time and wondered at the significance when the next scene showed a pile of rubble with the cross laying down over it. The thought words came: *"The Mass will be taken away."*

Later, at the Adoration Chapel, I was looking down on Jesus' Head while He was being crucified. He was saying, "Woman there is your son (us)" and to the disciple John, "Behold your Mother." The thought words came: *"We are her children and she is our Mother."*

Saturday, August 28, 1993:

After Communion, I saw a picture of several toddlers and then they disappeared. This was followed by a scene of what was best described as the *"Wrath of God"* and flames being thrust down on the earth. I asked if there was a specific message and I saw the words: *"Stop abortion."* (Note: N.Y. State approved the abortion clinic here today.)

Later, at the Adoration Chapel, I at first saw like a rainbow bridge with lights on at night. The next scene I saw a huge wind in the shape of a funnel cloud. This eventually twisted the bridge metal into a mess. I had the sense that this was in the U.S. someplace and the words came: *"Wrath of God."*

Sunday, August 29, 1993:

After Communion, I saw Christ walking toward me then I saw the earth encircled with symbols of all peoples holding hands around it. The last scene was like a picture of the African Continent. (We had a visiting black priest from Tanzania.) The thought words came: *"See Christ in all peoples."*

Later, at the Adoration Chapel, I saw a big wide cup overflowing with some liquid and felt the wrath of God was overflowing and asking for justice. The words came: *"Pray especially for unrepentant sinners."*

Monday, August 30, 1993:

After Communion, I saw a huge storm churning the ocean (Emily) and then I had a scene of a shadow moving across North Carolina and Virginia. The words came: *"Floods and destruction."*

Later, at Adoration, I saw some islands with certain islands being affected by considerable volcanic activity. In one city I could see smoke rising. I saw an Oriental woman. I then saw the word

Tokyo and knew it was Japan. I asked if there was a message and the words came: *"Prepare for the end times."*

Tuesday, August 31, 1993:

After Communion, I saw at first a circling of lights and maybe events—it was hard to discern what it was. I never saw anything like this before. After further meditation I received the words: *"Life review."* We will be asked then to *"Choose"* between God or the demons.

Later, at the Adoration Chapel, I at first saw a red-colored mountain and a cloud around it. After meditation, this image came to represent God the Father in *"The hilltop experience."* I then saw a quiet river flowing next to some trees. This came to represent Jesus' love in *"Beside restful waters He leads me."* The third scene was a picture of the dove with fire behind Him. This represented the Holy Spirit bringing *"The flame of knowledge."* A final scene showed a triangle with the thought word *"Trinity."*

Wednesday, September 1, 1993:

After Communion, I saw a picture of a grandfather clock at 7:45. The message came: *"Time is running out for repentance."*

Later, at the prayer group, at our house, during the "Crucifixion" decade, I saw a dove flying through the air and He came to hover over Jesus standing in the Jordan River. A voice said, "I baptize you in the name of the Father and the Son and the Holy Spirit." I then received a thought message: *"Receive the Baptism of the Holy Spirit."* I sensed this was meant for all of us.

Thursday, September 2, 1993:

After Communion, I saw an angel coming from above and I received the words: *"Remember to ask your guardian angel for help through these trying times."*

Later, at the Adoration Chapel, I saw cartoons on a TV. A message came: *"TV, sex, movies and materialism are leading man to damnation."*

Friday, September 3, 1993:

After Communion, I saw Christ get off His throne in heaven and come walking forward. The thought message came: *"I am coming to bring My sheep back to the home I have prepared for I am the Good Shepherd."* There was a beautiful feeling of the loving kindness of Jesus for myself and His followers.

Later, at the Adoration Chapel, I saw the "Eye of God" showering His wrath on the earth. The message came: *"Sinners repent or the chastisement will fall."*

Saturday, September 4, 1993:

After Communion, I saw a triangle representing the Trinity. Then I saw what looked like a ball of fire flying through earth's air. The thought words came: *"The ball of fire is coming, prepare your lives."* This message seemed to have more validity or confirmation by the fact that God (the three persons) is approving this chastisement.

Later, at Holy Hour, I at first saw a doorway to heaven. Then I saw the Shroud of Turin on the door (only the face) and Our Lord was crying. A message came: *"I am asking My children to come home. I am also asking My faithful to pray for the rest of My children to come back home."*

Sunday, September 5, 1993:

After Communion, I saw a gleaming triangle indicating the presence of the Trinity. The next scene I saw, looking up to heaven there were four lampstands with big burning fires at the four corners of the earth. At each I could see angels and I sensed they were ready to mete out God's justice for the sin of man. The thought words came: *"Prepare your lives."* During a Baptism, I saw the Pascal Candle burning three times its normal size and then after Communion, I saw it at normal size. I took this as a sign for this vision to be true. (Read Revelation 7:1-8)

Later, at the Adoration Chapel, I at first saw Jesus on the cross. Then I saw a Z from which I deduced that He is the Alpha and the Omega. The next scene was a superimposed image of Mary over Jesus. From this I sensed the message: *"Mary is one with Jesus."*

Monday, September 6, 1993:

In church, I saw a beautiful lady in a veil with a five pointed gold star on her forehead. Then I saw a huge hotel with many rooms and the message came: *"In My house there are many mansions."*

Later, at Perpetual Adoration, I saw an empty chair and the thought words came: *"The chair of Peter will be empty—pray for the Holy Father."* I felt the Holy Father may be exiled or there may be a major upheaval in the Church.

Tuesday, September 7, 1993:

After Communion, I at first saw a triangle representing the Trinity. Then I saw several hooded monks who appeared to be Franciscans. Also, I could see some old churches. The thought words came: *"Consecrate your souls to Jesus."* On asking for the significance of the monks—they are the caretakers of some of the Holy Places.

Later, at the Adoration Chapel, I at first saw like an image of an atomic bomb. Then I saw an all-encompasing yellow light shine down which seemed to blot out the image of the bomb. I received a message: *"A new life where man is in union with God and nature."* I sensed God will bring a new life to the earth—a life without anger, fighting, sickness, or death.

Wednesday, September 8, 1993: (Our Lady's Birthday)

At Sacred Heart Church, Marmora, Canada, I saw an angel and his name came to me—Gabriel. Our Lady was kneeling before him and the words came: *"Our Lord is asking for our yes."*

Later at the tenth Station at Marmora, I saw a bright object with concentric rings around it. Rays of light were radiating out from the center. The message came: *"Our Lord is asking us to center our lives around Him."* I asked Our Lady if she had a message for me and she responded: *"Consecrate your hearts and souls to me."* This was so she could give our gift to her Son.

Thursday, September 9, 1993:

After Communion, I had a very chilling feeling about building dark clouds—they seemed to be filled with evil. Then I saw a very dramatic scene of a demon coming towards me which I asked Jesus to remove. I had a strong feeling that demons are increasing their attacks on man and the words came *"Prepare for increasing demon attacks."*

Later, at the Adoration Chapel, I saw buildings in a city and then a huge dove representing the Holy Spirit appeared with red markings. A message came: *"An era of peace will come over the earth after it is purified by fire."* Then I saw a large building and it had huge flames all around it.

Friday, September 10, 1993:

After Communion, I saw several cliffs on the edge of an active volcano. Then the scene moved deeper to an image of what looked like hell where the souls were falling into it. I could see some demons there. I received the message: *"Myriads of souls are going to hell. We need to pray for souls headed to hell to give them the grace to turn their lives around."*

Later, at the Adoration Chapel, I saw an Indian maiden and it was Blessed Kateri Tekakwitha. I also saw the inside of some churches. She is asking us to visit Auriesville. A message came: *"To save our lives we must be ready to lose our lives."*

Saturday, September 11, 1993:

After Communion, I saw a series of images, the first was a cross. Then there was a cross over the altar with the priest offering Mass. Then I had a quick glimpse of Joseph Terelya and then the Pope. Finally, I saw a ringing bell. The thought words came: *"Freedom from sin."*

At the Adoration Chapel, I saw many lights twirling. Then they slowed down so I could see they were events happening like newsreels of our life. We will be outside of time viewing our lives. A message came: *"Prepare for the warning."* I sensed it could happen soon, but no date was given.

Sunday, September 12, 1993:

After Communion, I saw people kneeling in their pews and on the altar the priest was raising the Host. Then I received a message: *"Give praise, honor and glory to God. Kneel in humble adoration."* I felt very strongly the Lord wants us to honor Him with our reverence. Reverence to Him should come before any of man's laws or understanding.

Later, at the Adoration Chapel, I saw a crucifix with burning candles at each of the five wounds of Christ. I received a message: *"We must suffer for Christ on earth in carrying our crosses."*

After, I saw an image of Padre Pio who had the stigmata-the five wounds of Christ. (two hands, two feet and his side)

Monday, September 13, 1993:

After Communion, I first saw a triangle briefly. Then there were dark clouds and I saw a cross with a corpus lying on the ground with some refuse. The words came: *"Apostasy, ruin, evil will flourish."* I sensed this will be a dark time for the Church with many falling away to apathy, influenced by earthly distractions and increasing temptations from the demons. Some will even choose to follow other religions or believe in heretical misconceptions of the faith.

Later, at the Adoration Chapel, I saw a picture of the Apostles and they were teaching the people. I received a message: *"Go out as the Apostles and teach the word of God to those who need it."* I feel people have grown spiritually cold. They need the strong faithful to enliven the faith of those willing to listen. We must strive to bring the faithful closer to Jesus for protection against the evils of these end times.

At Holy Hour, I saw at first an image of Christ's Sacred Heart, then I saw a face which I felt was God the Father as an old man with a beard. A third image showed a dove with a peace branch representing the Holy Spirit. Then I saw massive flames on earth with darkness and people walking in the flames. A message came: *"During the three days of darkness the souls marked by the beast will be tortured by flames but not consumed—much like in hell for three days. Then they will be removed."* This is the purification of the earth making it ready for Our Lord's and Our Lady's triumph over Satan.

Tuesday, September 14, 1993: (Feast of the Triumph of the Cross)

After Communion, I saw a cross empty and then one with the corpus. I received a message: *"Wear a blessed cross with a corpus to protect us from the demons."* Afterward, I saw what looked like the face from the Shroud of Turin superimposed over the cross. The cross should play a big role in our Christian belief and wearing it gives Christ reverence and thanks to Him for saving our souls by His death.

Later, at the Adoration Chapel, I received a message: *"Water and fire are the elements for punishment due to sin."* I saw a huge blue wave of water appear to wash up along the whole eastern coastline.

Wednesday, September 15, 1993: (Feast of Our Lady of Sorrows) At church, I saw the Blessed Virgin with outstreched arms. She had a bright orange glow over her head. She said, *"I want to protect my children from the evils of this day and bring you back to my Jesus. I love you as a Mother and I want to shelter you with my mantle."* We can understand how her heart was pierced when her Son died on the cross and yet we are causing her more sorrow by so much sin against her Son.

Later, I again had a vision of Our Blessed Mother with an orange glow over her but this time I had a hard time seeing her face—it kept blanking out. I received a message: *"Forgive others as you would have them forgive you. I am sorrowful because my children have fallen away from God. Please pray that they will come back to My Son."* I feel Our Lady is drawing us to more fully understand the great commandment Jesus gave us—to love God and to love our neighbor.

At the prayer group, during the Sorrowful Mysteries, starting at the "Scouraging At the Pillar" I saw Our Lady in a picture of the Pieta. I received the messages: *"This was my ultimate sorrow to see my Son dead in my arms. I was crying over my children, especially those headed for spiritual death. I want you to ask for graces from me and my Son to heal your sorrows."* I felt a personal healing over an old sorrow of when Carol and I held our own son who had died in our arms.

Thursday, September 16, 1993: (Feast of Sts. Cornelius & Cyprian)

At St. Mary's in Waterloo after Communion, I saw a crucifix and then I saw the inside of a Church with some statues of men which may have been the martyrs Sts. Cornelius & Cyprian. I received a message: *"The martyrs are calling us to Jesus."* I felt strongly that we should give our thanks to God for our Faith and we should strive to keep it strong as did the woman in the Gospel who perfumed and loved Jesus. Note: The Communion Antiphon was identical to my 9-10-93 message—*"To save our lives we must be ready to lose our lives."* This was a confirmation of my decision to go to the Auriesville Shrine to answer Blessed Kateri Tekakwitha's calling.

Later, at the Shrine of the North American Martyrs in Auriesville, I saw Blessed Kateri Tekakwitha standing next to a cross. A message came: *"I am bringing you to Jesus and asking you to carry your crosses. Pray for the strength to carry it. Also, pray for grace from the Holy Spirit if we have to give our lives for the faith that the Holy Spirit will give us what to say and do."* We were surprised right then to have Benediction (We did not know it was scheduled at 3:30 p.m.) and the priest let us venerate the relic of Kateri. What a beautiful blessing. Note: Lena S. had two messages in the Ravine and we saw the Blessed Mother in a statue of Jesus on the cross in the Ravine where one of the martyrs died.

Friday, September 17, 1993: (Feast of St. Robert Bellarmine)

After Communion, I saw a priest giving out Communion. A message came: *"Love and pray for our priests."* We take them for granted so much and do not realize how important and spiritually dependent we are on them. They bring us Jesus' sacraments and keep the faithful united. We need to support them and help them in keeping their vocation.

At the Adoration Chapel, there was a loud noise from a lawnmower right when I wanted time for a message. I saw a blue candle burning. Then I had a beautiful tingling and I saw Our Lady dressed in blue crying—the lawnmower just stopped. I received a message: *"Pray for my priest sons, they are near and dear to my heart. Some of my priests will fall away and some will be martyred."* Our Lady is asking us to pray to her for the priests to give them the strength to endure everyday trials and the future testing which will really try us in the end times. The lawnmower started up again after Our Lady's message.

Saturday, September 18, 1993:

After Communion, I saw an empty cross with rays coming out from the center. I received a message: *"We must all carry our own*

crosses, some will be heavier than others. *Our Lady will be there to help us carry it. She loves her children and is crying for those blinded to the faith to return with our prayers."*
Then I saw a picture of Our Lady dressed in blue laying her hand on my shoulder and I could feel tingling radiating out from my left shoulder (where she touched me). She was giving me personal support for our trials with my daughter. This was so powerful I began sobbing profusely as tears of love came. Thank you, dear Mother. Now I know why you are constantly crying for your children to return to your Son.
Later at Nocturnal Adoration, I saw like a woman's head in a glass shape. I received a message: *"Pray for the removal of the sin of abortion in this country. It is an abomination before the Lord. This country will have a deep debt to pay."* Our Lady is asking us to direct our prayers to all pregnant mothers and the changing of our social morality. Otherwise, great catastrophies will strike this land. I then saw some red fetuses. *"Their angels are crying out to God for justice."*

Sunday, September 19, 1993:
After Communion, I saw a Bible and it would appear and gradually disappear. I received a message: *"More and more people will fall away from religion."* Our Lord and Our Lady are asking: *"Keep a constant vigil of prayer for the faithful to remain with God and for the fallen away to return to God."*
Later, I saw a pyramid and the message came: *"The Anti-Christ will come from Egypt (much like Jesus came out of Egypt). He will bring a false peace during an upheaval in the world. Prepare for the Anti-Christ—he will win many away from God."*

Monday, September 20, 1993:
After Communion, I saw a vision of St. Francis of Assisi. His message was: *"Jesus loves us very much. See the fruits of that love on the cross. Use your talents to bring Jesus' message to as many as possible."*
Later, I saw beautiful pictures of colors and gems and things I had never seen before. I received a message: *"There will be a new heaven and a new earth."* I then saw a huge abyss with orange color and demons and souls were being cast down into the pit. I

then saw a very brilliant yellow light from God the Father shine down on the earth. Everything was now in a beautiful state of peace.

Tuesday, September 21, 1993:

After Communion, for awhile it was blank as if no vision was coming. Then I could see Our Lady dressed in black with a shawl wrapped tightly around her like it was very cold. Then I saw a picture of Jesus on a cross and He was moving forward. The message was: *"Prepare for I am coming when you least expect it. I will refine all mankind with fire—the just will be protected and those against Me I will say to them I do not know you."*

Later, at the Adoration Chapel, I saw a crucifix standing before me. Then I saw scenes of a white horse, a black horse, and a red horse. A message came to me: *"The events of Revelation will be coming soon. Prepare! Pray! Watch!"* (See Rev. 6:1-5)

Note: In Revelation a white horse and rider represents WAR, a conqueror. The black horse had a rider carrying a balance and represents FAMINE. The red horse and rider had a sword to cause killing and represents STRIFE.

Wednesday, September 22, 1993:

In church again; it was awhile until I could see anything. Then I saw a formation of white angels shifting from left to right in a column. This was followed by increasing darkness and many demons were now in flight all over. A message came: *"The demons will be thick in the sky before and during the three days of darkness. Guard your lives. Prepare! Pray!"*

At the prayer group, at our house I saw many shields of arms representing different countries. A message came: *"A great war— the Battle of Armageddon—is coming. Peace, peace, then sudden destruction will be fulfilled."*

Thursday, September 23, 1993:

After Communion, I saw an angel praying before the tabernacle. The picture included the tapestry in the chapel and was very specifically our church. The message came: *"Give humble adoration to Me in all the tabernacles of the world. I love you."*

Later, I saw a picture of Christ the King coming in majestic robes of gold. His picture darkened and slowly diminished. I received a message: *"Christ the King is coming but first Anti-Christ will reign for a while. Do not take the mark of the beast. Instead keep close to God and ask the Holy Spirit to guard over you."*

Friday, September 24, 1993:
After Communion, I saw Jesus on the cross. Then suddenly a very bright light appeared on the cross and He appeared as in the Resurrection with a very bright burst of light rising to heaven. I received the message: *"The risen Lord is triumphant. He will bring peace to His people."*

As I came out of the house I was greeted by a shooting star on a starry night. At the Adoration Chapel, at 12:00 a.m., I saw a comet approach the earth and strike at the Atlantic Ocean leaving big waves where it hit. Great clouds of dust and smoke were sent into the air. I could even see underwater where there was a major disturbance as the comet hit the water. The message came: *"A comet will strike the Atlantic Ocean and it will send out huge tidal waves. The burning trail will send up huge clouds of smoke which will cloud the sun for three days. Prepare and have your life in order."*

Saturday, September 25, 1993:
At the Adoration Chapel, I saw a huge cross in the darkness. I could feel myself and others flying through space behind the cross as Jesus was leading us to the blue earth. We landed on earth and everything was beautiful. I received a message: *"I will lead you to heaven on earth. Peace will be all over the world. It will be like in Eden before the fall."* When I got in my car, the radio was playing and the song was: "A Brand New World" or lyrics to that effect— some confirmation.

Later, I saw a cross with corpus and a few light rays were present but the cross was dark. Then suddenly there was a strong light coming forth from the cross. I received a message: *"I am the Light of the World. My light of grace will pierce the darkness. I am enlightening your faith—pray to keep your faith's flame burning."*

Sunday, September 26, 1993:
After Communion, I saw a cross, followed by a glimpse of God the Father in gold and a dove of the Holy Spirit. I then received a message from Jesus: *"I am the eyes and ears of your*

faith. Through the eyes of faith you can see Me in the Eucharist and I bring you My love. Through My word, you hear in the Scriptures you can come to a full realization of My love for you in My dying on the cross. I am asking you to remain strong in the faith and keep each family member with Me as well."

Later, at the Adoration Chapel, I saw a man wrapped in bandages like Lazarus. Then I saw a bright light and sensed Jesus was there—I could feel a tingling all over. A message came: "*I am the Life and the Resurrection. He who believes in Me I will reveal the truth. And the truth will set you free.*" John 11:25

Monday, September 27, 1993:

After Communion, I saw a bright light break out of the sky and the voice of God the Father sent down a message:"*My wrath is coming from heaven. Your sins are an abomination before Me. They (our sins) are crying out for justice.*"

Later, at the Adoration Chapel, I saw a TV picture with some people on it and they gradually turned to demons. I received a message: "*The TV is being used by the demons to subvert the people. After the Anti-Christ comes to power, turn off your TV sets for he will control the people's minds even more powerfully through the viewing of him.*"

Tuesday, September 28, 1993:

After Communion, I saw people seated looking forward, then some lines of people on the road. A message came: "*Pray for My people to protect them from increasing attacks from the demons. The weak will need many prayers to withstand the coming onslaught of evil.*"

Later, at the Adoration Chapel, I saw some demons shimmering in the lower regions. Then I saw fire and souls were in hell and they looked like molten coals. They are there for eternity, never to see God. I received a message: "*Souls in hell are like molten coals. I am sending a message of fear of the Lord to those on the edge of hell to contemplate their decision for or against God. Love of the Lord is most perfect, but fear of His judgment can also be a means to choose Him.*"

22

Wednesday, September 29, 1993: (Feast of the Archangels)

In church, I saw choirs of angels in heaven. Then I saw a vision of St. Michael the Archangel radiant in his glory as he was throwing the bad angels into hell. Then I had a glimpse of Gabriel giving the message to Our Lady and finally an image of Raphael with Tobias in the Old Testament who dispatched a devil who killed Sara's seven husbands. I received a message: *"We are Michael, Gabriel and Raphael and we come as God's messengers to bring God's people back to Him to do His Divine Will. We constantly stand in God's presence giving Him glory and praise."*

Later, at the prayer group, I first saw a young man looking like an angel after the "Agony in the Garden" decade. An empty seat (15th seat) had a strong angelic presence and it appeared to be Myridia, our Prayer Group Angel, who made up the 15th being. The angels urged us to kneel at the "Crucifixion" decade. A message came then: *"Give honor and glory to Jesus in the Blessed Sacrament."* At the quiet time I had a brief image of Our Lady who said: *"Continue to give honor and glory to my Son—He is waiting for you."*

Thursday, September 30, 1993: (Feast of St. Jerome)

After Communion, I saw several church steeples and I received a message: *"I will protect My Church to the end of time. And the gates of hell shall not prevail against it."*

Later, at the Adoration Chapel, I saw an image of Our Lady in the sky over her apparition places and an image of the cross (Christ) over the Holy Places. I received a message: *"We are the Permanent Signs who come to give hope to those who must endure these evil days. Take courage—your faith has saved you."*

Friday, October 1, 1993: (Feast of St. Therese, Little Flower)

After Communion, I saw a nun, who looked like St. Therese, holding flowers (roses). I asked her for a message: *"Meekness and humility are desired by my Jesus. He is asking us to come to Him as innocent and dependent as a little child."*

Later, at the Adoration Chapel, I saw a nun who I assumed was St. Therese. She had her back to me and was leading me behind her until we came to an image of Mary holding the Baby Jesus. A message then came: *"I am leading you to my Jesus and His Mother so they can guard you from the evils and chaos of these future years. Listen to them and pray to them for strength."*

Saturday, October 2, 1993: (Feast of the Guardian Angels)
After Communion, I saw an altar with a little child and their guardian angel was next to them. I asked my own guardian angel, Mark, for a message: *"Stare at Jesus in the Host and tell Him how much you love Him. Then promise Him that you will strive to do His will. When you are in difficulty, do not forget to ask for my help."*

Later, at the Holy Hour I saw Jesus and my guardian angel Mark. I asked him for a message: *"Love Jesus in the Blessed Sacrament. See in creation how beautifully the Lord makes things. I am asking you and all to be eternally obedient to Him. I am also asking you to pray for sinners and ask their angels to make them (sinners) attentive to God's calling."*

Sunday, October 3, 1993:
In church, I saw a row of seats with no kneelers and at the seat before it, the people were kneeling at the time of Consecration. I received a message: *"Continue to give God reverence at the Consecration. For it is mercy I desire and not sacrifice."*

Later, at the Adoration Chapel, I saw the veil of Mary and then a very bright light near her heart area—I could not see her face. I sensed Jesus' presence. I received a message: *"Our hearts are intertwined as one. We see the evil threats that are imminent. Please pray to us for the strength to endure these temptations. For if the time is not shortened, even the faithful might be lost to the evil one."*

Monday, October 4, 1993: (Feast of St. Francis of Assisi)
In church, I saw St. Francis appear several times. I received a message. *"Come close to Jesus and He will refresh you. See God's influence in nature and understand His ways are not our ways. Prepare for the evil and chaotic days ahead."*

Later, at Holy Hour, I saw St. Francis in the fields next to his garden. I asked him for a message: *"I am not worthy to be a saint, it is only through the power of the Almighty that has made it so. You will be asked to be a soldier of Christ in the coming days. Stay close to Jesus in the Blessed Sacrament."*

Tuesday, October 5, 1993:
In church, I saw some pots and cauldrons brewing and a big cup overflowing. I received a message: *"My cup is overflowing and My justice will soon be meted out. Keep together in your prayer groups for strengthening each other through the coming hard times."*
Later, at the Adoration Chapel, I saw visions of Egyptian pictures on the walls of the pyramids. A message came: *"Anti-Christ is coming. He will take power during a major world chaos. The Black Pope and the Anti-Christ will reign together as in Revelation but their reign will be of short duration."* Read (Rev 13:1-18).

Wednesday, October 6, 1993:
After Communion, I saw a picture of an altar and the priest had a dalmatic robe on facing the altar. I received a message: *"There will be a major upheaval in the Church. Schism will flourish everywhere. This will come about as a result of the Pope issuing his latest encyclical."*
At the prayer group, I saw a brief image of John Paul II and had the words: *"The present Pope will go into exile."* Then I saw an image of the Black Pope as a demon incarnated. I then saw an image of our prayer group angel, Myridia. This was followed by an image of a cross with many faces of Jesus Christ all over the cross. *"See Christ in everyone."* I saw some circling lights again like in the life review. *"We will be tested by fire."* Then again: *"Events will happen in rapid succession."* Then Jesus said: *"I am pleased with your prayers."* Mary said: *"Thank you for responding to my call."* All these visions appeared during the Rosary.

Thursday, October 7, 1993: (Feast of the Holy Rosary)
After Communion, I saw the Blessed Mother in full image with a crown on her head. I received a message: *"I am the Queen of the Holy Rosary. I bring you my Son, Jesus, through the Rosary. I*

am asking those who can to say the fifteen decade Rosary for sinners and yourselves. In the future, this will be your most powerful weapon against evil when the Mass will be taken away."

At the Rosary Service, I saw Our Lady crying. I felt she wanted more of the children to come to the Rosary service.

At Terry W.'s prayer group at her home, Our Lady appeared again in a crown: *"I thank you for coming to say this Rosary today on the Feast day of the Holy Rosary. I am asking you to come closer to my Jesus and keep in constant prayer."* Then an image of Jesus appeared: *"My Mother is crying for you and praying that you will repent of your sins and return to Me."* Mary again said: *"I have come to prepare my children for my Son's Second Coming."* At the "Crucifixion" decade which I said, I received: *"They will look on Him whom they have pierced."* Mary again: *"I am asking you to come to my Son as a child with child-like faith."*

Friday, October 8, 1993:

After Communion, I saw a break in the sky and God the Father spoke: *"This is My Divine Son, listen to Him."* Jesus then said: *"In a little while you shall not see Me, for I am going to the Father. I will be coming in glory but first you must endure an evil time."*

At the Adoration Chapel, I saw a vision of a large bird representing the Holy Spirit. I received a message: *"I enable people to have love for God. I am constantly dwelling in you to maintain your being. Please ask Me to help preserve your faith. I have an abundance of virtues to give you in order to strengthen you through the coming evil times."*

Saturday, October 9, 1993:

At the Adoration Chapel, I saw a bright light almost like a Host coming on a cross. Then as the cross drew nearer I could see Jesus on the cross. His message came: *"I am continually being crucified throughout all time for I died once for all mankind. This act of dying on the cross for all has been your salvation. You have been redeemed from your sins if you would just confess and repent of them to Me through the priest. I will be coming a second time on the clouds just as I promised the Apostles I would return as I left them. Please keep your faith strong through prayer and endure just a short while longer. I am with you always."* Later, after Communion, I saw a hooded demon who appeared as the Black Pope. Then I had a glimpse of the Anti-Christ. I received a message: *"You will suffer through demonic forces for three and a half years. The faithful will be forced underground like the catacombs. Some will be martyred, but fear not, for I will strengthen and protect My little ones. In the end My Sacred Heart will triumph."*

Sunday, October 10, 1993:
After Communion, I saw at first a bright light above me as God the Father. Below Him I saw a cold rather ugly man who might have been a judge or magistrate. I received a message: *"They will tie you up and flog you in synagogues. They will bring you before judges. They will ask you to choose between men or God and you will be martyred for believing in My name. But even if you should die, you will be saved for your faith in Me and you will join Me in Paradise."*

Later, at the Adoration Chapel, I saw a large hill of water and I rose in some kind of boat over it and came down the other side. I received a message: *"Move inland away from the coast and to some high ground. Have a house where you can pull down the shades on the windows. Prepare, for My justice cannot wait much longer. Keep praying."*

Monday, October 11, 1993:
After Communion, I saw myself in an underground pit in the ground (20ft high by 5ft). I gradually rose up out of the ground with dirt sides on the pit. I then saw a picture of leaves on the ground. The message was: *"You will truly be underground for protection from the power of the demons who will be running rampant for several years. Stay together, My children, in prayer— you will not have long to wait."*

Later, at Holy Hour, I saw a long tunnel underground. I received a message: *"My faithful servant you must help people prepare for the coming battle of good and evil. The demons will tempt many people and they will be lost. But My faithful must be strong and lead the weaker ones back to Jesus in the Blessed Sacrament. We must prepare now for we will need to be strong against the demons in the coming trials."*

Tuesday, October 12, 1993:

After Communion, I saw what at first looked like a huge flying saucer in the sky. I received a message: *"The city of God is coming. A part of heaven will be brought to the earth. Men will rejoice when they see My day. All will see themselves as resurrected people—young and in full health. This is the hope which mankind looks forward to in great expectation."*

Later, at the Adoration Chapel, I saw a picture of a rose and a glimpse of St. Therese. She said she was there so I asked her for a message: *"I have come on behalf of the children—especially those abused and those aborted. The Lord is very upset with your country for the way you treat His little ones. I am here to warn you a great chastisement will befall your country if they continue to despise His little ones. Please do what you can in prayer and deed to turn back this judgment."*

Wednesday, October 13, 1993:

After Communion, it took awhile but then I saw a hill going down and there were little flames near the top and it grew to larger flames near the bottom. I received a message: *"The clouds of evil are reaching high to heaven. The stench of sin is pervasive. Woe to you O inhabitants of the earth—your judgment is coming. Your sins are so many yet you do not even realize you are committing them. Your blindness is no reason to stem the punishment, for you have the words of Scripture and the prophets."*

Later, at the prayer group, I saw a picture of Christ with a crown and the words came: *"Christ the King is coming to declare His Kingship and the conquering of sin—paid for by His death on the cross."* Then I saw Mary coming with a crown and the words were: *"I come as Queen of the Holy Rosary in honor of the month of October which you have dedicated to me."* I saw a dove bright and flying in the darkness and the words came: *"I come as Divine Love especially to nourish the flame of love for God to those newly confirmed."* I then received a message from Jesus: *"You will have much to suffer as I did and you will defend My name with joy."* Later, as I said the "Crucifixion" decade I received: *"I am thanking you for your reverence in kneeling for this decade."* I then could hear three knocks and had an image of Jesus knocking on the door: *"Please let Me into your hearts."* Finally, I saw Mary's face in the dark from a distance and she said: *"I will not be with you much longer, pray, for my Son comes soon."*

Thursday, October 14, 1993:
At the Adoration Chapel, I saw some Gestapo looking cops dressed in black with guns. Then I had several side views of what looked like the demonic eyes of the Anti-Christ. I received the message: *"The Anti-Christ will have eyes which you should avoid. He will be able to hypnotize your thoughts and gain control of your mind. He will have demonic powers and you should hide from him. He and the men he will influence will seek out the faithful and try not only to kill the body but to steal the soul from God if they are not protected."*

Friday, October 15, 1993: (Feast of St. Teresa of Avila)
After Communion, I saw very vividly a picture of a nun but at times her face was hard to see. I asked her for a message: *"My Jesus has found favor with you and this is the reason for your visions. He is the Almighty and asks for our honor, praise and respect. He is the reason for our being for which we should be most grateful. My Jesus will soon be coming again. Prepare and be on the watch."*

Later, at the Adoration Chapel, I saw several mouths talking but I only saw the mouth not the rest of the faces. I received a message from Jesus: (my love for Him was very strong this night.) *"It is not what a man eats that makes him unclean. It is what comes out of his mouth that convicts him. (Matt. 15:18) Men should not spend so much of their time talking but instead should be praying. Instead of running after material goods you should be seeking things that will bring you to heaven. Seek first the kingdom of God and everything else will be given you. (Matt. 6:33) That kingdom now is even close as I speak."*

Saturday, October 16, 1993:

After Communion, I saw a young lady who I assumed was St. Margaret Mary (feast day). I then saw a picture of the Divine Mercy. Where Jesus was standing bright rays of light were coming from His Heart. I then saw a picture of Jesus on the cross. I received a message: *"Christ Jesus is the center of our lives. He died on the cross so that all men's sins will be forgiven and He enabled all of us to reach heaven. His crucifixion is the greatest example of His love for us. He is reaching out to us from His Sacred Heart at each Mass. That is why receiving Him in Holy Communion is our most intimate way of coming to know Him."*

Later, during Nocturnal, I saw a bright illumined huge cross high in the sky. It was casting a beam of light like a spotlight back to earth. I received a message: *"There will be a miracle of a Permanent Sign with the cross in the sky. It will be visible to all and it will be a supernatural event to witness God's presence on earth. Those of faith will praise it and thank God for this precious visitation. Others will refuse to believe in it and will hide their faces from it."*

Sunday, October 17, 1993:

After Communion, I saw Jesus standing in the sky in a large image with a huge golden glow behind Him. Then there were many people in front of Him looking up to Him. I received a message: *"I am the vine, you are the branches. Apart from Me you can do nothing. I am asking for your love, praise and honor. In return I will shower you with My infinite love and graces. I am asking you to be thankful for My act of creating you and being your Savior. In return, I will welcome you to heaven for eternity with a splendor beyond your wildest dreams."*

Later, at the Adoration Chapel, I saw a large candle and a bright flame. In the middle of the flame I could see a dove and I recognized a visitation from the Holy Spirit. I received a message: *"I am the Spirit of Love. I have come to bring you strength and understanding. We (Trinity) are pleased that you brought the children before us in the tabernacle. You are truly fulfilling your mission of bringing souls back to us. Continue in this work and encourage others to help win souls back to us. The people will need to be close to God, for the future trials will truly require strength from prayer."*

Monday, October 18, 1993: (St. Luke)
After Communion, I saw a cross with no corpus and some very modern images which may have related to New-Age symbolism. I received a message: *"New-Age thinking and non-traditional teachings are an abomination before Me. Heresies and false prophets are to be avoided. Many such temptations will be brought by the demons to distract you from your faith. But you are to read and trust the Scriptures. Pray for discernment and keep faithful to My teachings as written by the evangelists."*
Later, I saw some skulls and sensed there was death all around me. I received the message: *"There will be a stench of death all around you. Men who are not in the Book of Life will be tortured so that the living will envy the dead. They will call to the mountains to fall on them to avoid the pain. The demons will cause many to lose their faith and draw them to all kinds of perversions. My little ones huddle in your homes in your prayer groups and pray for deliverance through these times. My faithful will survive it if they have trust in Me."*

Tuesday, October 19, 1993: (St. Issac Jogues and Companions)
After Communion, I could see possibly a Frenchman in a colonial hat, some Indians and finally I saw two missionaries dressed in black habits. There was a sense of calling from the Ravine at Auriesville. I had a message: *"Once martyred we felt the freedom from the bondage of our sins. While we are on earth, we are constantly under siege from the turmoil of temptations. Then when you are with the Lord, everything is loving and peaceful. We are asking you of earth to be strong in prayer during your future trials where you may be asked for martyrdom. Remain strong in the faith and persevere."*
Later, at the Adoration Chapel, I saw bright gold rays spreading out from a central core. I sensed this was God the Father coming. I asked Him for a message: *"My people have become more like the Israel of old who have lost their way in the desert. The people of today are rudderless—they have lost their spiritual di-*

rection. *A man who builds his faith on sand will never survive the onslaught of evil. You must form a foundation of faith on prayer and fasting. Tell My people to prepare themselves, for evil will worsen dramatically.*"

Wednesday, October 20, 1993: (St. Paul of the Cross)
After Communion, I saw what looked like a bishop with a mitre and then had a quick glimpse of the Pope. I received a message: *"Shortly, you shall see the beginnings of a schism in the Church. As more of the tenets of the Pope's recent encyclical become known, there will be more dissension. Some bishops will refuse to follow Rome causing an upheaval in the Church."*

Later, at the prayer group, I saw a beautiful gold opening in the clouds representing God the Father. He said: *"Hear O inhabitants of the earth, soon my Son will be coming to you again."* Then I saw an image of the Immaculate Heart of Mary but her image started to fade. She said: *"My vision is fading because I will not be with you much longer. I have come to prepare you for my Son's Second Coming."* I then saw and felt Jesus' presence. He said: *"Walk with Me on your journey of faith and I ask you to make Me a part of your everyday activities."* I then saw an image of Al Bello, (a member of our prayer group who was in Medjugorje) and a picture of Our Lady and she said. *"I am watching over and will protect my son (Al)."* I next saw an image of the Infant of Prague crying. He said: *"The statues are crying because My people have become deaf to My calls and messages to pray. Many have a spiritual darkness in their heart and need to be enlightened."* I then saw a huge brightness in the sky and the Angel Gabriel came in glory and said: *"Rejoice, I bring you great tidings of joy. I, Gabriel, stand before God and announce to you Jesus is coming again."* Finally, I saw a beautiful picture of Our Lady of Guadalupe. She said: *"Your country continues to persecute the unborn. I say to you if enough prayers are said, I will remove abortion from your land."*

Thursday, October 21, 1993:
After Communion, I saw a huge image of Jesus and He said: *"My people, what am I to do with you? You constantly ask for signs and messages. Yet you have not taken to heart and practiced what has been given you already. As a result of your*

stubborness there will be a time when no messages will be given you. Then before the great evil testing begins, warnings will again be given you."

Later, at the Adoration Chapel, I saw cars driving down a busy street with all kinds of lights. Then I saw advertisements of many products. I received a message from Jesus: *"The glitter of earthly things has distracted many from a good prayer life. People allow the daily activities to tie them down to the earth too much. They must remember why they were put here. If men are so taken up with themselves now in the "Green," what will they do in the "Dry" of evil times. If men fail to kneel to My name now, they will be brought to their knees later when I visit them with disasters. I am directing you and others to do what you can to wake My people up to the true heavenly calling everyone should be aspiring to. They need to be encouraged back to prayer, Scripture and the sacraments-especially Repentance.*"

Friday, October 22, 1993:

After Communion, I was traveling through a very well-lighted tunnel and then it came to complete darkness. I received a message: *"You will soon be entering into an age of spiritual darkness but it will not last long. It will be a difficult time for the Church and the faithful since demonic powers will be rampant. This is why I have been preparing My people to be able to withstand this great testing-time of the earth. It will be the reign of the Anti-Christ and his powers will mislead even those elect who are not prepared. Now is the time to store up holy objects such as blessed candles, holy water, crucifixes with the corpus, Rosaries and scapulars—for these things you will need for your protection and they will be hard to find.*"

Later, at the Adoration Chapel, I at first could see only a large narrow cross. Then there was an awesome strong blue light which eventually materialized to Our Lady. She said: *"My Son is coming as an Innocent Child. He will come in great glory and every knee in heaven and on earth will bend in His honor. There will be a great testing-time. The reign of evil will test your faith to its breaking point. But you must rely on Jesus' help through this time. I have given many messages to My favored ones to warn the people to pray for what comes. Even now I am asking My little ones to continue preparing the people for the evil which lies ahead. Thank you for responding to My call."*

Saturday, October 23, 1993:

After Communion, I saw an image of a big green hill and at the bottom was a dugout door in the hill like some kind of underground house. I received a message: *"You have seen right. (I had some words earlier in the Mass about men's icy hearts). Men's hearts will turn icy cold to My love. Already they are apathetic, wandering on their own. In the future the demons will turn this apathy into hate for those who believe in Me. You will be tortured and chased because of your love for Me. Pray the days be shortened for your sake."*

Saturday, October 23, 1993:

At the Adoration Chapel, I saw many dark shadows—some looked like people, others I could not tell but maybe they were demons. I received a message from Jesus: *"The shadows are those who have died but have not yet been judged. Many are the lukewarm who do not realize what has happened. Other shadows are some demons whose numbers are increasing. I have allowed them this time and shortly they will come to power. My little ones, you must follow the messages and pray for guidance through this evil age. Call on Me, the Holy Spirit, God the Father, My Mother, your guardian angel or the saints to carry you through this time. We will listen to your prayers and protect you. Some will be martyred though. Peace be with you."*

Sunday, October 24, 1993:

After Communion, I saw a mosaic of Jesus on the top of the dome in a church. Then I saw Him with loving eyes in the skies among the clouds. I received His message: *"At My Second Coming when I come in glory, those who have followed My commands will taste of My dinner. My love and peace will so surround you that you will become a part of Me in heaven. Your minds cannot fathom the joy of love I have in wait for you. This is truly the culmination of your quest for love and peace in My Kingdom. But before you can enjoy the Resurrection you must endure your own Calvaries. Pray for protection during this time."*

Later, at the Adoration Chapel, I saw a car from the inside traveling the highway. Then I could see the streets of Washington D.C. and the White House. I received a message: *"Your government will be the first to bring persecution to the Church here in this country. At first through demonic power, they will drive out religious schools. Then they will attack and eliminate the churches. Gradually, they will even seek out those displaying any religious ideas. They will force you into hiding like the Jews under Hitler and even torture the faithful for sport like in Rome. But fear not, they will have to answer to Me and they will be judged severely. For your part, pray for all souls to be saved, for saving your soul will not be easy."*

Monday, October 25, 1993:

After Communion, I saw empty pews in the church. I received a message: *"What am I to do with My people? They have Me to receive in Communion everyday but only a few are there. Their love for Me is so distant. Their icy hearts have rejected Me. I tell you, what little My people have in the Mass will soon be taken away. People love themselves and their possessions more than they love Me. They will soon reap what they have sown when My judgment and disasters befall them. Tell the people to pray and prepare for they soon will have to give an account of their misdeeds and lack of love for Me."*

Later, in church, I saw a series of lights passing in front of me very close and they gradually formed a circling saucer-like object. I received a message: *"Yes, the warning is coming soon. This will be a frightening experience, for some may die from fright alone. It will be a supernatural awakening to show people their sins as I would see them. It will be a review of your life experiences in a twinkling of time. For some it will be the last chance they will have to come back to My love. Please encourage all to come closer to Me in prayer. For after this, they may be more open to your message."*

Tuesday, October 26, 1993:

After Communion, I saw a man with a pair of binoculars looking curiously for something. I received a message from Jesus: *"You will look but you will not see them, for evil spies will abound. In the coming time of Anti-Christ, his disciples will be seeking out the Christians to kill and torture. It will be an evil age when all will seem lost. But be faithful and keep in hiding for your salvation is near. Once the devil's allotted time runs out, there will be a triumphant reign of My peace and justice and the demons and accursed will be bound in the great abyss of hell."*

Later, at the Adoration Chapel, I was on earth looking up into a beautiful blue sky when it seemed like I was moving into dark space. There were some bright objects moving about the heavens. I received a message from Jesus: *"There will be a conjunction of stars as at the Star of Bethlehem. Only this time it will be a sign of the Anti-Christ coming to power. It will be visible to those on the ground and the astronomers will witness it to the people. From that moment, the demons will be loosed to roam the earth and they will trouble men's souls. Evil will increase in men as a result and the faithful will be tested severely. At that time, you will understand all My warnings and prayer will be necessary to save your soul."*

Wednesday, October 27, 1993:

After Communion, I had a vision of thousands of angels opening up the sky as they were getting ready for a big event. I received a message: *"The angels are heralding My Second Coming. For a New-Age is about to dawn on mankind. It has been promised since I was raised up from the Apostles. This will be a judgment time for all when each person's deeds will stand before Me. For those who have done My Father's will, it will indeed be joyful to share My banquet. But for those who did not follow My Father's will, there will be the gnashing and grinding of teeth as they are thrown in the fires of Gehenna."* (Matt. 5:22)

Later, at the prayer group, I first saw a hallway with the morning sunlight coming in. God the Father said: *"Awaken My people from your spiritual slumber. You need to have more prayer in your life to show how much you love Me."* I then saw a Bible open in front of me and Jesus said: *"My word is before you in the Scripture but few take time to follow My example in the Gospels. Take time each day to read a passage and meditate on how to incorporate that into your lives."* I then saw a funeral bier being loaded into a hearse. I received a message: *"We should remember we are here on this earth for only a short time. We are to follow God's will and use our talents for what God intended us to do. Then when we understand where we came from and why, it will be apparent where we are going—back to Jesus."* Mary then visited me and said: *"I want to thank my little ones for coming to pray this evening. I and my Jesus are greatly pleased. With your fervent prayer we will watch over your intentions."* I saw some children glowing before me as if the life energy was radiating from them. A message came: *"You are obligated to see that My little ones are taught the true faith. Their souls are your responsibility and woe to those who lead them astray."*

Thursday, October 28, 1993: (Sts. Simon and Jude)

After Communion, I saw what looked like one of the Apostles. I asked St. Jude for a message: *"We Apostles were asked by Jesus to go and preach to all nations of His word. You in your turn are also asked to witness your faith to others in deed and example. Pray to me as I am the patron for hard cases. The people of earth will be faced with evil you have yet to experience. Pray and take courage for the Lord will watch over His faithful ones during the coming distress."*

Later, at the Adoration Chapel, I saw some pictures of cities with huge skyscrappers. I received a message: *"Man's pride has raised many tall buildings much like the Tower of Babel. He has become so taken up with the material things of this world that he believes he need only depend on himself. He does not realize that he needs Me for survival. But soon he will see how frail his possessions are. For several cities will be brought low and what will they rely on then. When they are brought to their knees through disaster, they will learn the hard way that I am the center of their lives. I nourish My faithful and give them all good things for those who follow My will."*

Friday, October 29, 1993:

After Communion, I saw an angel of God arrayed in His glory and the word "Michael" was impressed in my memory. I asked him for a message: *"I am Michael who stands before God and I announce to you that Jesus is coming again to receive His people.*

Also, before that time the demons will be allowed several years reign on earth. But I am sent by God to strengthen you during that time. For I assure you, God will never let you be tested beyond your endurance. He will provide you with the opportunity through prayer to protect your soul through this evil time. Have trust in the Lord for He will always be the greater power. Give praise, honor and glory to Jesus."

Later, at the Adoration Chapel, I saw a dove of peace being killed by an eagle in the air. I received a message from Jesus: *"My people are not ready to fight the evil that will come. You are lackadaisical in your prayer lives. Some are even reluctant to be with Me only one hour a week. When the demons will come, there will be so many as to blot out the sun if they had material bodies. You forget they still have angelic powers and could deceive even the elect. This is why I call on you all to a constant life of prayer so you will have the spiritual strength to overcome these future temptations. Stay close to Me and you will save your soul."*

Saturday, October 30, 1993:

After Communion, I saw friends saying goodbye to several people at a train station. I received a message: *"I tell you, you should be ready everyday to meet Me at the judgment. For no one knows how much time each of you have left. All the more reason you should take care of your spiritual lives and keep them in constant preparation. This includes frequent Confession, prayer and fasting. For you are asked to be perfect through My grace as your Father is perfect."*

Later, at the Adoration Chapel, I saw Jesus at first in the clouds and then He was walking on the earth. I then saw very bright objects coming down to earth and they appeared to be angels ready to harvest the souls. I received a message: *"It is the harvest time for mankind. Soon I will send My angels to gather up the tares and weeds to throw them into the fire, while the wheat of good souls will be gathered into My barn. Before this happens you and others can help My people prepare with your messages. They will have to choose between Me or the demons."*

Sunday, October 31, 1993:

After Communion, I saw people at Mass. Then I saw Jesus at the altar with the bread and wine and suddenly He became dazzlingly bright light which was almost blinding. I received His message: *"I give you My Body and Blood under these appearances of bread and wine. This is My most precious gift to you—My own self. My Eucharistic presence is My real presence and demands your honor and respect. My Holy Sacrifice is shared among the whole communion of saints including all present at the Mass. Through this sacrifice all sins have been forgiven. My request is that you follow the will of My Father in heaven and everything will be given you."*

Later, at the Adoration Chapel, I saw a separation—on one side was total darkness. On the other side there was light and a garden much like in Eden. During the message I saw a deep abyss where souls were falling into hell. I received a message from Jesus: *"Life is a choice which must be made by everyone. Some will choose to do nothing, others will choose evil acts. But you must choose Me as the center of your life if you are to be worthy of heaven. Some will be selfish and will follow fame and riches. Those who give Me lip service and do not love Me sincerely, will arrive at the judgment and I will say: 'I do not know you for you loved yourself more than Me.' It is only through the gift of faith and a good prayer life that you will come to My love which waits for you unconditionally. Those who remember Me before men and Myself, will enter into heaven. All others will enter hell where the road is wide."*

Monday, November 1, 1993: (All Saints' Day)

After Communion, I saw Jesus suspended in the sky and all the saints were underneath Him giving Him praise. I received a message: *"I call all of My people to be saints. For My yoke is easy and My burden light. If you would but follow My Father's will in heaven, you could be saints with My grace. Listen to My call and keep Me close to you by faithfully receiving My sacraments— especially Repentance."*

Later, in church, I saw a cross with a very bright light and on the cross I saw roses aligned both vertically and horizontally. Then

I saw a brief image of St. Therese the Little Flower. She gave me a message: *"Jesus calls all of us to be saints. The flowers on the cross represent Jesus' great love for us that He would die for us. Jesus in His call for our perfection wants us to return our love to Him. He wants us to mirror that love to those around us to give witness to Him. He is also calling us in these end-times to be soldiers and struggle in prayer to fight the battle against evil."*

Tuesday, November 2, 1993: (All Souls Day)

After Communion, I was under water with a veil overhead. To the side of me was a dingy grey area where I could see part of peoples' faces—they had a cloth over their nose and mouth because of the stench. They too suffered from flames and could not see God. I received a message: *"These are the souls who were not purified enough on earth. They suffer like those in hell except that they have been promised heaven one day. You can make sufferings on earth help alleviate this torture later. Also, you can pray with the saints to diminish the souls' stay in Purgatory. Many souls cry out for help to their relatives on earth but those on earth do not think of them. Please ask all to pray for the poor souls, for when they are freed, they will not forget you and will return the help and more."*

Later, at the Adoration Chapel, I saw a sea of grey clouds and there were some heads struggling to stay atop the clouds. This appeared to be the top most part of Purgatory where souls were the closest to being released to go to heaven. I received a message: *"These are the souls who will be with Me shortly. They will receive the most benefit from your prayers and will also soon be able to repay you for your help. These souls can barely glimpse My Kingdom in the distance. Their pain is being so close to Me but can not yet attain My full comfort and glory. Please pray for all the souls in Purgatory and you will be storing up treasures in heaven. My Mother visits these poor souls on her feast days to relieve some of their intense suffering. Do not forget your own relatives who may still be here asking for your help."*

Wednesday, November 3, 1993: (St. Martin de Porres)

After Communion, I saw what looked like St. Martin helping some poor children. He gave me a message: *"Our Lord said 'the*

poor you will always have with you.' But do not become compla-
cent towards the poor—always be willing to reach out and help
those less fortunate around you. You must be willing to give of
your time as well as your money to your neighbors. Then when
Jesus comes and asks if you saw Him in the hungry, the naked,
the sick and those in prison, He will say 'since you did this for
the least in My Kingdom, you did it for Me—enter into My rest.'
But if you fail to help others and cling to your possessions out of
selfishness, He will disown you before His Father."

Later, at the prayer group, I saw several icons of our Blessed
Mother. She said: *"I am bringing you to my Son in all that I do.*
He is asking us always to find room in our hearts for Him." I then
felt and saw Jesus and He was carrying the Blessed Sacrament in a
monstrance. He said: *"I have given you Myself in the Blessed*
Sacrament so that I can be with you always to give you hope in
being with Me in eternity." I saw a vision of Pope John Paul II and
Mary said: *"I am blessing my Son (Pope) and leading him with*
my Jesus to guide My Son's flock through these turbulent years."
I had a vision of the computer simulation of "Virtual Reality." Jesus
said: *"Man has become so prideful in his own creations thinking*
science is a God in place of Me. Man will soon learn that his
reliance on himself will be an act of futility." I then saw a picture
of St. Joseph as he said: *"I come as a comfort for those who are*
dying and also for the many who will die in the coming evil age.
You will need prayers and heavenly help to endure it." Another
vision appeared of St. Joan of Arc with her sword. She said: *"Those*
who live by the sword, shall die by the sword. Man is constantly
killing each other much like Cain at the beginning. Peace can
only be achieved through prayer and the laying down of arms."
Finally, I sensed a red banner and felt the presence of the Holy
Spirit. He said: *"I am the Spirit of Love and I come to show thanks*
to your prayer group for its faithfulness through all these twenty-
two years. Your treasure in heaven will be great."

Thursday, November 4, 1993: (St. Charles Borromeo)
After Communion, I saw St. Charles dressed in black robes.
He gave me a message: *"I am appalled at the way people treat*
religion in this day. They have little root in faith and do not seem

to live it in their daily lives. The people should learn from the example of the saints to be more humble and less concerned with the things of this life. Jesus should be your constant focus and pleasing Him our everyday task. As a part of His Church we should strive to set people on fire for the love of Jesus."

Later, at the Adoration Chapel, I saw many unusual events and then the view backed-up and it appeared that I was seeing TV programs. Jesus gave me a message: *"TV programming in general is not giving My people good example. There is too much sex and violence which seems to be glorified by the viewers. This is leading My people astray and wasting time that could be spent in prayer. The 'r' rated rental movies also are an abomination and give scandal to your children. It might be better to avoid the TV and movies altogether. By not buying these evil things, it may discourage their sale. All things as these which distract you from Me should be avoided, especially when in excess. Keep your focus on Me in prayer and all good things will be given you."*

Friday, November 5, 1993:

After Communion, I saw the heavens split from the top and God the Father came forth in His glory. He gave me a message: *"'I Am' is not happy with His people's behavior. You have not sought out My help with your daily troubles. As a result you will wander about in confusion without direction and be susceptible to the temptations of the demons. I am giving you another chance with My 'warning' to realize your errors and understand you need Me for both earthly and spiritual survival. If you still continue to reject Me, many chastisements will befall you since there will be no reason not to know what is expected of you."*

Later, at the Adoration Chapel, I saw some hooded dark shadows with some eyes showing. Then I saw some with skulls showing. I received a message: *"The demons will continually be increasing in their numbers. Once they have taken over most of men's ruling positions, this will allow the Anti-Christ to gain control. During this time of hiding, prayer will be your constant weapon against the evil ones. The Rosary and blessed candles will be needed to survive. Many will be severely tested but I will be triumphant in the end."*

Saturday, November 6, 1993: (Joan Segrue Wedding)

After Communion, I saw a wedding couple and Jesus standing on the side. I received a message: *"Love is the bond which unites all mankind. My love for My Church is like the bond in marriage. My covenant with man is like that in the marriage contract—love forever. When there is love among My people, all creation is in harmony. When people are at odds, only war and strife will result. The love in the family is important since this is where peace starts—it is the basic unit of My people. For those who are married, love your spouse as I love My Church with unconditional love."*

Later, at the Adoration Chapel, I saw a dark sky with a row of doves and they all flew into a bright light. I could feel the presence of the Holy Spirit. He spoke to me: *"I am the Spirit of Love. I come to help you bring peace to the earth. Through your example of prayer and fasting continue to help bring souls back to Me. During the future evil times you will need to pray to Me for discernment that you can recognize faithful Christians apart from the evil impersonators. You will recognize your own with the mark on their foreheads—God's own elect. The others with the mark of the beast should be shunned for at that time they will be lost and a spiritual threat to you. Pray and be on the watch."*

Sunday, November 7, 1993:

After Communion, I saw a bright sun with clouds around the middle opening in the sky. God the Father spoke to me: *"Judgment time is coming soon. I love My people but they have given a deaf ear to Me. With signs, prophets, and My Son's words I have done everything in My power to bring My word of love to them. Still man persists in unbelief or ignores Me. If man would make one forward motion toward Me, I would forgive Him and give Him grace to know Me better. But I will not force My love on anyone, they must make that decision for themselves. But on that day when My Son comes, all those who are not ready will be sent to hell, while the faithful will be welcomed into My bosom."*

Later, at the Adoration Chapel, I saw beautiful gold vestments and very many gold cups and utensils. There were several bishops in different scenes but I was most dazzled by all the gold and brass. Jesus gave me a message: *"There are some of My bishops who are much taken up with the pride of their position and apathy in action. These are the ones who should be leading My people and showing them how to do My will. They should be encouraging a good prayer life and heavy use of the sacraments—especially Penance. But because they are not very active, many souls are going astray. The bishops and the people will be ripe for following the temptations of the evil one. I am therefore asking the strong faithful to offer much prayer and fasting to inspire these weak bishops and lukewarm Catholics. Bring back the former zeal for My love that they all should yearn for."*

Monday, November 8, 1993:
After Communion, I saw a huge church. Then in front of it in a row outside I saw gargoyles or faces like demons. I received a message: *"Your churches and Masses you will not have much longer. For the demons will grow in strength and eventually force the churches to close. At that time you may have underground Masses for a while, until the priests are also found. In the end of the evil age you will huddle together to say your Rosaries—this will be your only weapon against evil. This time will be short and My Kingdom will soon come in full glory for you to share."*

Later, at church, I saw a darkness, then the scene changed to a picture of a Jewish synagogue with the Torah scrolls opened. Jesus gave me a message: *"You (plural) are My faithful remnant—you who stay close to Me in prayer and who give Me honor and glory. God the Father, God the Son, God the Holy Spirit and Mary are most appreciative of your help. I rely on My close friends to teach the children and to give good example to the rest of My people. Please guard your faith from the evil one by constant prayer. The devil will be attacking My remnant even more in these days because He wants to destroy your mission of keeping My people strong. For I rely on you as I do My son John Paul II and My priest sons. You will not wait long My children for My glorious return. Be faithful and watch in prayer."*

Tuesday, November 9, 1993: (St. John Lateran)
After Communion, I saw a small church with a prominent cross on top of it. I received a message: *"I am happy this day that all My people see themselves as a living Church, for all of you make up*

My Body. This is why there should always be a cross with My Body prominently displayed on the altar. For if you identify yourselves with Me, you must also identify yourselves with the cross. I am the capstone and the cornerstone. I give you reason for living and becoming a part of Me. If you are close to Me, then pray constantly and offer up to Me all your petitions and cares of each day."

Later, at the Adoration Chapel, I saw a car driving in the road and it gradually speeded up and then ran right into a bright light. Then in another vision I saw a huge fire which engulfed the land I was seeing. Jesus gave me a message: *"Events will speed up dramaticly as the demons take power. Because of My people's sin and lack of prayer, there will be many chastisements sent to your land. You will be tested by fire such that it will seem like a raging inferno. Those houses where prayer is said constantly, I will protect from the flames—but woe to those houses that do not pray. The fires now in the west will pale in comparison to what will be coming. Some of this can be mitigated by prayer but not all. Start as many prayer groups as possible to stem the tide of the coming evil—for it will exact My justice. I love My people always and am waiting for your love, but the lukewarm I detest."*

Wednesday, November 10, 1993:

At church, I saw a large building and then a hole in the wall. It came to me that this represented the "Eye of the needle" Our Lord talked about in the Gospels. Jesus gave me a message: *"For the rich it will be almost impossible to enter into heaven unless they give up their lust for money. You can not have two masters. If you love money, you will not have room in your heart for Me. Riches and fame are fleeting in this life and useless at the judgment. You would be better to store treasures in heaven than on earth. For where you store your treasure is where your heart lies. Amen, I tell you I am your Most Precious Treasure. Find Me in My Kingdom and you will have treasure for eternity. So do not worry over the things in this world for they should not distract you from putting your trust in Me."*

Later, at the prayer group, I first kept seeing many crosses. Jesus said: *"The cross is your life. You must suffer as I did if you are to be My disciple. So do not complain at your testing but bear it in patience because it will become your salvation."* I then saw a man with a very grotesque face dressed as a Pope. Jesus said: *"A demon possessed bishop will gain power over the cardinals and will exile My son John Paul II. This will cause strife in My Church but keep courage."* I then saw an image of the Statue of Liberty and I received: *"Your spiritual freedom will soon be challenged. You will have to pray in private for religion will be scorned and even draw punishment."* I saw some bingo cards and received a message: *"I am sad, My children, that you must rely on man's greed for money to help finance your schools. You have seen My feeling toward the money changers in the temple. Your schools will eventually close because you have such little faith."* Our Lady came with a beautiful warm feeling and she was wearing a crown of roses: *"I come my little ones to comfort you in your time of trial. I bring my Son's graces to strengthen you for saying my Rosary."* I saw some robots walking rigidly and received: *"Do not follow men in what they do just to be liked by all. For I call you to a higher life of love and grace which do not follow the ways of this world. Be faithful to Me and consecrate your life to Me."* I then saw a beautiful light coming and it was Our Lady. She said: *"I am the woman dressed in the sun. I come as the new Eve to prepare you for a new creation when my Son returns. Pray constantly and be vigilant to save your souls."*

Thursday, November 11, 1993: (St. Martin de Tours, Veterans Day)
After Communion, I saw a soldier in very old days. I received a message from St. Martin: *"In my day soldiers were poor and had a hard life. I could see Jesus in all the people I encountered. Once I came to Jesus, I had to do everything possible for those faces of Jesus I saw. You all are called to be soldiers of Christ in the Holy Spirit. Do as well as I did at the tasks the Lord has directed you to do in His name."*

Later, at the Adoration Chapel, I saw some images of women movie stars and then I saw a movie going on in a theater on the big screen. I received a message from Jesus: *"Movies and entertainment should be selected carefully for its moral content. Movies over the years have degraded in morals. Sex and violence appears to sell well to most of the patrons. You have become like frogs slowly being boiled so that your hearts turn cold and you do not even realize when you do wrong. I tell you to pray for discernment and avoid immoral entertainment. All those connected with making the bad movies will be more liable to judgment since they benefit monetarily from corrupting men's souls. This is why recently some of their possessions have been taken from them—some in fires, floods or other disasters. They will taste My judgment most severely."*

Friday, November 12, 1993: (St. Josephat, martyr)

After Communion I saw a light shinning down on a man which looked like the saint for today, St. Josephat. I asked him for a message: *"Martyrs are truly with God in a special way. We love Jesus so much that the things and people of your life would not stop us from adoring Him. We were asked to give the ultimate gift of life back to Jesus. This is no easy decision for it takes great courage and grace from the Holy Spirit. I pray in the coming evil trials that the faithful will keep holy and if it be God's will for you to be offered martyrdom, that you stand up to evil and proclaim your unyielding allegiance to Jesus no matter what anyone will do to you."*

Later, at the Adoration Chapel, I saw a picture of our flag in the darkness and gradually it disappeared. Jesus gave me a message: *"Your country will soon lose its identity and its freedoms. This will come part as a punishment and part due to the reign of Anti-Christ. The demon forces will soon take control of the international forces. As a result national identities will be lost and the evil force will dictate food and work conditions. This is when the mark of the beast will be required for food and money. You must pray fervently to Me and God the Father for help in these times. Evil will so seduce the people that many will fall away from the faith, since they have little prayer life."*

Saturday, November 13, 1993:

At Mt Carmel House, a home for the dying, I was greeted by Our Lady of Mt. Carmel dressed in brown with outstretched arms. I also saw the faces of people who were those that died here. I asked Our Lady for a message: *"Service is what I ask from all my children to help their neighbors—especially those who are less fortunate than others. I want to thank all of these people present for all they have done for the patients. They truly have helped to prepare those who died to meet my Jesus. I have a special place in my heart for these workers who will receive a great treasure in heaven. For they have seen my Son in all the dying faces. They live the Beatitudes. When my people see Jesus reaching out through the poor, the sick and the dying, blessed are they who see to my Son's needs."*

Later, at Nocturnal Adoration, I saw a great darkness and a large flaming comet came across the sky. At the same time I saw a long underground tunnel with people inside. I received a message from Jesus: *"Your salvation is in sight. Soon you will see the bondage of sin and Satan's reign come to an end. It will be much like the exodus story at the time of the destroying angel coming to kill the Egyptian first born. This time My angels will come to carry out My justice on My people. They will slay the people without the Lord's mark on their foreheads—much like those saved with the lamb's blood. They will thrash the tares with a flaming sword, but My faithful will enjoy My eternal peace and glory."*

Sunday, November 14, 1993:

After Communion, I had a vision of the writing on the wall "Mene, Tekel, Peres." This comes from Daniel 5:25-28. Mene-means the days of our country are numbered. Tekel-we have been weighed on the scales of justice and have been found wanting. Peres-our country will be divided and given to another. A second vision was of a man swinging a sickle. Jesus gave me a strong message: *"Your country will soon be facing My judgment yet few are spiritually ready. More prayer is needed for the harvest is great but the laborers are few. There are many signs which already have been given. My Mother has pleaded with you many times—especially over the sin of abortion. Now is the time for action because you have very little precious time. Your mission is to bring My people back to Me in prayer. It is your responsibility to help carry this out in the best way you can. It is important to solicit as many as possible to help in this task. It will be difficult because of man's cold hearts. Through prayer and fasting this mission is your last before My judgment comes and I triumphantly return."*

Later, at the Adoration Chapel, the two lights over the Blessed Sacrament were out and it was a little dark. In a vision I could see a very luminescent cross in the sky which could be the "Permanent

Sign." Jesus gave a message: *"My light in the heavens is a gift to you. You have asked for a sign and a sign will be given you of supernatural origin. This is a grace and a strength to you for this evil age. It is a witness that My Mother's apparitions are true and not much time will be left before the chastisements come. Pray and give witness of your own on the apparitions to let My people know that I want them to return to Me before it is too late."*

Monday, November 15, 1993:

After Communion, I saw some lights coming in the distance as a train went by. Then it was like traveling closer to a light at the end of a long road. Jesus said: *"I am the light of your salvation. Everyone is drawn to My peace and beauty but only those who are My elect will enter into My presence. If you do My will and follow My life as written in the Gospels, then you will be My disciple. Then you can come into My light and enjoy everlasting peace."*

Later, I saw a huge door with very ornate markings on it and it was opening part way. Then I received a message from Jesus: *"This is the doorway to heaven. Every soul must come through this door if they are to enter. In order to enter you must prepare your spiritual life first. You should have frequent Confession, daily Mass and Communion when possible, and reverent prayers from the heart. In following My will you should also do many works of mercy for your neighbor who mirrors My image. If you do these things, the door will open freely for you. Others who are not the elect, will be refused since I will not recognize them from their lack of prayer."* After this message the door opened and I saw a very brilliant blue light and Jesus came to greet me wearing a crown. There was an instant feeling of joy and peace which I could not forget. Then the image ceased.

Tuesday, November 16, 1993: (1st Reading Eleazor martyred)

After Communion, I had a vision of a prisoner being brought down a long hall. Then I saw an executioner with a big axe striking down in front of me. I received a message: *"All of you at times are called to witness your faith in front of others—to stand up for your beliefs even though it might not be popular. In the coming evil age this will become more of a reality and your life may even*

*be threatened by the evil-inspired people who will be in control
for a time. Pray to the Holy Spirit for inspiration in what to say
and have the courage if asked to even die for your faith. You will
be a powerful witness to all the faithful around you."*

Later, at the Adoration Chapel, I saw about ten children come
running toward me. Then Jesus gave me a message: *"Send the
children to Me for I love them in My presence. You all are the
caretakers of My little ones who are so precious to Me. See to it
that they are taught the faith and are led to the sacraments. You
must come to Me as children with childlike faith—without wor-
rying about how men will think of you. But woe to those who
abuse or mislead My children, they will pay severely. The unborn
too should be protected for your country's sin of abortion weighs
heavy against you. Again I ask, come to Me like little children so
I can fill you with My love and peace."*

Wednesday, November 17, 1993: (Feast of St. Elizabeth of Hun-
gary)

After Communion, I saw a young girl kneeling and radiant
with love. I asked her for a message: *"The poor are a gift to you
by Jesus. They are a test of our selfishness of our time and wealth.
Jesus has directed us to help His people in their distress. It is up
to us to carry out His will and do what we can for the less fortunate. For in helping others we will gain a reward in heaven.
The things of this world are to be freely given and not hoarded.
Jesus gives us many gifts and He in turn expects us to share
them with others."*

Later, at the prayer group, I first saw Mary come in a vision
which seemed like a reverse image as in the Holy Shroud. She said
*"I come to lift my children up in their inner spirit in their hearts.
You must protect your spiritual life with daily prayer and leave
your hearts open to listen to my Son's will for you."* I then at the
"Nativity" decade was visited by my son David's angel (He died in
infancy): *"I represent your son David and he sends his love and
asks you and your family to pray to him for daily help in your
troubles. He is celebrating all births especially Jesus' coming at
Christmas."* I then saw Mother Cabrini whose feast day was Saturday. She said: *"I too as St. Elizabeth have a deep love for the poor
and the helpless. I come to send you my help and invite you to*

return to my shrine in Denver. There are more graces waiting for you at my spring." Jesus came and gave me a vision of a priest. He said: *"Pray sincerely for more vocations to the priesthood. Without enough prayer and encouragement of souls, it will be difficult to have more priests sent to you. You will need them more dearly in the coming evil age."* I had a vision of St. Michael the Archangel. He said: *"I am coming to help all those who pray to me to support you through these trying times. With my help and your prayer I will protect you from the demon powers."* I received another message from the Holy Spirit: *"I am the Spirit of Love and I come in Christ's image to shower your prayer group with graces and My gifts. Pray to Me often to lift up your hearts to God always."* My last vision was Jesus showing me a scene with President Clinton and Jesus said: *"Your country is in danger from leaders who are leading you astray on many moral issues. Pray for your country and for your leaders that they will follow God's ways instead of man's ways."*

Thursday, November 18, 1993: (Dedication of St. Peter & Paul Basilicas)

After Communion, I was distracted at first but before the Blessed Sacrament I had a vision of what could have been a bishop or clergyman with strange green glowing eyes as if demon possessed. Jesus said: *"There are evil-intended bishops and cardinals already infiltrated in My Church. They are the ones influenced by demons who are sowing seeds of dissension. There will as a result be many rifts among the clergy in defilement of the unity I desire for My Church. I urge you to pray for your priests and bishops that they will not go astray."*

Later, at the Adoration Chapel, I saw a picture of the Pope with some great celebration. Then I saw snakes slithering around the altar and the statues. Jesus said: *"The Holy Father is being tested both physically and spiritually by some evil clergy around him. They are keeping him from fulfilling his mission to lead the Church in unity. They will try hard to remove him from office either attacking his health or claiming some false scandal. By exiling him they hope to replace him with a man called the 'Black Pope' who will be possessed or influenced by demons. Pray for the Holy Father and the unity of the Church in Me."*

Friday, November 19, 1993:

After Communion, I saw a priest in the sanctuary standing behind some flowers and the flowers faded away. Then the priest was saying Mass later. Jesus gave me a message: *"You will not enjoy the Mass much longer for it will be taken away. Men will slowly fall away from religion as their hearts grow colder to Me. As religion falls in disfavor, the government will harass the churches till they close. As the evil age approaches they will even seek out the priests to kill them. You will be left only with your Rosaries to pray to your Father in heaven. Prepare and be ready to keep faithful despite men's evil intentions toward you."*

Later, at the Adoration Chapel, I saw the universe with many stars and Our Lady started coming to the earth through the stars and gently landed on earth. She gave me a message: *"My little ones I come as a loving Mother to caress and nurture you back to good spiritual health. I love you all and I do not want to lose even one of you to the evil one. But I have given you many messages and signs and still many of the faithful do not believe. People have become so taken up with the world that they have forced my Son out of their hearts. As a result I can no longer hold back my Son's judgment destined for your country. Please pray to keep the faithful remnant close to my Son. Strike out where possible to save as many souls as possible with your prayers and your example. I am at your side to help bring you my Son's peace. Please follow His will for your life."*

Saturday, November 20, 1993:

After Communion, I could see many people with big long binoculars staring forward. Jesus gave me a message: *"Your lives will be intruded and watched by government officials. Your privacy will be invaded. People will be so controlled financially that their decisions will be few. This is why religion in the future will be so controlled. For many will be more concerned about survival than have room for Me in their hearts. With a lack of prayer I will bring them to their knees at their own hands. They will flounder about until they realize without Me they can do nothing. So pray to keep close to Me and save your soul."*

Later, at the Adoration Chapel, I saw Jesus on the cross and the next scene I saw a tremendous inferno behind the cross. Jesus gave a message: *"I detest sin in all its forms but most of all from those sinners who have no remorse. The reason for the flames is to witness many souls are going to hell. If they saw hell and the result of their sins, it may be different. But these condemned sinners are lusting for the things of this earth. They worship this earth and have no regard for Me who died for their sins. Because they have chosen not to repent, their judgment becomes final. Their sins are murder, abortion, fornication, rape, incest, robbery and many others. Please have people pray constantly to make reparation for so much sin in the world. The scales of My justice are far outweighed by sin over those praying, fasting and offering up their pain to Me. The chastisements as a result will be coming to purify this earth to make it a new creation."*

Sunday, November 21, 1993: (Christ the King)

In church, I saw Christ in a crown on His throne. Then the scene changed to Jesus walking forward with outstretched arms. He said: *"Those who want to be first in My kingdom must be the servant to all My people. I have shown My love for you the most by My death on the cross for your sins. A friend has no greater love than to give up his life for his friend. By My example of helping the sick, the hungry, the dying, all that are in physical or spiritual need, please do as I do in your own life. By helping others you will store up treasures in heaven. As the Church year closes, I am asking you to think of how you are readying yourself for the final judgment. I love all of you and am urging you to pray constantly to keep in touch with Me. Your journey of faith should be an ever increasing love for Me and an understanding that this is why you were put here on this earth."*

Later, at the Adoration Chapel, I saw a picture of Jesus in the crib as an infant with a brilliant light spreading out from Him. Jesus gave me a message: *"I am coming again more than just at Christmas. For My Second Coming will be sooner than you think. But before I come, there will be an evil testing-time. For as I had to endure My Good Friday, you too must meet your own cross before you can see My Resurrection. I need many souls to hold up My faithful remnant during these trials. You will be asked to lead souls back to Me and guide them through this time. Pray and keep a close watch on your spiritual lives."*

Monday, November 22, 1993: (St. Cecelia)

After Communion, I at first had a tingling feeling of a spiritual presence. I saw a picture of St. Cecelia and asked her for a message. At first I sensed a 'no' answer and I was unsure what was happening. It appeared Jesus wanted to give me a message so St. Cecelia gave way. Jesus said: *"I am bringing this message so you can realize its importance. There are fewer and fewer of My faithful sending up prayers for making up reparation for sin. Many of My stalwart souls have passed to the grave and they are not being replaced. Fewer young people are as faithful to prayer now. It is therefore important to ask for more prayers than ever. It is like a need for love—as giving to a blood bank. Please make My wishes known to My people."*

Later, I saw tall flames with some demon faces and I was told this was hell. Jesus said: *"Time is short to save souls for many are falling into the flames of hell. The materialism of this world is worshiped like a God instead of giving Me the glory. I have told you many times of the danger of living just for this world alone. Without Me you can do nothing of lasting consequence. You cannot take anything from this world into eternity so any attempt to love these things are futile. I am the center of your life and living to follow My will is your only purpose on this earth. So pray, keep close to Me, and bring souls to Me."*

Tuesday, November 23, 1993:

After Communion, I saw the outline of the forty-eight states and a great fissure broke it down the middle of the Mississippi River. Jesus gave a message: *"Your country is like the kingdom of iron which became divided. Because of your preoccupation with materialism and your insensitivity to abortion, your kingdom also will fall under the weight of its own sin. You have brought your own destruction upon yourselves since you have lost sight of asking strength from Me. If you put your trust in Me as on your coins and as your forefathers, your blessings would continue. But as it is you have depended on yourselves only so now you will reap the whirlwind."*

Later, at the prayer group, I saw Mary coming in the sky and she said: *"I played a significant role in my Son's first coming and even now I am also acting on His behalf to prepare you for His*

Second Coming. Watch and be ready." I then saw a picture of Jesus as an infant. He said: *"You can see My face in all infants as their innocence shows forth their image of Me, their creator. Protect these little ones from abuse and you will be loving Me in your actions."* I saw many angels coming forth in a golden yellow light. They were praising God as Jesus was coming at Christmas. I then saw a picture of Jesus in a crown of thorns. He said: *"My Kingdom is seen most through the pain My people suffer and the pain I continue to suffer for men's sin. Do not waste your pain—offer it up in reparation for sins."* I then saw a picture of a priest and he was very joyous. Jesus said: *"Pray for My priest-sons for they are going through great stress during these times. Also continue to pray for vocations that men will want to offer their lives up to Me."* Mary again appeared and she said: *"I want my children to know that they receive many graces from me at all my places where I am appearing and have appeared. I only ask that each have faith in my Son as I bring His message to my people."* My last vision I saw many people looking up into heaven. They were praising God for sending a supernatural miracle.

Wednesday, November 24, 1993:

After Communion, I saw from the bottom of the cross looking up at Jesus on the cross and His glory was flowing out and His Father was receiving Him. Jesus said: *"At the appointed time everyone will have to die and face their judgment before Me. It will be a summation of their life's struggles. For what you will have done on earth will judge whether you are worthy of heaven. At the final judgment the goats will go to the left into the abyss of hell while those judged to be lambs will enter into the eternal bliss of My Heavenly Kingdom. For this is why I came into the world that My dying on the cross will save you and you will have life to the fullest."*

Later, at the Adoration Chapel, I saw Mary with the Infant Jesus and she said: *"I am coming with Jesus in preparation for Christmas. I have a deep love for all my children. My Son on the cross directed all of you to be my children through the disciple John. I treasure this task that I should look after and help my little ones in bringing you to my Son. I am constantly looking for ways to keep you close to my Son. Through the Rosary your prayers are sending bouquets of love which pleases my Son very much. Keep faithful and thank you for responding to my call."*

Thursday, November 25, 1993: (Thanksgiving)
After Communion, I saw looking up a church aisle and the priest was raising the Host. Jesus gave a message: *"I give you My Body and Blood in the Eucharist for which you should be most grateful. Today is a day to be most thankful for the many blessings I have bestowed on you. Your life, your faith and the many close friends and relatives should be your most treasured gifts before the things of this world that are secondary. The freedoms you enjoy also are a blessing but with increasing sin they may be fleeting. Giving your prayers up to Me would be a most fitting thank you from you. For a good prayer life is a most treasured prize."*

Later, at the Adoration Chapel, I saw a picture of reindeer pulling a sleigh and Santa Claus. Jesus gave a message: *"I am not pleased how men concentrate on the material things around My feast days such as Christmas. Giving gifts is praiseworthy but not in excess and not when the shopkeepers take advantage of it. The focus should be on giving glory to Me on My Day of Incarnation—not on material things which do not give glory to God. You need to have your spiritual priorities in better order. Prayer and things of heaven should be more important than the things of this world which will never last."*

Friday, November 26, 1993:
After Communion, I saw a bare wooden cross with bones and skulls around it. Jesus gave a message: *"I see 'dead men's bones' in your future. Many of your people are not ready to die but one day you all will be judged. For if you are not spiritually ready to die, you also will have trouble living in this life without Me. If you do not recognize Me before men, I will not recognize you before My Father in heaven. I say to you if a strong man knew an enemy was coming, he would protect himself. Likewise I tell you to be on the watch for I will come when you least expect it."* Jesus is telling us to be constantly prepared to die because we never know when our life will be required of us.
(PERSONAL BELOW)

Later, at the Adoration Chapel, I heard a wind and I saw a brilliant light circling slowly and finally it stopped at an image of a dove representing the Holy Spirit. He said: *"I am the Spirit of Love and I come to give you My gifts of knowledge, courage, and fortitude. You will need to be strengthened because men will test you on your messages. But I will give you what you are to tell them. Your messages are indeed sent by Godly intervention and are not just your imagination. You are being given these gifts in thanksgiving for your many years of keeping close to Jesus. As for the messages, they will be publicized at a future appointed time which you will know later. Keep close to God in prayer and continue to follow His will."* This was in response to my spiritual director's request as to why these messages were being received.

Saturday, November 27, 1993:

After Communion, I saw a bare cross at first being carried forward and later on the altar I saw a cross with the corpus on it. Jesus gave the message: *"You cannot adore the cross without My Body on it. For those who want to follow Me, they must pick up their cross of pain and bear it with Me. You must carry it all the way to Calvary and be sacrificed on the cross with Me. By enduring your long suffering you will save your souls. For only through pain and prayer are you cleansed of sin and made humble enough to be a part of Me. I long to have you with Me and I ask that you carry this burden of life just for a while and then you will experience a reward you will treasure forever."*

Later, at the Adoration Chapel, I saw some objects going by me at a very fast speed. Then I was in a car traveling with traffic through a lighted tunnel. Jesus said: *"Today, My people are moving about at too fast a pace. With such haste men are only taking time to get by in life. They are not making enough time for prayer or time to listen to Me. At the beginning of your day, offer up your every action to Me as a prayer throughout the day. Then I will be at your side through all that you do and you will be following My will for you as well. Also, I am here to help you if you would but ask. I will answer your prayer in time if it is in your best interest. So take time out of each day to show your love for Me and you will be rewarded."*

Sunday, November 28, 1993: (1st Sunday of Advent)

After Communion, I saw a Star of Bethlehem with some emphasis of a cross in the star. Jesus said: *"O come My people, return to Me while there is time. I again am coming in the Christmas celebration but also not long I will be coming the last time in the Second Coming. I love My people as one big family and I ask your families to pray together. Now, more than ever, I am asking for constant prayer. Advent is a great occasion to get people more focused on prayer. So be on guard, pray and be watchful for no one knows the exact time of My return."*

Later, at the Adoration Chapel, I saw a moving picture of Our Lady coming down to earth from the sky with a bright light around her. She said: *"I come to prepare my little ones to receive my Jesus during this Advent season. You should make a special effort to be close to my Son in prayer. The closer you get to Him, the closer you are to heaven. In addition to prayer I ask you to help one another especially those in need of food, clothing or shelter. For in helping the needy you are helping my Son. Continue consecrating yourselves to my Son and follow His will for you."*

Monday, November 29, 1993:

After Communion, I saw a very narrow and spindly looking cross with no corpus. Jesus gave a message: *"My people how weak is your faith in Me. This thin cross before you represents the depth of faith a good share of the people have. For many their faith in Me is almost superficial. They struggle to Mass on Sunday out of habit and then rush to their cars as if they cannot afford Me any more time for the week. These lukewarm Christians are the ones in severe need of prayers. They need to be more deeply rooted in My love. In the end, if they are tested, they will not withstand the trials because of their weak faith. Those who continue to give Me lip service will be shunned at the heavenly gate for they really do not know Me."*

Later, I saw a picture of a flame on the Advent wreath. Jesus gave me a message: *"I come as a flame of love burning brightly and wanting you to be a part of this flame. This Advent you need to nurture the flame of faith in your soul with prayer. If care is not taken, it can be snuffed out by neglect or apathy. To keep your faith burning, reach out to others to spread My love and My word. In that way the light of Christmas will glow even brighter in unison with the Star of Bethlehem."*

Tuesday, November 30, 1993: (St. Andrew, Apostle)

After Communion, I saw an older man with a beard who represented St. Andrew. He said: *"All of you and myself are called by baptism to be Jesus' disciples. We are personally invited by Jesus to be His ambassadors of His word to the rest of His people. You should take this calling seriously and do what you can by your example and instruction to bring the faith to others. You, personally, are being gifted to bring an even better understanding of Jesus' message to His people. Please pray and keep close to Jesus so from strength you will be able to go out and preach His message."*

Later, at the Adoration Chapel, I saw a picture of a bishop at a distance and then the scene turned dark so that I could hardly see him. I could not identify who it was. Jesus had a specific message: *"Be on guard My faithful ones for some of My shepherds are like wolves in sheep's clothing. Some are misleading My people and are conspiring against My son John Paul II. They do not always follow the Pope but do as they please. The strong faithful will need to pray for discernment to understand their errors. The Holy Spirit will help you and I will lead you also to the true faith untainted by misinterpretation of My Gospels. Be watchful and pray for the bishops that they will be true to Me."*

Wednesday, December 1, 1993:

After Communion, I saw a vision of Christ coming forward in a crown of thorns and the words "Christ Crucified" were impressed in my memory. Jesus gave a message: *"My sole purpose for coming into the world was to be crucified and die on the cross so that your sins would be forgiven and you could have the right to enter heaven. This is why I am coming at Christmas as a perfect act of love and to follow My Father's will. For concern for My people is all consuming. I have made you in My image and I care for your every need. All I ask is that you accept Me into your hearts and make room for Me in your lives through prayer. Then through the eyes of faith you can thank Me by your praise of My glory in heaven. I am asking you to come to Me every day of your lives."*

J. JESUS T.
SUMMONED THE
TWELVE AND
BEGAN TO SEND
THEM OUT
TWO BY TWO.

Later, at the prayer group, I saw a picture of Mary with child on the donkey traveling to Bethlehem. She said: *"I traveled long ago to bring Jesus to the people of David in Bethlehem. Now I travel again to earth to bring you my Son at Christmas."* Again I saw Mary at the crib scene holding her hands out to me. She said: *"As I cared for my Son's needs as an infant I am reaching out to you also to help you in your trials on earth."* I then saw a picture of Jesus as a young boy teaching. He said: *"I will confound the wise and raise up those with childlike faith. Be humble and give your life to Me."* I then heard some angels come from heaven. They said: *"Joy to the world your Savior comes. Prepare and make ready for your visitation is at hand."* I then saw an hourglass and the sand was running out. Jesus said: *"Your time is slowly coming to a close. Many signs of My coming have been fulfilled. Read the signs in the heavens and pray to be delivered from this evil age."* I then saw a boarding house with some lights on inside. Jesus said: *"I am asking you to make room for My homeless. Shelter those whom you can and you will be making room for Me also."* Finally, I saw a branding iron in the furnace with strong flames around it. Jesus said: *"You will be branded for Me with a cross on your forehead for all those that are faithful. In this sign you will see those who are true to My word and can be trusted."*

Thursday, December 2, 1993:

After Communion, I saw shoes of people walking. Jesus said: *"In order to have compassion on others, imagine walking in the shoes of them and try to envision the problems they are going through. Imagine just a little the rejection I went through while on earth—how I was hurt by the people I came to save. You yourselves will suffer rejection when you believe and proclaim My name. But be at ease, your faith will be your salvation."*

At the Adoration Chapel, I saw a bright light and it showed up a heart. Then I saw Jesus coming with His Sacred Heart showing: *"I come in joy for My people as they prepare for My great feast of Christmas. People have an extra sense of love and hospitality at this time. I would love it to continue throughout the year as well. I have a deep love for you and want to put My arms around you (plural) and hug you. I would like to keep you from evil influences but I give you free will so that you can freely choose to return to My love. Keep close to Me so when the last trumpet sounds My glory, you will be ready."*

Friday, December 3, 1993:

In church, I had a vision of looking down from a building to see a cobblestone road with people walking by. The next scene I was on the ground looking up at a castle. Jesus gave a message: *"My Kingdom is before you on earth since I created it with very delicate detail to everything in it. Everything was in harmony before Adam's fall. Now, after the fall, things are in disarray and the hate of man is visible in many ways. Even though man has abused My Kingdom, it is not too late to make amends and change his ways. But, for change to occur, man must accept Me as his Lord and Master. He must see that without Me he can do nothing. So by either the hard way by experience or through faith, man will come back to Me if his free will so chooses. I ask you all to pray for each other to build up your spiritual strength."*

Friday, December 3, 1993:

At the Adoration Chapel, I saw a picture of a man in clothes of an older day. St. Francis Xavier agreed to give me a message: *"I am a missionary for Christ and it was Christ's words 'go and preach to all nations' that I took personally. I too felt strongly that my mission was to bring back souls to Jesus. This in essence should be everyone's mission but only a few carry it out. You have a very appropriate missionary land here in the United States for they have many distractions to tempt people away from Christ. Many prayers will be needed to soften the hearts of this stiffnecked people. Keep up your prayer efforts despite your time constraints. It is worth every moment that you spend in prayer."*

Saturday, December 4, 1993:

After Communion, I saw an older priest whom I did not know. Jesus gave a message: *"My priest-sons are always My life-blood to My people. For they are the ones who bring Me to you in the Eucharist and the other sacraments. This is why they are so precious to Me and should be to you. Treasure your priests for the graces they bestow you through Me. They are acting in My place on earth. So I tell you pray for your priests because they are under constant attack from the evil one. Also, pray for more vocations since their numbers are dwindling. With more prayer, you will also be more deserving of receiving more priests."*

Later, I saw an old man with a long beard sitting alone. Jesus had a message and the words came *"The poor and the lonely."* He said: *"I come this Advent season to ask your help especially for the poor and the lonely. In this time of family and friends, those who are alone are tested dearly. Please visit and comfort anyone who is alone for they are starving to be joined with My Body the Church. Also, the poor are in need of your help always. Those who have everything and give gifts from their excess may expect gifts back. But if you give to the poor, they can not pay it back and you will receive a reward in heaven. Pray for all My people, for everyone suffers their own trials. Give comfort to all you meet and share My love with them."*

Sunday, December 5, 1993:

After Communion, I saw God the Father calling down from heaven to His people in the desert. Jesus gave a message: *"I am calling out to My people who seem to be lost in the desert of life on this earth. At times you seem to be without direction, but I come to give you that direction through prayer. By focusing your life on Me and following My will for you, you will enjoy life with a deeper sense of inner peace. Once you are one with Me, you will no longer be anxious over the things of this world. For you will understand how your future life in heaven will be eternal joy with Me. Pray and join Me this Advent in greeting Christmas with love for everyone."*

Later, at the Adoration Chapel, I saw some bells in a church tower and I sensed the word *"Bethlehem."* Jesus gave a message: *"I was born poor in a lowly stable in Bethlehem. We did not have much but we shared a good life in love. It is not necessary to have many riches to survive. And you will not be judged on how successful you were. You will be judged though on how you use your talents for the glory of God. Do not be like the man who buried His master's money, but do My will in using what I have given you. It is important to realize your real purpose is to love Me and help your neighbors. Pray often to gain strength for this life long work."*

Monday, December 6, 1993:

After Communion, I saw a red-colored sky at the dawn. The words a *"New creation"* came and Jesus said: *"With each Christmas I give you a new creation, the beginning of a new era. This celebrates the New Testament because it is an enrichment with love and a fulfillment of prophecy from the Old Testament. The prophecy in Isaiah of the Messiah's coming was brought to life in My first coming. And even more meaningful to you, I will be coming again shortly as foretold in the Gospels. So be ready and pray for your Deliverer will come on a day you least suspect."*

Later, I saw an ornate cabinet and in it was stored the "Torah." Jesus gave a message: *"I have made a covenant with My people in the days of Abraham that I would be your God and you My people. I now renew that promise at Christmas as I come to reveal My promise that the Messiah will save His people. I have made a new covenant with you through My Eucharistic presence in the bread and wine. In this new covenant there will be the forgiveness of sins through My death on the cross. With My presence given to you I also offer you My peace. For this is one of the themes of Christmas—peace on earth and goodwill to all men. In appreciation of My gift to you I ask you for your gift of visiting Me before the Blessed Sacrament."*

Tuesday, December 7, 1993: (St. Ambrose feast day)

After Communion, I saw a bishop in a red vestment holding a staff. St. Ambrose gave a message: *"I too have struggled to bring souls back to Jesus. This is a life-long work all of us should be participating in. My personal experience with Augustine was a delight in my eyes. Bringing him to the faith was fulfilling the Gospel in bringing home a lost sheep for Jesus. Augustine went on to be an inspiration to the rest of the faithful. This is the reward of leading people to Jesus. They become on fire with Jesus' love and want to share it with others. This fits in with Advent as we help others to greet Jesus at the crib of love."*

Later, at the Adoration Chapel, I saw the entrance to a dark tunnel and then the word *"Unknown"* came to me. Jesus said: *"Do not be anxious about tomorrow for today has enough troubles of its own. Many people are taken up with frivolous concerns. I say to you put your priorities in perspective and weigh your spiritual life first. Then you will see that to keep your prayer life in order should rank first. I wish to comfort My people in this time of Advent and have everyone happy for My feast of Christmas. So put away your complaints and whining and concentrate on the beauty of this feast by being at peace. Be joyful and others will be happy with you."*

Wednesday, December 8, 1993: (Immaculate Conception feast)

After Communion, I saw Our Lady coming dressed in white with rays of light shining forth from her Immaculate Heart. She said: *"I am the Immaculate Conception, the new Eve who through my Son brought you your salvation. My obedient 'yes' is your inspiration to follow the Lord throughout your life as my example. Please continue to pray and be faithful to my calling for you to stay close to my Son. I am the Virgin foretold by the prophets who will usher in a new era of the Lord's promise of redemption. Thank you for responding to my call."*

Later, at the prayer group, I first saw Our Lady come dressed in black. She said: *"I am dressed in black because I am sorrowing for the sins of this country which is dedicated to My Immaculate Conception. Pray your people will see their errors."* I then saw a saintly woman who revealed herself as St. Ann. She said: *"On Mary's birth we dedicated her to our Lord at the temple.*

Only later did I learn of My daughter's gift of no original sin." I then heard some singing of *Silent Night* especially *"...round yon Virgin Mother and Child."* Then the words of Ahaz were given: *"I will give you a sign a Virgin will conceive and bear a Son."* I then saw some crosses and Jesus said: *"You have received your new cross. Wear it in faith. You all should take up your crosses of life and bear them patiently till I return."* I then received a vision of St. Joseph. He said: *"The Virgin Birth from the Holy Spirit was my trial before men. But I bore it joyfully since our Savior was brought into this world."* I then had a vision of a gold light overhead and there was a huge ring of angels looking down. They were preparing to celebrate the Lord's coming at Christmas. My final vision was that of Mary wearing a crown in the splendor of heaven. She said: *"Men have added a crowning touch to my Son's bequeathing me of no original sin by accepting as dogma my Immaculate Conception. Thank you for the many Rosaries you are sending me this night."*

Thursday, December 9, 1993: (Blessed Juan Diego feast)

At Holy Name of Jesus after Communion I saw a bishop's miter and a shroud of cloth was being held out before him. I asked the bishop for a message: *"I was pleased by Our Lady of Guadalupe for having visited me with her miracle of roses and the image on the tilma. This was an inspiration to the Indians around my diocese. Our Lady was presented with child and she was fighting the practice of killing infants at the time as offerings. Even in your country abortion still cries out for prayer and Our Lady's help. Pray to Our Lady and Jesus that people will see the value of life over their comfortable living."*

Later, in church, (Fr. Newcomb was laid out in state at night) I saw a cross of light on the altar and Jesus gave a message: *"It is good that you are here to celebrate My priest-son's passing away. I love My priests so much it is like loving a part of Myself. They bring you ever so close to Me through the Eucharist of the Mass. My priests give Me so much pleasure in the devotion of their lives to Me. How beautiful it is to have them lead My faithful. I am so overjoyed with them it is so hard to express it to you in earthly terms. But their spiritual value is immeasurable. So I ask you*

*again to pray for your priests, especially the ones dearest to you
and whose Masses you attend."*

Friday, December 10, 1993:

After Communion, I was out in space looking at the blue globe
of the earth. I could see several layers of red and then there were a
lot of demons that descended on the earth. Jesus gave a message:
*"At the appointed time, the demons will attack the earth. But fear
not these abominable things will happen, for I will protect My
faithful. Some will be martyred. The layers of red are the demons
who will be unleashed from the various levels of hell. Their coming down to earth will be at the time of the Anti-Christ. The demons will claim their own. This will be part of the purification of
the earth. Then those close to Me will be brought forth to enjoy
heaven on earth with no death or sickness. Pray that you will not
be tempted to follow the demons for you must choose Me or them."*

Later, at the Adoration Chapel, I saw a white light and a fainter
blue light in the distance. Then I began traveling through a tunnel
with the two lights at the end. Gradually, I came before Jesus with
Mary at His side. Jesus said: *"Everyone will pass through this
way some day in their life. It will be their judgment day. It is good
to make people aware that this waits in store for them. That is
why I encourage everyone now to prepare their spiritual lives.
Keep close to Me in prayer and come to the realization that to be
in heaven you must give your will over to Me. So when you come
to heaven you will be prepared and you can intimately become a
part of Me as all the saints and angels are. It is a beautiful, peaceful place with no more worries or troubles. All your time will be
eternally appreciating My gift of existence to share My glory. For
all I have will be yours—infinite love, knowledge and a sharing
with all the community in heaven. No more pain, sickness or death,
just eternal splendor in My Beatific Vision. Pray that as many
souls as possible will come to Me and believe. Be evangelists and
save souls from everlasting pain in hell."*

Saturday, December 11, 1993:

After Communion, I saw Father Jack saying the Mass and he
was seated in red vestments. Jesus said: *"I come to you in the*

breaking of the bread in the Eucharist during the Mass. This is a special gift of My presence to those who are worthy and do not have mortal sin. This is a permanent memorial until I come again in judgment. It is a time when I become a part of you through the body of My Church and you become a part of Me when you give your will over to My will. It is good that you go to Confession at least once a month or more often if you commit a mortal sin. Please avoid the sin of sacrilege. If you have mortal sin, do not receive Communion for this is a defilement of My Sacrament. So pray and keep close to Me and you indeed will be worthy of Me."

Later, at the Adoration Chapel, I saw a picture of Jesus dead on the cross and then the next scene I was seeing Him laid out in the tomb. Jesus gave a message: *"Winter is the season of preparation. If the seasons are thought of as your life, then winter is the time to think of dying. Many people die suddenly or are not spiritually ready. I tell you during this winter think of how you can prepare for your death. Would you change your life much if I told you that you would die soon? So take advantage of the time you have with praying to store up treasures in heaven. Also, good works will help in this matter as well. So go through life prepared spiritually to die every day. Then you will not be caught unaware, if I should come just for you or at My Second Coming."*

Sunday, December 12, 1993: (Feast of Our Lady of Guadalupe)
After Communion, I saw a beautiful vision of Mary and then later a picture of the Guadalupe image on the tilma. Mary gave a message: *"Peace, be still. I am coming to comfort my people and make way for my Son at Christmas. Put aside your fears and anxieties for the peace of my Son will come around you if you listen for Him. My people are too taken up with your worldly things and are missing the point of Christmas—my Son's coming. Years ago man was also concerned more with physical comforts than His spiritual welfare. I came on Tepeyac Hill to free my children from their killing of the infants. I come again to witness against those killing their babies even today. Now they have given up the babies for the gods of materialism and financial gain by the doctors. Soon a punishment will be coming for thwarting my Son's plans for these unborn. Pray that His fury*

will be eased. Also, pray and help these potential mothers to have their babies and not kill them. If not, they will live to regret their decisions."

Later, at the Adoration Chapel, I saw some bright lights shining down from heaven. I then received the words: *"Woman dressed with the Sun."* Our Lady gave me a message: *"Continually I give the same message, John —pray, pray, pray. Still my children do not listen or understand. They do not realize without prayer they cannot communicate with my Son. If they do not open the door of their hearts, my Son will not force Himself on them. His love is ever-waiting but you (plural) must make the first step. My Jesus is becoming impatient with people's attitude toward their creator. People will have to choose between the things of this world or the things of heaven. So pray My children and see now the value of your prayer over wasting your time with the distractions of this world. Prepare your hearts to receive my Son at Christmas as He comes to you."*

Monday, December 13, 1993: (Feast of St. Lucy)

After Communion, I saw a statue of a young girl and she admitted to being St. Lucy. She gave me a message: *"Jesus came to me as a light in the darkness. I grasped His light for my own so I could be a witness of faith to those around me. Martyrdom was all I could offer my Lord that best showed my love for Him. In this way I became a light for Christians of my day. You (plural) too can be a light of faith to your fellow Christians through prayer and sacrifice."*

Later, I saw many arrows and they all pointed toward Jesus. Jesus gave a message: *"Christian men and women need more direction in their spiritual lives. Too often members even within the same faith are at odds over interpretations of Scripture or traditions. I call on all My people to strive for unity in their meetings and beliefs. If helping each other is one way to please Me, then getting along and accepting all should be your goal. Now in Advent peace and friendship should be uppermost in your thoughts in preparation for Christmas. Please pray for each other that all men will strive to live in harmony together."*

Tuesday, December 14, 1993: (St. John of the Cross)

After Communion, I saw a man with a long bushy beard in Carmelite brown clothes. St. John said: *"I had a hard life but it was of my own choosing so I could offer it up to Jesus. He was the center of my life and I tried to model my sufferings after Jesus' acceptance of His trials. The earthly things of this life should not distract us from following our spiritual destiny to be with Jesus after this life. So I urge people to build an inner strength in prayer to keep ourselves humble before Jesus and adore Him as much as possible in the Blessed Sacrament."*

Later, at the Adoration Chapel, I saw Jesus on the cross and the cross was moving forward. Flames were behind the cross and souls were being drawn out of the flames to follow Jesus. Jesus said: *"The cross will set you free if you pick it up and follow Me. I am talking of freedom from sin and its punishment. Many see a weakness before men if they honor the cross. You have to humble yourselves before men and not let pride or earthly distractions keep you from Me. Even though you want to have full control over your lives, it is giving your will over to My will that should be your goal. When you do what I will for you, it will do your soul more lasting good and lead you to heaven. Pray that you will listen to My calling and keep close to Me in faith."*

Wednesday, December 15, 1993:

After Communion, I saw the Holy Spirit in the shape of a bird in flight then later hovering as a bright white dove. He said: *"I come as the Spirit of Love at Christmas bringing the spirit of light with Jesus. I have brought the Savior to Mary through My power. I am the breath of life to Jesus the Babe of Bethlehem. The darkness of Adam's sin is now shattered with My grace and the light of My coming with Jesus. For we are one as we bring salvation to all mankind. This is the reason for celebration at Christmas time. Offer up your prayer of thanksgiving to God for sending His Son to be with you."*

Later, at the prayer group, I saw the Holy Spirit coming again as a dove. He said: *"I come to bring the spirit of My love to the world at Christmas. The love of God for His people is personified with the coming of Jesus to forgive their sins."* I then saw a vision of the earth and a stream of light or graces was coming down to the earth and focused on Mary with the angels as she conceived Jesus. He said: *"I came into the world to dispel the darkness of sin and give My people hope and love to bring them back to Me."* I then had an intuition reference to the Revelation that talked about Satan trying to devour the child from the Lady dressed with the sun. This was to emphasize how Herod tried to kill the Baby Jesus but the Holy Innocents had to pay the price. Then Jesus gave a message: *"I am bringing My Kingdom to earth at Christmas to start My reign and victory over sin. You shall know that evil cannot blot out My light and My will shall prevail."* At this time the vision was of the Three Kings who brought their gifts to honor Jesus' kingship. They brought frankincense to give Him adoration of His glory. They brought gold which represented the lasting of His promise to forgive our sins always if we repent. They brought Him myrrh which represented the burial ointment in anticipation of His death. Then Mary gave witness of her birth of Jesus. She said: *"I give glory and thanks to God that He has allowed me to be His handmaid in bringing my Savior into the world. Our hearts are like Siamese twins with one heart that can never be separated."* I then saw the angels bringing the shepherds and their lambs to Jesus at the crib to honor Him as the Good Shepherd who accepts all of His children.

Thursday, December 16, 1993:

After Communion, I saw a vision of Jesus sitting on His throne wearing a crown and the picture of heaven was filled with jasper and all kinds of gems and beauty as described by John (Rev 4:3-6) in the Book of Revelation. Jesus said: *"My Kingdom comes at Christmas. It is open to all who want to believe. I am calling all My faithful to awake from their lives of sin and follow My will for them. With prayer and repentance they will share in My banquet table. But woe to Him who refuses My invitation for it would be better that He was not born, since He will be condemned to hell fire for eternity. So embrace My love and receive Me willingly and I will not disappoint you but shower you with grace and peace you have yet to experience."*

Later, at the Adoration Chapel, I saw large billowing clouds of smoke from some huge fires—possibly a large war or oil wells burning. I also had a feeling of imminent disaster coming. Jesus gave a message: *"A grave war with possibly a large size will occur shortly in the Mid-East area. The clouds you saw involve large forces at war and if enough prayer is not said, it could involve atomic weapons. War is a punishment for sin and men in this area are having increased hostilities toward each other. If men cannot live peaceably together, then war is inevitable. Pray for peace to minimize the effects of this war for it could spread into a world war with so many angry camps of men wanting trouble."*

Friday, December 17, 1993:

In church, I saw an outline of the continent of Africa very clearly. Jesus gave a message: *"The area you have seen in the vision will be a hot-bed of activity in the future much as it has been. Men are continually fighting each other even as I come at Christmas to bring you My peace. Peace has been elusive because there is too much greed for power, money and material possessions. Until men realize these things are not important to their final resting place, turmoil will continue. Men have brought all of their problems among themselves and need to ask for My intervention for real peace to come about. Continue to pray for peace since little prayer is coming for this cause."*

Later, at the Adoration Chapel, I saw like a partially visible stairway to heaven. Jesus as an infant was being escorted by angels to Bethlehem. Jesus had a message: *"I am coming as an infant with peace and innocence. The angels are rejoicing as man should be. This was and is today the beginning of your redemption with My Incarnation on earth. I am personifying your sin and offering it up to My Father who now will see fit to forgive you. I am asking all of you at this time to help and comfort one another so peace will reign in every household. If you start working on peace at home, this will help towards affecting world peace. If you could increase your prayers for peace, this also would help. So this Christmas make this effort to greet My peace with your own peace contributions."*

Saturday, December 18, 1993:

After Communion, I saw a flow of snow and it was melting. Jesus gave a message: *"As I come this Christmas I still see many cold hearts who are still ignoring or rejecting Me. I come to melt these hearts with My love. You can help in the reception of My love by being cordial to these cold hearts and praying for them that they will be open to receive Me. In the end more will be invited to visit Me at My crib and those who accept My call will be rewarded with My graces to strengthen them through the trials of earth."*

Later, at Nocturnal Hour, I saw children playing with toys. Jesus gave a message: *"I am asking you to bring the children before Me at the crib. See to it they are brought up in the faith so they can know My love for them. For I call all My people of all ages to come and visit My peace so I can forgive their sins and receive them back purified like innocent children. For indeed unless you humble yourselves as little children you cannot enter into My Kingdom."*

Sunday, December 19, 1993:

After Communion, I saw a Scripture book open and someone was reading it. A Scripture verse came as Luke 4:18-21 "The Spirit of the Lord is upon me because He has anointed me; to bring good news to the poor He has sent me; to proclaim to the captives release, and send sight to the blind: to set at liberty the oppressed, to proclaim the acceptable year of the Lord, and the day of recompense. Today this Scripture has been fulfilled in your hearing." The significance of the last statement is especially felt at Christmas-the fulfillment of the Messiah. Jesus said: *"I am the Word of God. I have come that man may have light in the darkness. For God has visited His people and know that before you came to be, I loved you. My love is overflowing and at Christmas I come radiant as ever to share My peace and embrace you with My love. Receive Me as you would receive your King in splendor and glory. For though I come humbly in a manger, it is to all of My people that I bring salvation of your souls. Give thanks to God that this is wonderful to behold."*

Later, at the Adoration Chapel, I was seeing a partial vision of Our Lady—she kept disappearing. She said: *"I will not be with my visionaries much longer since I have already given you warning of my Son's coming. This Christmas is important for mankind to prepare for the many trials to come. As for your friend do not be disappointed if it is my Son's will to take her. I bring you my Son's love since our hearts are as one. Pray for peace in your world to greet my Son with hope. He will conquer all in His good time. Thank you for responding to my call."*

Monday, December 20, 1993:

After Communion, I saw Mary coming and then I saw the angel Gabriel kneeling before her. Mary said: *"Behold I am the handmaid of the Lord be it done to me according to your word. These are the words I announced to tell of my Son's First Coming. Since that time we have been of one spirit. I do my Son's will in everything He asks me. Even now I am fulfilling His request to prepare you for both His coming at Christmas and His Second Coming. Jesus is everything you would ever want to experience. He is perfect love. Once you know of Him, you also will want to please Him always and do whatever He tells you. So pray now that you will follow His will and become a part of Him. Thank you for responding to my call."*

Later, at the Adoration Chapel, I saw golden clouds and what appeared as God the Father in the clouds. He said: *"This is My Divine Son, listen to Him as He comes to you. I love My people as does my Son. It is His witness and example I send you to have hope and know how to live a life that pleases Me. I have sent my Son as a fulfillment of My first covenant with the Jewish people. He has brought salvation and forgiveness of the sins of all— Gentile included. With My gifts of love and forgiveness I only ask that you repent and accept Me as your God. In that way I may give you all your heart yearns for. Keep praying regularly to continue your strength to follow Me."*

Tuesday, December 21, 1993:

After Communion, I saw an elderly lady who greeted me. St. Elizabeth said: *"Blessed was I on that first Christmas that my Savior and His Mother visited me during my trial. For when the babe leapt in my womb, I knew then my Savior was coming to greet me. It was a special experience I will forever treasure. Now the Lord comes again at Christmas for you. Be joyful and thank Him for the many gifts He has given all of you. Mary brings Jesus to you so tenderly—listen to her calling and obey her Son. For Jesus is calling all of you back to Him in repentance for sin and to share His love with you."*

Later, at the Adoration Chapel, I saw some lights in the heavens and then saw a swirling galaxy and the beauty of the planets. Jesus gave a message: *"I am King of the Universe. My love for you is so immense that I have come down to be a human and have died for your sins. I would have died even if there was only one human. If you were to imagine yourself coming into a dog and could not speak, you can begin to understand a little of how much I love you. To take on your pain, sorrow and human trials was My way of showing you My understanding of your human condition. So I come through My love and graces at Christmas to lift you up to a higher level of being and help you understand how beautiful the place is that I am preparing for My beloved. I keep asking only that you pray and give your will over to Me. When I receive you, you will have such peace that nothing else will matter but My love."*

Wednesday, December 22,1993:

After Communion, I saw a heart-shaped object and then Jesus gave the message: *"My love is all-consuming. At Christmas the angels sing of My glorious coming to earth each time. It is a celebration of My love for mankind. I want to envelop all of My people with My graces and show them how much I love them. If people would just take a moment to thank Me, I would visit them with My gift of love they could feel. But love needs two parties— you must make the effort to receive My love in faith. Once you accept My will, heaven will await you."*

Later, at the prayer group, I saw a picture of Mary at the crib kneeling before her Son. She said: *"I present my Son every Christmas as a constant gift to His people for their salvation. You should be grateful for His condescension in becoming a man."* Then I also saw St. Joseph looking at the crib from the opposite direction. He said: *"My parentage of the Christ child was under question but my lineage to David was meant to be. I committed myself to bringing up my Savior in the best way I could."* Again I saw Mary this time holding Jesus in an icon. She said: *"Behold my Son. We come to show you the road to heaven through prayer and love of God."* Jesus was next seen in a picture receiving the children. He said: *"I receive you as children of God guided by My Mother. My love reaches out to you to warm your hearts so that love will make this world desire peace."* I then saw a huge red sun dawning and Jesus said: *"Each Christmas is the dawn of a new chance for you to appreciate My love for you. I call out every year at this time hoping you will grasp My light and that you will see My way is the only way for you to reach heaven."* The angels came as we kneeled for the "Crucifixion" decade. They said: *"We are the sentries who stand guard at all the tabernacles and Masses where the Body of Christ is present. We thank you for your reverence of Our Lord at the Crucifixion—it is indeed sacred."* I then saw Mother Cabrini holding a wooden crucifix. She said: *"Your country is in great need of prayer for there is little thanks being given God for the many gifts He has given you. You have squandered His blessings so I ask you to pray hard to make up for the many indifferences to Jesus."*

Thursday, December 23, 1993:

After Communion, I saw the desert and received the words "Herald in the Desert." St. John the Baptist gave the message: *"I am a herald in the desert. I come to announce the Lord's coming both at Christmas and when He will come again. My message to repent then still applies now in a world where people have forgotten the word sin. When the evil one can make people believe there is no evil or sin, then there would be no reason for a Savior. But as it is O happy fault, sin entered the world by Adam. But Jesus comes at Christmas to dispel the darkness and ransoms our sins with His Body and Blood. So prepare ye the way, the Lord comes again."*

Later, at the Adoration Chapel, I saw a half moon symbol with a face and a word came "Witchcraft." Jesus gave a message: *"There will be an increase in evil about you. For many will fall into the spell of the evil one who will sell them material goods for their souls. As a result these evil people will work for evil and persecute My faithful. Be on guard for these events and prepare spiritually to resist them. For they will test your faith even with martyrdom. Pray to Me and the angels for spiritual protection."*

Friday, December 24, 1993:

At the Adoration Chapel, I kept seeing a house on a hill and the vision zoomed in more on the house. Jesus gave a message: *"I am coming to Bethlehem now at the manger in a stable. This coming is the beginning of your salvation. The importance of this stable then makes this like a house on a hill for all to see God's glorious gift to mankind. This same house may also be a representation of your future home in heaven as My death on the cross allowed this for you. Be thankful therefore of this most precious gift of salvation. I am also asking all My faithful to pray more for peace and conversion of souls to heaven. Put aside your earthly distractions and spend more time in prayer so you can better use your time for both your benefit and the souls being prayed over."*

Later, at midnight Mass, after Communion, I saw a vision of Christ on the cross coming down to earth. Jesus gave a message: *"I come to bring salvation to all men by My death on the cross. My coming to earth was the start of your redemption story for this was the sole reason for My coming. My love for you continues to draw Me to My people and offer forgiveness of their sins. By repenting of your sins you humble yourself to be open to Me. I continually ask you to follow My will because I know the weakness of your human condition. Only through prayer and sacrifice can you stay close to Me and realize your destiny is to be with Me in heaven. But by your free will you have to choose to follow Me. Otherwise you will wither and die as does the branch without the vine. So be joyful on this Christmas for I offer you heaven if you would but make room for Me in your hearts."*

Saturday, December 25, 1993: (Christmas)
After Communion, I saw Christ as the Infant of Prague dressed like a King. Jesus gave a message: *"I come as King of My Kingdom on earth in splendor and majesty. The angels are announcing My arrival. I bring all of you My peace and love forever unconditionally. I bring you My presence now and in My love I instituted the Eucharist so I could always be with you in My Sacrament. Treasure My true presence in the Eucharist you receive at Mass. Visit and adore Me in My presence in the Blessed Sacrament kept in all the tabernacles. Pray and give thanks to God for the many gifts I have given you."*

Later, at the Adoration Chapel, I saw the Star of Bethlehem shining and Jesus came down from the star. Jesus gave the message: *"I am the Light of the World come down from heaven. I come so My light will pierce the darkness of sin. My light shines brightly to strengthen My faithful and give them hope in this evil age. I am the word of God who was and is still being rejected. My word is life for your soul. Those who receive My word receive Me and My Father who sent Me. Pray and spread My word to all willing to hear it and take it to heart. For many are called but few are chosen."*

Sunday, December 26, 1993: (Holy Family Sunday)

After Communion, I saw a vision of the Holy Family of Jesus, Mary and Joseph. Jesus said: *"I come in My Holy family today to greet all My people and to encourage all families. We are representing a model or example for all families to follow. As a child I followed My parents' wishes in accord with My Heavenly Father. Only when My mission called, did we separate. But I still respected and helped My parents when the need arose. So also your families should respect each other and live in harmony. Today the family is coming under much attack and abuse. Pray for families to stay together and avoid divorce. I still treat homosexuality as an abomination and liable to Gehenna. Correct your fellow Christians in these matters when necessary in the discernment of the Holy Spirit."*

Later, at the Adoration Chapel, I saw some family members working together. Jesus gave a message: *"I come to comfort My families and lead them to My peace and love. Family members should work together and help each other. Avoid fighting and criticizing each other. Instead pray together and look for opportunities to encourage communication and understand each other. By working to create harmony in the family, your family can contribute to world peace. Continue to follow the example of My Holy family."*

Monday, December 27, 1993: (St. John the Apostle)

After Communion, I saw a book which looked like a Scripture book and then a picture of a young man that could be St. John. He gave a message: *"I am John the one whom Jesus loved and I come to ask all of the faithful to be apostles. By your baptism you are given a priestly role to evangelize those around you to Jesus' promises. Look to Jesus who has come at Christmas to spread*

His word by your example and teachings to others. In doing so you will share in the one mission of the Church to save souls. Pray to Jesus and the Holy Spirit for direction in your lives."

Later, at the Adoration Chapel, I was out in space and could see ballistic missiles flying ready to strike the ground. Jesus gave a message: *"World War III hangs in the balance as a punishment for men's sins. The clouds of war and hatred are getting darker. Men are not praying enough for peace—on the contrary, they increase their greed for power and prestige. Until men humble themselves and pray to Me to restore order, wars will continue and will get even worse. Without Me you can do nothing to stop these events. So send many prayers up for peace and harmony or you will reap the whirlwind of war."*

Tuesday, December 28, 1993: (Holy Innocents)

After Communion, I saw an altar and a man was standing holding a sword to the ground. Jesus gave a message: *"Beware of those wolves who come dressed as lambs. Their outward appearances show them as crying 'Lord, Lord' but inside they are plotting evil intentions. They speak to Me with their lips but their deeds are abominations. The plottings of men to afford their own comfort comes at the expense of other's lives. Many times the weak and defenseless are abused by those in authority who flaunt their power over men. But I tell you they will receive a just reward for their crimes. The angels of the unborn stand before Me witnessing the murdering of today's innocents. These sins are crying out for justice and shall be avenged. My people will bring punishment on themselves when they reject Me and I leave them to flounder by their own devices. I urge you to pray and make reparation for the many offenses being committed in your country."*

Later, at the Adoration Chapel, I saw rockets going through the sky. Then planets or round bodies were passing. It seemed like a dramatic state of chaos. Jesus gave the message: *"Your punishment that I have held off is about to befall you. I am warning you to prepare spiritually and physically. You will need much prayer and fasting to endure the next four years. Wars, insurrections and evil will prevail for a time. But I will protect you if you call on Me. Your petty problems will pale in comparison to what will come. Now is the green time but shortly the dry trying times will begin. The faithful should stay together to help each other. These coming end times have been prophesied in the Scriptures. Blessed is he who reads the signs of the times. The visions you saw are a foretaste of the bad omens in the sky. Pray constantly for you will need to be strong during this time."*

Wednesday, December 29, 1993:

At the prayer group, I first saw Our Lady as a young girl. She said: *"I come as the Mother of my children as announced by my Son to John from the cross. I wish to guide and care for you in leading you to follow my Son. I thank you again for your many Rosaries this evening."* I then saw Jesus as a young man teaching in a synagogue. He said: *"This new year I ask you to make some prayer intentions. Assign a time each day so that you can make prayers of petition or thanksgiving. Be faithful to a prayer regimen to protect your interior life with me."* I then saw St. Michael the Archangel with his spear coming to earth. He said: *"The Lord has commanded me to come and protect and lead you in the coming battles with evil. Prepare your arms of prayer, fasting and repentance."* Jesus again gave a message as I was seeing a picture of a calendar: *"This is an important year coming which will see many prophecies fulfilled in time from many visionaries."* I then saw a proverbial "Couch potato" sitting on a sofa with a crown on his head. Jesus said: *"My people have become very comfortable and have insulated themselves from the world's problems. I tell you to move out of your comfort zone and reach out to help others in need. Go the extra mile with your friends to provide your time, talent and money for them."* Another vision was like many battle shields coming together in constant wars. There will be much strife over the hatreds of man. A final vision came of a young nun, St. Therese the Little Flower. She said: *"Our Lord has asked you many times to help your neighbor. So now I echo that call to visit the sick, visit the imprisoned and grieve with the families of the dying. In this way you will store up treasures in heaven for the life we are awaiting."*

Thursday, December 30, 1993: (Jeanie Memorial Mass)

At 6:00 p.m. Mass, after Communion, I saw Jeanie alive and moving and she was dressed in a black blouse. She gave me a message through her angel: *"I am happy to see all my friends are here. It is very heartwarming. I want to thank you and Carol for being such great friends for me. I also want to wish my family and friends well through you. I especially want to thank Father Dave Bonin for his wonderful eulogy—it was inspiring. I want you all to know this place I am in is such a beautiful light and peace that I could not even begin to paint it. God has been so gracious to me. I thank you and will pray for all of you."*

Later, at the Adoration Chapel, I saw some gold colors and I saw what looked like the image of God the Father I have seen. He said: *"I love My little ones. You are like My precious sons and daughters—the apple of My eye. I love all My creatures and especially man since I made Him to My image with free will. Sometimes man has problems choosing to adore Me but you have to come to Me by your own choosing. As you consecrate yourself to Me you can become a part of Me even while you are on earth. I am happy to receive you whenever you can make time to pray and talk with Me. Make a habit of keeping close for lovers need to see each other often. I am asking you to be strong and pray for strength for this coming year."*

Friday, December 31, 1993:

After Communion, I saw the letters "St P" and then saw the floor inside of St. Peter's Basilica and realized St. Peter wanted to give a message. He said: *"Greetings, my fellow Christians. I am speaking to you as the first Pope directed by Jesus to spread His Church to all nations. Many of our people are at odds over petty quarrels in the Church. Only Christ should be most important and what He wants us to do on earth. That is, we are to do His Father's will and keep His commandments and evangelize those who need the faith. You are to follow only what Christ taught— not other misinterpretations which the evil one is trying to put in place. So pray, My children, to follow the Church faithfully this new year."*

Saturday, January 1, 1994: (Solemnity of Mary, Circumcision)

After Communion, I saw physically a ray of light come in the church and shine through the Station of the Cross of Our Lady with Jesus on His way to Calvary. I then had a vision of Our Lady in her peaceful beauty. She gave a message: *"My Son's birth comes as your gift of salvation. He lowers Himself to be a man so He can take on your sins and allow you to enter into heaven with Him. All of you are sent here to be reunited with Him in glory. At the temple I was told a sword of sorrow would pierce my heart grieving for my Son's death. But it was meant to be to forgive man's sins. You yourself will go through a sorrow of having to give up your control over your body and the things of this world to become one with my Son. In order for you to get to heaven, you must lose your life and be consecrated to Him and give Him your all."*

Later, at the Adoration Chapel, I saw a few glimpses of a young woman and Jesus but mostly I saw a bare cross. Jesus spoke a message: *"I have come to free you from your sins but right now I want to emphasize My peace and love. This is a time of joy when I became one heart with My Mother. She gave birth to Me as a man and has not ceased trying to bring her children to Me. We have a close loving relationship that has never changed since. Today, I want to share this love with all My people for I yearn to have all of you with Me in heaven. But I will not force My love on you. I ask you to pray much to understand your part in My plan for all mankind. You all are being called to a higher life than this on earth."*

In church, I saw angels coming down to Mary and there with Mary was the dove representing the Holy Spirit. He said: *"I am the Spirit of Love and I witness to the Incarnation of Jesus by My overshadowing of Mary. At the moment of conception I was one with Jesus. Later, at birth I am still one with Jesus and Mary. This is an event that happened once in time yet lives on outside of time. Where Christ is, God the Father and Myself are also. This Christmas season I inspire people with love for the Infant Jesus. I also help those inclined to believe to have a deeper faith and love for God through prayer. Receive my breath of love in your hearts and continue to praise God."*

Sunday, January, 2, 1994: (Epiphany)
After Communion, I saw the Three Kings riding on their camels. Then at that time the star seemed to come right down into my face and the light blotted out everything. Jesus gave a message: *"Receive Me into your hearts for I am being manifested to you this day. The Magi and the shepherds adored Me and brought Me gifts. I am the King of this earth and over everything in the universe. It is appropriate that everyone praise Me and give Me adoration. I ask you (plural) now to come forward and give Me your gifts of heart, mind, and soul. In doing so I will welcome you to be a part of Me. Your salvation will be My gift to you. Then you can share My love in the peace of heaven forever."*

Monday, January 3, 1994:
In church, I had the words 'Mother Seton' in my mind and had some flashbacks to Emmitsburg. She did give a message: *"The poor are always in need of your help. Make a little effort to notice them more and look for ways to help them. At the least you can offer them prayers and some donations. Do not begrudge them help since you are really helping Jesus through them. Your attitude to giving of yourself should be positive because you never know about the fortunes of this world. You could find yourself in a poor position one day and be thankful for someone's help."*

Later, at the Adoration Chapel, I saw a woman, whom I did not know, laid out at a funeral. Jesus gave a message: *"You should try to stay in a state of grace always for you do not know when I will call you to judgment. Be always prepared to die on any given day for I will come as a thief in the night. Those who commit mortal sins should seek Confession as soon as possible. Unless there are some unusual circumstances of My mercy, most souls called home with mortal sin will be sent to hell. So be on guard and go to Confession often to stay prepared. If someone loves you and you do them an injustice, you are quick to ask forgiveness. So also, do this with Me, the one you love. I do not want to lose even one soul. You are too precious to be lost. So pray to stay close to Me."*

Tuesday, January 4, 1994:

After Communion, I saw a cup as at Mass representing the Eucharist and it came closer into view. Jesus gave a message: *"I give you My Body and Blood in My real presence in the bread and wine. This is My most precious gift to you in every Mass*

where I am offered. This is My memorial to you to show that I am always with you. When you receive Me in Communion we are spiritually joined as one—even more perfectly than the angels. So treasure this opportunity and receive Me as often as possible—but only without mortal sin. The image of spreading the bread in the miracle of the loaves and fishes witnesses My great love for all My people to be loved and taken care of through My overflowing generosity to you."

Wednesday, January 5, 1994:

After Communion, I sensed Our Lady was there and the crib scene again came into view. She said: *"My Son comes with His great love for all His people. He loves you with an unconditional infinite love because He is love personified. He wants to receive you as often as you can greet Him. In your everyday situations ask Him to be a part of your life. He will help you in everything you ask Him. His love is so consuming, He wants to be with you always. Receive Him in Communion as often as you can and greet Him in your tabernacles or where He is exposed. My Son is a gift to you so take advantage of His graces and help."*

Wednesday, January 5, 1994:

At the prayer group, I first saw a beautiful angel in 3D color—very clear. I then had the feeling it was my son David's angel. His message: *"I am happy to be with you again to give you encouragement on the eve of my birthday. Since I have seen you, you have grown more in the understanding of Jesus' ways. Give my love to my mother and my sisters."* I then saw a brilliant light shining down on earth and Jesus gave a message: *"I am the Light of the World and the darkness of sin is dispelled. I am the light of life in your souls that gives you your being. By My death I have given you the right to share in My light in heaven."* I then saw Mary dressed in the light of the sun. She said: *"I come dressed in the light of my Son. It is He who shines from me as we both share our love with you. Continue your prayers for the world is in great need of them."* I then sensed the Holy Spirit was present in many flames. He said: *"I bring you My flame of love to warm your hearts. I bless all of you with My graces for your prayers this evening. Stay with the light of Jesus, your Savior."* I then saw beautiful gold rays of light coming from God the Father. He said: *"I have given you light by day with the sun and light by night with the moon and stars at creation. I have made you in time by My will and offer you the light of faith to reach heaven."* I then had a picture of a priest and it was St. John Neuman. He said: *"We all share the light of Christ and need to stay close to Him. We do that by use of the sacraments given by the priest. This is why I pray to God to send more priests to your land which is in deep sin. You also should pray for vocations."* I then saw a nun and it was St. Teresa of Avila. She said: *"I have a great love for the Infant Jesus because this is how He appeared to me. He is King even in His most humble birth. He brought us salvation for which we are eternally grateful."*

Thursday, January 6, 1994:

At the Adoration Chapel, I saw a fleeting image of our flag and it gradually disappeared. Jesus gave a message: *"Your country will fall on hard times during this year. Financial disaster will trigger internal strife possibly with some food shortages. The current president will lead the country into some poor choices because of his moral problems. The poor finances will be a contrived affair. People will be enticed into the stock market only to see it fail. This will set your country up for control by the Anti-Christ who will soon come to power. Be ready and pray for God's help to carry you through this evil time. All these events will be part of your punishment for your sins of abortion."*

Friday, January 7, 1994:

At Sacred Heart Cathedral I saw some well-lit huge caves. Jesus gave a message: *"The underground Church in your country is not far away. People will soon persecute you for your belief in My name. You will be tested and rejected much like I was. But be at peace, for I will purify the earth shortly. Pray for spiritual strength through these times. I will protect the souls of My chosen ones. But you may have to endure some physical hardships."*

Later, at the Adoration Chapel, I saw some long trenches and many people were being buried in mass graves. Jesus gave a message: *"Many people will die from wars and persecutions. Some will be persecuted for religion, others for old hatreds. Because of the increased sin in the world, wars will come. The spiritual conflicts will increase when the Anti-Christ comes on the scene. So pray constantly for the strength to endure your coming trials. But know that I have gone before you and I have suffered these things. If you are to gain heaven, you must suffer as I did. Continue to visit Me and be with Me as often as possible."*

Saturday, January 8, 1994:

After Communion, I saw a bright star in the distance which gave the appearance of the Star at Bethlehem. Jesus gave a message: *"I am the light who has come into the world and the darkness grasped it not. My people did not accept My divine origins. They could not understand or comprehend My Incarnation as a man. Consequently, they rejected Me and called Me a blasphemer when I made references to divine powers. They did not understand that I could love man so much as to become a man and die for your sins. It is sad that with all the prophecies My own Israelites did not recognize Me as the Messiah. The reason most did not believe and even today is because they lacked the gift of faith and the grace to receive it. So pray for your people to have the gift of faith so they can save their souls."*

Later, at the Adoration Chapel, I saw a dollar sign and Jesus gave a message: *"Man was not made to serve money. I am your Master. You cannot serve money and be My disciple. If you store spiritual treasures in heaven, they will be given you on judgment. If you pile up wealth here on earth, it will gain you nothing on judgment. So direct your lives to serve Me and you will always be at peace. If you live for money, then you always worry about keeping it from theft and corrosion and have no peace. Without My help you will wander aimlessly with only greed driving your emotions. If you put your trust in Me, I will give you graces to endure all your tests. So pray always to keep close to Me."*

Sunday, January 9, 1994: (Baptism of Jesus)

After Communion, I saw physically the sun shining down and felt God the Father would give the message. I then had a brief glimpse of the baptism of Jesus. God the Father said: *"This is My beloved Son upon whom My favor rests. Listen to Him. My Son has come to take away the sin of Adam and Eve. This allows the forgiveness of original sin in the sacrament of Baptism. Together with that original sin, My Son's death will forgive all sin since it was an act for all time. This is also a manifestation of the Trinity—Myself, My Son and the Holy Spirit. All Three Persons in the one true God show you the way to heaven by showing you Jesus' life as your example to follow. So pray and be Christ-like in your activities and you will gain heaven with all its glory.*"

Later, on the way to the Adoration Chapel, we saw the sun in a strange view where rays were shooting straight up from a setting sun. It also had sundogs on either side. I then had a vision of like a Host with pulsating rings of light emanating outward. God the Father gave a message: *"I am sending you some heavenly signs in the sky. They are divine gifts for My faithful. The rays heading toward heaven are a sign to lift your thoughts to heavenly things. These are to direct you to save your souls. Do not be so taken with the horizontal distractions of this world. Care for your neighbor as My Son directed but do not do things solely for monetary gain or just to please someone. The cares of this world are not to lead you away from God. You will know those things of spiritual value based on whether they lead you to God or away from God.*"

Monday, January 10, 1994: (Funeral Mass for Mary Harris)

At church, I saw some glimpses of Mary's face as I knew her. She was talking with me as I greeted her: *"Yes, I am happy to see you, John. Please give my love to Cliff, Greg and Theresa. I want to thank my friends of Mary for coming. Father Mull's homily was very nice and appreciated. Yes, I am in heaven. It is a most beautiful place where now I can adore Jesus and love Mary— they are inseparable. Yes, (with one of Mary's famous laughs and a wink) I did ring the bells for you. I will be praying for all of you. You will be happy to be with me here some day. Yes, I feel like a young spirit free from my body.*" During the Rosary before Mass we all heard very light tingly bells ringing briefly.

Later, I received the words "Welcome to my Love" and I saw Jesus reaching out to me. He said: *"I bring you My Eucharistic love. My Sacred Heart is burning with love for all of you. If you could but understand how much I love you. By dying on the cross for your sins you can see the beginnings of My sea of infinite love. I invite you always to come into My love by your presence before My Blessed Sacrament. I want you to become a part of Me by giving your will over to Me in following My Divine Will. In that way you will intimately experience My love for you and see how I have a specific plan for each of My precious souls. When you receive Me into your hearts, your hearts burn with My love. If you look deeper into My love, you would see how the least little offense hurts Me. With the eyes of faith you are drawn to do all that is pleasing to Me. So pray that My love will become a part of you and we will never be separated."*

Tuesday, January 11, 1994:

After Communion, I saw an elderly man sitting and he appeared to be waiting. Jesus gave a message on "Death"*: "I have died for your sins and I have opened the gates to heaven which were closed by Adam's sin. For many death is a hard event to handle. But it is more the unknown which most people fear. Know that I have gone before you in death and have prepared a beautiful resting place for My faithful. For those who believe, death is a transition to a glorious life of praising God with the entire community. I offer you hope and not to worry for your love and peace will quench any anxiety you have. So pray and believe that I am the resurrection and the life and all will go well with whoever goes forward into My Kingdom."*

Later, at the Adoration Chapel, I noticed the candles were burning low and Jesus gave a message: *"Time is running out before My coming return. But before My return there will be an evil influence for a short time. The days of the Anti-Christ will soon be upon you and at that time evil will appear to be in control. But do not lose heart, I will protect My faithful's souls. There will be a purification which will cause much loss of life and struggles on the earth. The beast will have a short reign but it will soon collapse. After this time I will usher in an era of peace you have yet to know. So pray and keep watch over your spiritual lives."*

Wednesday, January 12, 1994:

After Communion, (Reading was calling of Samuel-Here I am Lord.) I could see Our Lady coming in a glorious radiance but I could not see her face very well. She gave me a message: *"This is an appropriate time to encourage all my special children who are receiving my messages or those of my Son. You all are privileged and should be grateful for the gifts you are receiving. Give thanks to God and be sure to guard your prayer lives since my chosen ones will be more tempted. You who are endowed should also realize there is a deeper responsibility of faith that comes with the messages. You are to lead lives which are witnesses to my Son's glory and be examples of His love. So guard your spiritual lives closely and relate these wonderful happenings to my faithful."*

Later, at the prayer group, I first was greeted by Jesus as a young boy. He said: *"I love you all as My extended family. You all mean so much to Me. I want to see you love one another in your families. Also, pray together to keep your families together and not separated by hate."* I then saw Our Lady with outstretched arms. She said: *"I am happy to receive your love-messages as your prayers find their way to heaven. I will see to it your prayers are answered if it be my Son's will. Keep praying together for you give strength to each other in your prayer groups. Thank you for responding to my call."* I then had a very strong picture of Mary Harris. She said through her angel: *"I want to thank you all for remembering me at the funeral Mass. I also was very thankful to be a part of your prayer group. I will continue to pray for all of you."* I then was visited by my son David's angel. His message was: *"I come to comfort my mother on the anniversary of my death. I am here to help you if you would but ask."* I then saw the flames in the candles growing long and the Holy Spirit came as a dove. He said: *"I am burning with love for all of you. I want to shed My graces on you this evening to strengthen you in your prayer. Pray to Me for the virtues you mentioned and they will be given you."* I then saw some infants and Jesus gave a message: *"These are the infants who should have been born according to My plan for them. But men and women of your country continue to throw these gifts of life in My face in disregard of My plans. For this your country will pay dearly. Please pray and do what you can to bring this abortion law down."* Finally, I saw Jesus with His Sacred Heart and His love could be seen pouring out from His heart. He said: *"I am yearning for your love always. I am ever ready to receive you any time of the day. You can remember Me even with a few words or offer up your actions. I have many graces I would love to shower you with, if you would just ask Me for them."*

Thursday, January 13, 1994:

At Holy Name of Jesus I saw the heavens open up and the Trinity manifested Itself in a circle above me. Jesus said: *"I follow the Father in everything I do, We are One. The Holy Spirit is an outpouring of our love to My people. We are joined as One even though this is a mystery for you to understand. Our place at the Baptism was again a manifestation which every faithful may not have appreciated but we all were there none the less. Pray for understanding to all Three Persons in God that We may become a part of your life."*

Later, at the Adoration Chapel, I heard a phone ringing and Jesus was calling my attention to Him in the Garden of Gethsemene. He said: *"I call upon you to give Me your problems, your anxieties, your injustices and any other thing that has your spirit down. I will offer them to the Father as your prayer and they will gain merit instead of despair. You need to concentrate more on seeking My love and how to share your love with Me. For your spiritual life needs to be refreshed much more than the time you give life's distractions. Also, look for ways to help and encourage your friends. Do not be laboring them all the time with your problems. So look to the Scriptures for how to lead your lives as true faithful and loving people of God."*

Friday, January 14, 1994:

In church, I saw an earthen dug out tunnel. Jesus gave a message: *"You will be persecuted for My name's sake. At first you will be harassed only verbally for being a Christian. As time goes on it will be more increasingly difficult to conduct your affairs. As they eventually seek to put you in prison, you will find yourself hiding from the authorities of the day. No matter what evil intends to taunt you and persecute you, I will be there to help you through it. It will not be long and I will bring this sinful lot to a bitter end. Then My peace will reign and My people will see My glory. Take heart and keep praying to guard your souls."*

Later, at the Adoration Chapel, I saw a picture of Lenin and then I was looking straight up at a large hammer and sickle. Jesus said: *"Russia will become involved with internal struggles and eventually will be involved with a major war. The old tyranny of Russia is not dead and may come back to power despite the west's attempts to encourage reforms. There have not been enough prayers to completely rid Russia of Communism. The power of evil still resides there and will continue to cause political strife. Pray more for peace in the world so evil will not have so much control."*

Saturday, January 15, 1994:
After Communion, I saw Our Lady like she was greeting the children at Fatima. I asked her for a message. She said: *"Yes, my son, I come to ask you to use my Jesus' sacramental gift in Confession. I am re-emphasizing the Gospel and homily words for all sinners to avail themselves of my Son Jesus' love in forgiveness of your sins. He died for your sins so it is only fitting that you receive Him in this sacrament to keep your souls clean and keep you close to Him. Jesus is ever ready to receive your request to be reconciled. Sin still continues to offend Him and you must frequently make restitution to Him. Many of My children neglect this gift of Confession because they are afraid to tell their sins to the priest. But tell these souls to think of the priest as Jesus and to ask for Jesus' mercy on them. You must not neglect asking forgiveness since it is indifference to sin which will gradually force you away from Jesus and you will be lost."*

Later, at the Nocturnal Hour, I had a vision of a band of wheat and Jesus said: *"I am coming for My harvest—to separate the wheat and the tares. My angels will come and gather up the tares to be thrown into the fires of the great abyss. The wheat of My faithful will be given heaven on earth after the great purification. You will then experience what the earth was meant for man at the time of Adam. No death, suffering or disease—just love for Me and being a part of My will. After the final judgment you will be joined with your body in heaven in the last resurrection. This is the glorious hope which every Christian lives for—to share eternity with Me—free from all earthly cares or evils."*

Sunday, January 16, 1994: (PERSONAL)
After Communion, I saw a large image of Jesus come into view with yellow light all around Him. I said in light of the readings: "Speak Lord, your servant is listening." He said: *"You are being called to a higher life beyond the things of this earth. Therefore,*

I am asking you to put away some of your more earthly habits and concerns. Focus more on your prayer life and I will take care of you in My love. The distractions of this world will not help you in the next life. So pray in earnest from the heart and help people with your messages who can understand them. It is this mission I have given you that should be your main concern. Your responsibility to be a good example comes as My love yearns for you to go deeper into My love."

Later, at the Adoration Chapel, I saw at first a scuba diver below water. Then I saw some rivers high on their banks. Jesus said: *"You will first be tested as a country by severe ravages from the elements. Man has not acknowledged a connection between his sin and apathy to Me with the extremes in the weather. I will indeed make it known to Him. The punishment due for the sins of abortion will not go unanswered. Later, you will experience even worse events which I will tell you beforehand. Again prayer is needed to lessen any of the pending punishments. The more you can get people to pray from their heart, the less all will have to suffer. So be watchful as these events unfold."*

Monday, January 17, 1994: (Day of 6.6 Richter earthquake in Los Angeles 4:30 a.m.)

After Communion, I saw first an image of a bishop and then an image of Bishop Sheen. Jesus then said: *"My shepherds are becoming lackadaisical in general as regards to bringing My sheep closer to Me. They lack the zeal to inspire their people to love Me more. They should encourage the sacraments, especially Confession, as well as a better moral life built around prayer. Some of My outspoken sons are doing well but the rest are either against Me or not defending Me as with abortion. Pray that they will see their mission and stand up for My principles on the major moral issues."*

Later, I saw the tops of buildings in a city and beautiful trees and everything was peaceful. Jesus gave a message: *"The wickedness in the west is being avenged. The people of this area are full of hatred. They make movies glorifying sin, there is abuse of sex, and there is an idolatry of the things of earth. This people fails to realize their purpose on earth—to come to Me and give up their will to Me. I am humbling them by taking away their things and making them see that without Me they are nothing. In their need they are being brought to their knees and they will be forced to help each other to survive. This same abandonment of worldly things will happen to many more of your people. You have an expression 'an act of God'. Indeed, you will be learning the meaning of these words. I love My people and I give you My mercy often but sin has become so rampant that now My justice must be fulfilled. Pray always to keep your souls lifted up to Me for I am what your soul is always seeking."*

Tuesday, January 18, 1994:

After Communion, I saw a young boy dressed in a white robe with a hood and presumed it represented David who was anointed King in today's readings. Jesus said: *"It is true that it is the heart which I look into to see the eyes of the soul. For there dwells how a person really feels about those around them. I ask you to study your own hearts and if they be cold toward God and man, you should have a wake-up call. Indeed, you need prayer and love in your heart if you are to be My disciple. So put on heartfelt mercy to God and man for this is what I desire of you. Make your hearts burn with love for Me and I will take care of you always."*

Later, at the Adoration Chapel, I kept seeing an image of Lenin on banners and flags. Jesus said: *"I am emphasizing My message on Russia because the war Russia will become involved in will have far-reaching complications. The old guard of Communism will continue to try and take charge. War may occur either with China or Israel unless more prayer is forthcoming. This war could reach to a world war since many countries are at odds with each other. Peace will not happen on its own. Men must seek My help or they will reap the consequences. Many times I have told you how war comes as a result of men's sins. So be prepared and pray much to lessen the ravages of this future event."*

Wednesday, January 19, 1994:

After Communion, I could see an altar and a cross but there was no corpus on it. Jesus gave a message: *"You do not see the body on the cross since it represents men who do not have Me in their minds or hearts. Some of My chosen show Me affection but many need to be reminded constantly. If My people really loved*

Me, they would have My picture around them. They would be saying little love prayers during the day. If you loved Me, you would visit Me often in Mass or before the Blessed Sacrament. Because most are forgetful of Me, I will strike down the things they adore in My stead—for I am a jealous God. I love you and I am trying to show you My love always but it is often hard to get My people's attention. So bringing man to His knees with difficulties may be the only way to wake Him up to My presence."

Later, at the prayer group, I first saw a prayer service like a Billy Graham crusade. Jesus said: *"My people need to be evangelists to spread My Good News to My people. You should have the zeal to convert sinners as do some of the other Christian beliefs. Pray to the Holy Spirit for what to say to friends who may be open to your teaching."* I then had a view of our old chest of drawers and I was thinking of the upcoming baptism. Jesus said: *"I have gifted you with children. I ask you to celebrate this gift of life and share with the parents in bringing them up in the faith. I also want to remind you to cherish this new life and protect the unborn from the abortionists who only want to kill to gain money."* I then saw a black flag—a shadow covered our flag and a blizzard of snow was falling around it. Jesus said: *"I will visit your land with many extremes in the weather. The hot and the cold are like the lukewarm in faith who need to be pushed more into action. Many prophecies have foretold these extremes as a warning of hard times to come."* I then saw Our Lady of Guadalupe. She said: *"I come to remind you of your country's standing abortion rule by your Supreme Court. As long as abortion is allowed, you will experience much pain and loss of the blessings given your land. I renew My pledge to take away abortion if you would direct enough prayers to this cause. I will take your prayers tonight as a down payment."* I saw some oriental structures and a Chinese man appeared. Jesus said: *"Many problems with trade and human rights will cause much strife in China. This could lead to a desire to expand their borders for financial survival. It could lead to war as a result."* I then had a vision of Dr. Kevorkian and a sense of connection with euthanasia. Jesus said: *"Mercy killing will progress from the abortion mentality. People will want to assist suicide for the terminally ill. This will frustrate My plan for suffering souls who give their pain for the sins of others. Without this My justice will come sooner. Pray that people will under-stand the true value of life and see that I am the Master of your lives."* I again saw Our Lady of Guadalupe. She said: *"I am com-ing to ask your prayers for the Indians of the Americas who have had their land taken and have been put on reservations. Recently, in Mexico these people have shown their frustration in life's pov-erty. Pray that they will be helped."*

Thursday, January 20, 1994:
After Communion, I saw an image of an open window with darkness all around it. It was likened to a window of opportunity. Jesus said: *"Now is the acceptable time to come to Me, My little ones. If My people would see through the signs of the times, they would see a chance to come into My love through prayer and repentance. Little by little this opportunity will be slipping away. As evil will increase, those influences will stifle future opportu-nities to be saved. So come now and accept My glorious invita-tion to the wedding feast."*

Later, at the Adoration Chapel, I was seeing images of diabolic dictators such as Adolf Hitler and Sadam Hussein. Jesus said: *"For a while I will test My people with physical hardships and losses of their possessions. This may bring some souls back to Me. But still man thinks he can achieve everything by himself without Me. For this reason there will come a great evil tribulation where evil will seem to be in control. I am only allowing this testing period to show man he cannot fight evil without Me. With evil, man will not alone be able to overcome it. It will be a time when man will be forced to turn to Me or join the demons in hell. There will be a clear choice for him to decide. No longer will the luke-warm coast along—they will be forced finally to live for Me or whither on the vine without Me. This will be a time when prayer and My mercy will be your only salvation."*

Friday, January 21, 1994: (Feast St. Agnes, Virgin, Martyr)
After Communion, I saw several visions of a young woman and believed St. Agnes would give the message. She said: *"We are drawn to Jesus by the bonds of heaven which He has purchased for us with His blood on the cross. The things of heaven should be what we strive for always, for they will lead you to eternal life*

with Jesus. You should avoid the bonds of earth's distractions for they will only lead you to earthly desires and cravings of the body. But you must be lifted to a higher plain of life with Jesus. He is the one of our dreams and desires. Pray to stay close to Him." After this message it was ironic that the last prayer before Mass ended referred to forgetting the "bonds of earthly things"—exactly the words in the message. This was a confirmation of St. Agnes' words to me.

Later, at the Adoration Chapel, I had a vision of some devastated streets as from a hurricane or tornado. I then saw a blizzard of snow raising havoc on some city streets. Jesus said: *"You will experience trials with the weather which have yet to occur. Record cold, heat, rainfall and snow will befall you. The weather is a reflection of the spiritual chaos in the lives of many. This is a worsening of the testing time which is coming upon you. Before long more people will realize that they are not the masters of their lives—I am. They will also see that life as they know it will no longer be predictable. This is partly the reason for the testing—to wake man up to the power of God and the respect that I deserve. For My faithful who read these signs, know that I will forever protect those who do My will. Earthly things will be taken but I will give you the grace to endure these times. Keep faithful to My ways and your reward will be great."*

Saturday, January 22, 1994: (Roe v. Wade Anniversary)

At Holy Name Our Lady came in a vision holding the Baby Jesus. She said: *"As my Son was at odds with the authorities in the Gospel, so you will be contrary to the morals of those in power in your day. When your country elected to accept abortion as law, it was a dark day in my Son's eyes and My own. Your law no longer is in conformance with the laws of God. When a society turns its back on any of its citizens, even the unborn, that society is doomed to destroy itself eventually. This is the road your country has chosen and this is the reason my Son's justice will be visited upon you. The innocent faithful must not lose heart. My Son will protect your souls and purify the earth in His time and manner. Pray often that you try to understand and obey my Son for He will do what is best for His people."*

Later, at the Adoration Chapel, I saw a large rainbow circling the moon. In a vision I saw a large line of white lambs standing looking for Jesus. Jesus said: *"These are My little lambs who suffer persecution in the womb. They are on the firing line ready to be slaughtered to please men's convenience and an attempt to hide their disgrace. In the end the disgrace of abortion is worse than any problem those women imagined they would help with this act of killing. My plans for these lives are being thwarted before they can even begin. This disgusting selfishness will reap more pain over time as well as spiritual suffering. The pain of guilt will always be with these women no matter how much they are forgiven, if they seek forgiveness. It is important to try and counsel young women to understand the importance of the life they are trying to snuff out. Please pray that more women will have a change of heart and realize it is My plan for these lives to continue no matter what hardship it may mean."*

Sunday, January 23, 1994: (Baptism 12:00 Mass)

After Communion, I saw a lady laid out in a funeral and then I had a picture of a cemetery with many tombstones. Jesus had a message: *"Prepare your lives and repent for truly this life is passing away. I tell you your time is short to get ready for the evil tribulation which is about to befall you. Once events start it will be difficult to repent later. I have said it before but I am re-emphasizing again. Now is the acceptable time to come to Me and give your life over to Me in full trust. I will take care of you—do not fear. It is a time of warning much like Jonah's. For most of the people are too absorbed in things and themselves to remember Me. Pray constantly as I continue to exhort you, for your prayers are necessary to keep your love connections open to Me. Keep close to Me and continue to ask for My help during this perilous time."*

Later, at the Adoration Chapel, I saw the tomb where Our Lord was buried. But there was no body. Then I saw Jesus walking there and He said: *"I am the Life and the Resurrection. Those who believe in Me shall receive eternal life. Though you walk in the valley of darkness, I will be at your side. Though you be tested by the evil one, My angels will protect you. I ask you to have but the faith of a mustard seed. Then I will give you every good thing if you follow My commands. For I ask only for a belief in Me and help for your neighbor. Then you will receive a prophet's reward in heaven. All My faithful will be eligible for this gift if they just follow My will. So I ask you not to fear and do not be discouraged by the coming events for I will be at your side watching over you."*

Monday, January 24, 1994:

After Communion, I saw a cross with Jesus and then I saw the cross from the back. Jesus said: *"Many have indeed turned their backs to Me and have forgotten My rightful place in their lives. This has happened most in your country where affluence has created a "Me" generation who believe they can do everything on their own. Even their neighbors become distant because no one lifts a hand to help others. While they have an abundance of things, My name is no where in sight. Therefore, I tell you when their things are taken from them in hard times, it will be a test to see who they cling to. If they still do not seek Me then, it will be both a spiritual and physical disaster. Man must recognize Me before men before I will recognize them before My Father and forgive them."*

Later, at church, I first had a picture of Jesus on the cross. Then I saw Jesus being struck in the face by the soldiers. Jesus said: *"I have prompted you indeed about My on-going persecution on earth. You (plural) also will share in this persecution for the evil of man is witnessed most in the abortions being done in your country. It was a curse enough for these abortions. Now they are torturing My faithful even for taunting the sinners' consciences and troubling their potential customers. You have already been told how this persecution of My body will continue. For those who did not understand the previous messages, now they can see for themselves how the immoral politicians will lord their will over you. I tell you pray more fervently now, for these men will increase your difficulties till you will have to go underground to avoid their harassments. Fear not, I will protect you and they will answer to My judgment. Pray for their souls and for a change in their hearts before they become so cold that Satan will sift them."*

Tuesday, January 25, 1994: (Feast of St. Paul's Conversion)

After Communion, I saw a bright light and a lot of excitement in people. Jesus said: *"I sent Paul before you as an example to follow. It is easy to criticize and persecute others when they are in the minority. You have had it easy for many years in that you could worship on Sunday and follow Me without trouble. Now I will be offering you a test to be one of My disciples, for the faith will no longer come as easy as before. Like Paul you will be persecuted for believing in My name. Already those who stand up against abortion are being harassed. This will continue even against those who are Christian. So pray and take courage, your faith will save you."*

Later, at the Adoration Chapel, I could see learned men and the word *"Experts"* came to me. Jesus said: *"Many people consider themselves experts in certain skills or fields. As a result, they may overflow their feeling of confidence and think they are gifted in other areas as well. I tell you knowledge of this world is useless unless you know the faith and follow My will. For I will confound the wise and I will raise up the humble. It is mercy and repentance I desire. Those who want to do things on their own will fall on their face eventually. You must conform your will to Mine. Then I will help you use your skills to fulfill My plan for you and contribute your worth to society. It is only when you are in concert with Me that I will give you success. But do not think piled-up riches will help you. You have been gifted for only a short time. In the end, all must suffer as I did to merit your crown in heaven."*

Wednesday, January 26, 1994:

I received Communion at home while I was sick. I saw a very strong vision of a U.S. Navy officer with his uniform and hat on. Jesus gave a message: *"There will be a serious incident involving your navy ships which will involve some loss of life. The repercussions of this could turn into an incident like the Bay of Tonkin years ago. You could get dragged into a war that will not be desired. I am warning you to prepare and pray for your people that your leaders will act correctly."*

Later, at the prayer group, I first saw Our Lady dressed in white and she was amidst the darkness. She said: *"The issue of abortion has divided your land. Yet it is just another sign of the battle of good and evil. You are killing millions of unborn each year with no letup. Is heaven to not see this? Pray your Rosaries that it be lessened."* I then saw many angels and they were bright lights coming down from heaven. Jesus said: *"My angels are ready to bring down calamities among you. How long do you expect Me not to raise My hand against your sins of abortion? This sin—more than any other—will cause you My strongest punishment."* I then saw a naked little child. Jesus said: *"I asked My Apostles to bring the little children to Me. These are My joy and woe to those who abuse them. Their abuse will not go unpunished. I ask that you help where possible to send aid or help the hungry and unclothed children."* I then saw a picture of an eagle that became wounded. The Holy Spirit said: *"I am the Spirit of Love and I see your country is wounded deeply with sin. Your sins are so many that they are dragging you down so that God has left you on your own. Woe will it be to those who go through life without God's help."* I then had a picture of God the Father and He said: *"'I Am' has come to ask mankind to change his ways. If you continue on your way of killing and sexual abuse, you leave Me no other choice but to judge you and purify the earth."* I then saw St. Therese the Little Flower come and she said: *"All of heaven can look down and see the evil of your day and all of us are in disgust of the disrespect for life. We all understand how Jesus will not let it continue much longer. There will be a supernatural intervention."* I then had a picture of some Arabs. Jesus said: *"The Arabs will be an instrument of the evil one in fighting My faithful. They will cause much destruction in the Holy Lands as in the days of the crusades. They will be involved in the War of Armageddon."*

Thursday, January 27, 1994:
    After Communion, I saw some old woman praying as a statue of Our Lady was being carried out. Our Lady said: *"My Son asks you to be the light of His word before your fellow men. His word is not to be kept silent but spoken often so it will shine to the rest of the world. Your world is cold and dark with sin abundant. So please pray that the light and heat of faith will be accepted by His people."*

(Night of ice storm) Later, at the Adoration Chapel, I saw a bright dawn with radiant light. Then as day approached a huge white cross appeared in the sky. Jesus said: *"My warning for all of you is coming soon. This will be a time when every soul will see their lives as I do—in full detail. It will be a brief review of your life. No one will doubt that it is from a supernatural origin. Certain men may reject it but they cannot deny it will happen. From this point on, events will quicken as the evil tribulation will gradually unfold. Pray and repent for this will try men's souls to the limit. Ask for My help and I will protect your souls from the demons. This will last but a short time and then My glory will be bestowed on the earth."*

Friday, January 28, 1994:

Later, after Communion, I saw Our Lady coming and then I had a brief glimpse of Maria Esperanza (The mystic of Betania, Venezuela). Mary said: *"I am happy to see all of my children together saying my Rosary. You are indeed my loved ones. I am thankful to my children for wanting to make this pilgrimage to my daughter's place of apparition. All pilgrimages carry special graces since I know the spirit of love and endurance you must go through. I will be watching over your safety on your trip. Pray to me for any help you may need for any adversities. Pray my Rosary often and you will keep close to my Son as well."*

Saturday, January 29, 1994:

After Communion, I saw a bright orange cloud open up in the middle of the sky and God the Father came forward. He said: *"Nathan in the reading talks of the sin of David. But the country of plenty that is identified in this story is your country with its many blessings. Unfortunately, the ewe lambs being offered up are represented in your many abortions. I am asking your people to repent of your evil and stop the murdering of My innocents. Your judgment will be heavy for these sins and even more so if you continue to defy My plans. Go tell your people to follow this message—to those who will listen. For those who fail to heed My message, they will be grouped with those to be purified from the evil tribulation. Those judged unworthy will indeed be sent to hell with the demons."*

Later, at the Adoration Chapel, I saw several people kneeling in prayer. Then later I saw some trees in beautiful blue skies. Jesus said this would be a *"Love message."* He said: *"My people come to Me in prayer for many reasons. I hear and apply all your prayers to the best benefit of your intention. I would ask only that you pray for those things if it be in My will. For I see the good for each soul in a broader perspective. Therefore, I will store up your treasures for those things or people when it is the proper time and circumstance. Many people feel I do not answer their prayers. Mostly, I may answer them in a better way which may be different from your view. Other times people may have a high price for helping them. You may have to fast, suffer and pray long for those souls farther away from Me. In any case keep praying to stay close to Me and help your friends. Along with answering prayers, I give you many blessings in your jobs, your friends and even some creature comforts. Be thankful for them but do not indulge yourself in them. For your main purpose is to love Me and your neighbor. In that way you will be fulfilling My plan for you."*

Sunday, January 30, 1994:

After Communion, I could see a wife, her husband and some children. I then saw a break in the sky and Jesus came forth and said: *"I have great love for all who belong to My Body in the Church, especially the little ones. I have given you Myself in the Eucharist so you could share in My love always on earth. My love reaches out to you unconditionally and it is as deep as the sea in My eternal waiting for you. It is you who must come forward to accept Me, I have made you to be a spiritual being seeking its creator. You must pray for strength in spirit to overcome all obstacles that keep you from Me. It is only when your spirit rests in Me that you will experience My peace. Continue to think of Me often."*

Later, at the Adoration Chapel, I saw many people who were at the edge of hell as they were gradually sliding down into the pit. God had asked them to choose Him or the demons and they could not make up their mind until it was too late. Jesus came and said: *"I come to continue to warn My people of the judgment that awaits them. Some have become so wrapped up in worldly things that they fail to acknowledge My presence. They have made the world and themselves gods to worship instead of Me. I am asking you to help and give example to these people. Pray for their hearts to come back to search for Me. Even in pain and difficulty with which I am testing them, pray they will see their real purpose in life. This earth is a testing ground but all that is in it will be passing away. People cannot wish to stay here, they must strive to see Me or be cursed. Pray that some will see the light before it is too late.*"

Monday, January 31, 1994:

After Communion, I saw a continued vision of empty pews. Then I heard God the Father say: *"At the end will my Son find any faithful left? Many are falling away from going to Church. Even at times it is hard to find a priest to say the Mass. Of My people who do come, many give Me lip service. During the week I rarely hear from them. My people need to wake up and read the signs of the times. My judgment time is not far off, yet few are properly prepared. Sound the call to My people to be on the watch and repent for you have little time left.*"

Later, I saw a priest dressed in white at first and we were entering into a beautiful white ramp which was bright without a light source. It was then I could see a beautiful earth as we all could see it. It was restored to its former beauty. Even at night there was a glow from God that lit the night. Jesus gave a message: *"This is a view of what heaven on earth will be during the reign of peace which will be My Mother's triumph. You will see Me clearly and your joy will know no bounds. Peace will permeate you with My love. You will experience no sin or temptation. You will not worry about what to eat or wear for everything will be provided. You will be able to pray unimpeded by merely opening your mind to Me. Life will be glorious for you then as it was initially intended. This will be a beautiful time of fellowship as the whole community will be of one mind directed by My will. This will be a foretaste of heaven which will come at the end of time as you know it. Pray and offer sacrifices that you will be worthy enough to merit this gift of My love to My chosen.*"

Tuesday, February 1, 1994:

After Communion, I saw Jesus standing at the altar and then a large white Host took the spot where I saw Him. Jesus said: *"I give you My Body and Blood in the Eucharist at every Mass. You should be eternally grateful for this freely given gift of mine to all mankind. This is My way of drawing you closer to Me to share My love with you. The breaking of the bread has become a symbol for unity in My Church. Please honor this intent as I ask My people to stay together as one faith. You all are intended to be My one flock and if you ask for My graces, I will keep you together."*

Later, at the Adoration Chapel, I saw some leaves on a potted plant and then I saw a lot of snarled traffic with many cars. Jesus gave a message: *"You have many misplaced priorities in this life. Many have let worldly cares get them upset and discouraged. These things of the world are imperfect in many ways yet you expect them to be flawless. I tell you—set your mind on heavenly things and you will not be disappointed. For if you loved to pray as much as you loved worldly things, life would be much easier for you. If you listen for My love and repent of your sins, then all things will be given you. You must seek Me first and realize this is your first priority. Things that are eternal are what your soul craves. Do not clutter your mind with earthly obsessions but follow My directions in the Scriptures. Then you will have My lasting peace and see the joy of My love."*

Wednesday, February 2, 1994: (Presentation in the Temple)

After Communion, I saw an old woman dressed in a veil over her head and an older man kneeling in an alcove of an older church. I then saw the outside of an old church which I took representing the Temple. Jesus said: *"In My Presentation this was the beginning of the fulfillment of the Old Testament. Being brought forward, I was consecrated with My people of Israel. This was My marriage to the Jews and Gentiles in that I now would be carrying out the very prophecies of the Messiah. But instead of an earthly King as many had hoped, I come as King of the whole earth and heaven. My mission was to die for your sins and afford everyone the opportunity of eternal life in love with Me. My gift to you is Myself so you could have love personified in Me. I reach out to you every day, please take the opportunity to show your love in return."*

Later, at the prayer group, I first saw Our Lady from the side holding up an infant child. She said: *"I too have a deep love for the children as does my Son. These are precious gifts given to the world to show you how helpless you once were. My Son wants you to come to Him with the innocence of these little ones."* I then saw Brad and Jeanette with Kayleigh and then Christina with Donna and Herm during their presentations at Baptism. Our Lord said: *"Grandparents take a special delight in their grandchildren with a deep pride. All grandparents should give thanks to God for these blessings of children. I look over all My children as you do with great love and pride of having you with Me."* I then saw a scene at the "Presentation" decade of a vision of the presenting of Jesus outside the Temple much like in the Fr. Peyton films. Mary said: *"It was Simeon who foretold my sorrow as I held my Infant Jesus. I treasured the time my Son was with me on earth. But even more so I treasured how my Son was given to us as a blessing to take away your sins."* I then saw a vision of students with their teachers in the church for CCD. Jesus said: *"Blessed are those who teach the faith to My little ones. They will have a special treasure in heaven."* I then saw some children who were maimed and abused by war. Jesus said: *"Woe to those who kill and abuse My little ones. It would be better that they should be thrown in the sea with a great millstone about their necks."* Again I saw some naked and hungry children. Jesus said: *"All over the world My starving children are crying out for help. Use your gifts I have given you to help alleviate their suffering."* Lastly, I saw again some fetuses actually being aborted. Jesus said: *"Many times have I called your attention to the ruthless killing by abortion. You will not have much longer to wait for My answer to your abuse."*

Thursday, February 3, 1994: (Feast of St. Blaise)

After Communion, I could see a priest in an old church and I had feelings for the church we visited in Dubrovnik. St. Blaise said: *"Men continue to want war in this area even though war has not gained anything for them. All war does is increase the anger between the warring factions. Please pray for peace in this area and all over the world. Man has not learned from history.*

Pray that men will see the error of their ways and allow God to show them His way is the only way to peace through love."

Later, at the Adoration Chapel, I saw actors singing as if on TV. Jesus gave a message: *"Many people make actors or famous people their role models even though they may not lead exemplary lives. You cannot do things just to please your peers especially if it is against My law. I tell you to follow My life in the Scriptures or model your lives after My Mother or the saints. The world concerns itself with money and they advise to learn from those who are ahead in money matters. I tell you to improve your spiritual lives by following the ways of those more spiritual than yourselves. In this way, you will learn to improve heavenly strivings rather than those of the world which are passing away. Pray and do things to build your spiritual skills and save your treasures in heaven, not on earth."*

Friday, February 4, 1994:

After Communion, I could see a priest serving Mass. Jesus gave a message: *"Remember to keep the Mass dear to your heart. I am offered to you every day. It is My gift of Myself to you to treasure. It is My way of drawing My Church together into one body. Give the Mass reverence and see to your loving duty at least every Sunday and more if you can attend during the week. I tell you the Mass will one day have to go behind the scenes of the authorities. I ask you to preserve it for as long as you can for you need My graces. Ask for My graces and I will give them freely. For as long as you have priests, seek to have the Mass wherever possible. You are preserving My presence as long as you preserve the Mass."*

Later, at the Adoration Chapel, I could see a light out on the altar and a candle out. Then I saw Christ on the cross and a little later only a bare cross. Jesus said: *"My sacramental presence will not be with you much longer. In many churches already I am banished to side altars or in other rooms instead of on the main altar for everyone to see. Because My people have little love and respect for Me, what little you have will be taken away for a time. If you really loved Me in the tabernacles, you would visit Me often to show Me your love. The evil tribulation must come to complete the purification of the earth. For My faithful, pray your*

Rosaries and ask Me to protect your souls. In a short time your faith will be rewarded with My glory. Do not be discouraged."

Saturday, February 5, 1994:

After Communion, I saw some individuals praying alone and then Jesus alone praying in the Garden. He said: *"It is good for you to set aside time for prayer alone so you can communicate to Me and the Father without the world's distractions. It is important to build up your interior life with the strength from prayer from the heart. In order for you to be strong and evangelize My people, you need a base of strength from your interior spiritual life. Follow My example in the Scriptures—how I prayed to the Father before all the big events in My life on earth. Now with the strength of evil against you, you must pray in earnest to overcome the evil one's distractions and confusion of the world."*

Later, I saw Jesus very clearly on the cross. I could see He was in agony from the pain of His wounds and struggling for each breath. Jesus gave a message: *"How long must I suffer your sins? The many sins of the world weigh heavy on Me and continue to crucify Me. Many sins of lies, murders, and rapes continue unabated and are increasing. But the one offense which troubles Me most is the sin of indifference. Some people's hearts have grown so cold that they cease to have a right conscience and do not have any sense they are sinning. If you do not even recognize sin, how can you repent and be sorry? For these do not even want My saving power, they do not need a Savior. I tell you I have only come to save sinners. Please pray hard for these hopeless sinners that they will think of Me and see their imperfect reasoning. These trouble Me most, since I love them but they refuse My love."*

Sunday, February 6, 1994:

After Communion, I saw some men walking in suits, I did not recognize them. Jesus gave a message: *"It is true I asked before to pray for your leaders. But today more than ever they will be deciding whether to pursue more involvement in some on-going wars. Even though there are many injustices, it is not clear that escalating a war with more factions is the solution. It is better to avoid war and work on helping at the peace table. Pray for less involvement or your people may live to regret their decision, if this turns into a world war."*

Later, at the Adoration Chapel, I saw like some battles in war with planes being shot down and bombs going off with some huge explosions. Jesus then gave a message: *"Those who are eager to get into war may get more than they bargained for. Civil wars are not easy to settle and may only raise anger at the intruders. Much loss of life may occur and any gains will be hard to determine. I tell you prayer for peace and non-involvement are your best alternatives. To try and solve people's problems with a bigger war will not work. This war could draw in unforeseen combatants which may widen the hatred and the killing. An escalation in bombing will only cause more destruction and loss of life. So pray this war does not expand or it indeed will be more than any party wanted."*

Monday, February 7, 1994:

After Communion, I saw Our Lord standing a little at a distance in a white robe with a bright light on Him so His clothes dazzled. Jesus gave a message: *"I have redeemed you from your sins and I have conquered death and the evil one. Yet you must suffer as I did to achieve your eternal reward. Your everyday trials will seem to worsen as you will be taunted by the non-believers. There will come a time when being identified with My name will cause you persecution. I am warning you before it comes so you can prepare for the coming spiritual battle. There will be hard times but the evil will be to such an extent as you have never seen. Keep close to Me in the Eucharist for as long as you have Me, and pray your Rosaries always for strength in those days."*

Later, I saw a door which had a golden light to it. It was pure light with no flaw and it stood before me. Jesus gave a message: *"This is the doorway to heaven through which all must pass. This is the separation of time and for those who are worthy, it is My path to eternal love and life with Me. I am showing you this so that you will prepare yourselves for life's heavenly choice. Everyone during their lives focuses in on either doing things for God or for just themselves. In your actions each day you are either choosing to follow God's will or your own. If you love Me and wish to enter heaven, you should choose to follow My will and My commandments. Anything else is the distraction of the evil one. I ask you to pray and keep close to Me, for by loving Me and doing My will, you will save your souls."*

Tuesday, February 8, 1994:

At church, I had forgotten it was Tuesday because of my jury duty and I saw a priest at the altar. Jesus said: *"You have been forgetful in a small matter but there are many in your world who have forgotten Me altogether. Some even outwardly have rejected Me. These people have been allured by the devil's glorifying the cares and pleasures of this world. In doing so, they have neglected their purpose on earth to come to Me and be tested true. For those who do not love Me and can not see Me in creation, they will be judged unworthy and cast into hell with the demons. My faithful must wake up these people through prayer and example before it is too late. I place on you a responsibility to help save souls for those willing to convert."*

Later, at the Adoration Chapel, I saw several people sitting on comfortable chairs and couches. Jesus gave a message: *"Life was not intended to be easy for you. It requires some trials since this life is a testing time of your faithfulness to Me. It is unfortunate that people are afraid to help each other for fear of being vandalized. But I tell you to still help your brother in need, for I am still with them. Do not try to just take the easy way out but make an effort to do as I would do in your stead. In other words, reach out to feed the hungry, shelter the homeless, and clothe those in need. For if you do it to the least of My people, you do it for Me. Also, pray and evangelize sinners for their spiritual hunger must be fed as well. In doing these things you will be following My will instead of your own, for this is the perfection I seek of you."*

Wednesday, February 9, 1994: (A blustery winter day)

After Communion, I could see a very snowy street with bad weather. Jesus said: *"I have told you before how I will test you with the weather. It will be so unusual that man will question— what is this visitation of hard times? Man will have to recognize this is unusual bad weather in this part of the world. If he does not realize he is being tested, so as to bring him to understand he* is not in control—I am; then will his punishment be spiritual as well. For some have believed on seeing Me or the things I do. But those who have seen My deeds and still will not believe, they will be cursed twofold since they were visited with a choice. They will burn in the deeper recesses of hell. So pray and lift up your spirits for your redemption is at hand and My glory will soon visit you."

Later, at the prayer group, I saw the word "Chastisement" and Our Lady said: *"In many of my apparition sites I have given messages concerning the coming chastisement which will purify the earth. It will be a great testing time but you can stay close to me and my Son with the praying of my Rosary."* I then saw a woman with a dress with glittering gems all over it. Our Lord said: *"You must not be drawn to the glitter of things in this world. All things have a purpose but you must not idolize these things and give them so much time as to take time from Me. For heavenly things are your goal and you should store up treasures in heaven with your good works."* I then saw some Oriental people and a Buddha statue. Jesus said: *"The people of the East will be involved in a large war which will greatly affect the world."* The flame was tall on the candle and the Holy Spirit said: *"I am the Spirit of Love and I bring My graces to My faithful to strengthen you through the trials of the coming evil tribulation. Receive them with joy and treasure them in your need."* I then saw several battle shields and also I saw some atomic bombs going off. Jesus said: *"Men continue to harbor hatred among themselves. It is inevitable that this will lead to a world war in concert with the evil one who will be instrumental in carrying it out. If enough prayer is not said for peace, even nuclear weapons will be used."* I then had a brief vision of like a flying saucer which I believe is the sign I have seen for the warning. Jesus said: *"The warning is coming soon and men should prepare for this vision of grace to see their sins. After this, evil events will quicken. So pray for strength from the Holy Spirit to endure this time."* I finally saw a huge serpent about to strike the earth. Our Lady said: *"The serpent in the Anti-Christ will be coming upon you. This will be his short reign but it will conclude with my crushing of the serpent's head. After this, my time of triumph will be ushered in as I have told you in many of my messages."*

Thursday, February 10, 1994:

After Communion, the priest, Fr. Jack, gave me two Hosts towards the end of the line. The words came to me *"A double portion."* Jesus said: *"For those who are faithful to Me through these times, I will give them a double portion of My graces. You will need My grace to withstand the evil one and his temporary reign. He will do his worst to annihilate mankind but his hand will not harm those souls pledged to do My will. You may suffer bodily but your prayers and faith will help you to reach My glory which you will share in due time."*

Later, at the Adoration Chapel, I saw some headlights like they were searching. Then later I saw a man and we were riding on top of the clouds. Jesus said: *"Man is constantly searching for what he desires. Some men seek riches, food or sex. These are the appetites and pleasures of nature in the body. Still others seek out those things of heaven and how to improve their spiritual lives. I tell you those who seek the things of this earth will never find peace. On the other hand, those who seek Me and love Me and do My will, these will find true peace as I will reward them. So in your search of life, seek those heavenly things that will raise up your spiritual desires and you will find what you seek—My love. Your immortal spiritual nature was created to adore and love Me.*

I am your goal, what your soul seeks the most—to be with Me in the Eucharist. So pray and show others that the spiritual goal is eternally rewarding not like the passing things of earth."

Friday, February 11, 1994: (Feast of Our Lady of Lourdes)
After Communion, I saw Our Lady close up and she was beautiful and dressed in white. She gave a message: *"I am asking you to be very sure to say your three Rosaries each day for peace. No matter what else you are doing this is of primary importance. Your world is on the brink of total war. Not enough prayers for peace are being said. If this is not forthcoming, then without the prayers you will be doomed to a disastrous war. Satan is strong right now and he is striving to destroy you. You must get on your knees and pray dearly. For those who have been to Lourdes I still revere my grotto and the work done there. But I ask you to live my messages or my Son's hand will fall shortly."*

Later, at the Adoration Chapel, I saw Our Lady and she was high, looking down on me. Then I saw like a Star of Bethlehem and Mary said: *"I brought my Son into your world and I am His herald for His Second Coming. His glory will be shown shortly. But first my faithful will be tested to the limit. Those who keep the faith during this evil time will truly be rewarded an extra measure. For there will be wars and rumors of wars as evil will reign for a time. But this is all part of my Son's plan for the purification of the earth. I ask you to pray hard to endure this evil age and ask God's help to save your souls. Your souls are your biggest concern. What happens to the body is of little consequence in the end since it will pass away in time. Those that pray together will save themselves."*

Saturday, February 12, 1994:
On my way to church the door ripped my jacket and in the first reading the Northern King of Juda was trying to keep the people from Jerusalem by having idols of calves placed in two of his cities to worship. I received the word *"Pride"* and Jesus gave the message: *"You must not be prideful of the things you own or your position in life. These gifts of mine have been bestowed on you but they can be taken away as well. Do not idolize things to the point you depend on them for they will pass away. In fact I will be*

testing your country by taking away your wealth since you have squandered My blessings with abortions and killing. So direct your lives to prayer and My love for those things of heaven are what you should take pride in."

Later, at the Adoration Chapel, I saw some penguins walking. Jesus gave the message: *"For those who have faith, your messages need no explanation. As people question them, they will soon see their fulfillment. Those that doubt, should read better the signs of your times. Events will continue to hasten and men will indeed understand that these are the end times talked of in Revelation for this time. Those who do not respond to My warnings now will have more to endure later. If people do not ask for My help, they will truly be lost. As events unfold, surely most will see the validity of your messages I and My Mother have given you. You are right to follow your spiritual advisor's suggestions to prove you are sincere in carrying out My plan for you. Pray constantly for My guidance, for I will not lead you astray but help My people as well."*

Sunday, February 13, 1994:

After Communion, I saw like a strange light flash across the sky much like Our Lady's foretelling sign before World War II. The readings were about curing lepers. Jesus gave a message: *"My people have yet to realize how they are suffering from the leprosy of war. War has and is disfiguring many nations with no real cause but greed and hatred for each other. Without a sincere wish by man to ask for a cure by enough prayer for peace, man is destined to wallow in his sores of war. He has to make an effort to want My help or My graces will not be given. I offer them freely but without asking, it is a refusal of My love. Without My help it is very possible an unwanted war will ensue. Prepare for hard times if this continues."*

Later, at the Adoration Chapel, I saw a winter scene and there was a large hill covered with snow. Then in the next scene I started traveling real fast like I was riding a jet and the ground was going by rapidly. Jesus gave a message: *"Do not fear when things will happen. I will warn you just before they do. It is not anyone's place to know why and when I choose to do things. It is enough for you to guard over your souls and see to it they are spotless*

HL.WALBVRGA

M.W.BECHTOLSHEIM.O.S.B.   ABTEI ST.WALBVRG

SAINT WALBURGA
PRAY FOR US

*...ommitted a serious sin,
...giveness. Regardless of
...t any time. So be always
...en you will not be found
...to heaven. The Lenten
...can grow more in your
...e so see how you have
...vantage of this time to*

*...e's Day)
...aped objects. Jesus said:
...love you. I am Infinite
...ou to understand. My
...ost loving act for you.
...Lent. My love for My
...man in a good Catholic
...u—you need only ask
...nd you will be blessed
...e your fellow man. In
...l My people together."*

Jesus gave a message:
*...have sent My Apostles
...on. I have entrusted to
them and their successors the keys to My Kingdom. I have left
them the power to consecrate the bread and wine into My Body
and Blood. This Eucharist is My daily loving presence to you
where My love reaches out to all. My Church means so much to
Me that I call for your prayers to preserve the unity among its
members. Also, pray for your priests that they will continue to
give My true teachings to the faithful. To preserve My Church
you must take care to pass on this gift to your children. It is your
responsibility to encourage them to stay with the true faith and
teach them the doctrines in the Gospel. If they refuse My teaching, continue to pray for them as My St. Monica did for her beloved St. Augustine. It is important never to give up, but keep
praying for conversion. I am constantly seeking to bring all My
children to Me by their own decision. You can act as My instrument in fulfilling My desire."*

Tuesday, February 15, 1994:

After Communion, I saw a tower rising up as the tower restaurant at Niagara Falls. Jesus said: *"I am calling you to another Lent to prepare your spiritual lives for the day when you will be resurrected from this earth to heaven. Take care to root out any stubborn vices that you could make penance for this Lent. This should be a time for inspection of how you could purify your life for Me. Use this time wisely for extra meditation on how to please Me with prayer and good works. Many problems abound in the world because there is not enough prayer or peace. Encourage the peacemakers or war will destroy you."*

Later, at the Adoration Chapel, I could see some modern art and the word came *"Confusion."* Jesus gave a message: *"Many people are confused with the things and people of this world. Too often people are only taken up with their immediate earthly tasks. I am asking My faithful to look beyond the world's events to think of their Creator and what He has in store for them. I am asking My people to search on a higher plane to seek why they are here and where they will go. You have been made in My image to love and adore God and thank Him even for your very existence every day. Seen in this light you can offer up all your trials to Me each day and I will help you and lighten your load. For those who love Me and consecrate themselves to Me, they will receive a proper reward. Peace of mind and My love will be with them always. So this Lent concentrate on the deeper meaning of life and you will experience the joy of My love."*

Wednesday, February 16, 1994: (Ash Wednesday)

After Communion, I saw some people standing in line and I received the words *"Sackcloth and ashes."* Jesus gave a message: *"Today you start your Lenten observance with the distribution of ashes. Let it remind you how your body was created from dust and will return to dust. You will take nothing from this world but your immortal soul—so treasure where your soul is headed. This is the acceptable time now for your country to do as Nineveh and repent of the evil abortions you have committed. Without a turning around on this issue, many calamities will befall your country. My justice hangs in the balance. You are the ones who will decide your own fate. Without prayer and praise of God I will pull back My blessings and we will see how you fare by yourself, if that is what you wish."*

Later, at the prayer group, I saw Jesus standing in a white garment and He was sad. Jesus said: *"I am waiting in the desert as I still suffer the abandonment of many of My people. This Lent offers you an opportunity to walk with Me through the forty days I spent in the desert praying for all My people past, present and future."* I then heard the saying: *"There is lamentation in Rama where Rachel is weeping for her children who are no more."* Jesus said: *"The children who were killed in Bosnia were graphic and brought great distress. But where is the grief for all the unborn babies you are killing every day. I warn you this will not go unpunished."* I then saw the Olympic rings and Jesus said: *"It is good these games draw all countries together. This has tremendous hope for world peace and an understanding among all peoples."* I then had a vision which looked like the Divine Mercy. A ray of love shot out from Jesus which headed right for my heart. He said: *"I bring all of you tonight My blessing of graces to fall on you and answer your prayers in My own way. Be open to receive My graces, for I do not force them on you but freely give them to you."* I then saw the dove of the Holy Spirit and He said: *"I am the Spirit of Love and I too shower My faithful with graces, love and virtues. Pray to enlighten your souls with the lessons from this Lenten devotion."* I then saw a great light and Jesus said: *"Darkness of sin covers this land. But I am the light which dispels this darkness because I have overcome it. Come during this Lent to get closer to Me in your interior prayer life so you will shine My light on others."* I then saw Mary at a distance with a light about her and then suddenly I could see her in conflict with Lucifer the devil. She said: *"For a time there will be a great struggle with the power of evil. But fear not I and my Son will protect you as my triumph over Satan will soon come."*

Thursday, February 17, 1994:

After Communion, I saw the word *"Money."* Today's reading talked about *"Choose life."* Jesus said: *"Today's message of choose life has been the theme of your messages. Man seems to constantly fall back on his weak human nature and thinks of earthly things rather than those of heaven. Your profit should be seeking*

Me, for those who seek only money will be wanting all the time and never at peace. Your soul's destiny is your main decision. With prayer and asking for My help you will be directed toward heaven and heavenly things. These are what I desire for you and the plan My will has in store for you if you 'Choose' it."

Friday, February 18, 1994:

In church, I saw a black owl looking around. Jesus gave a message: *"Many of My people think they are 'wise' in the ways of the world. How they fail to realize how little they really know. Things of this life will not last, so knowing them is of very little value. The dangerous part is that people become too prideful and laud it over others. It is just these whom I will humble, since in spiritual life you must come to Me as little children. You will find how little you know as My understanding is given you with prayer. So one Lenten intention might be to not be so boastful even of what little knowledge you have. Otherwise, you will quickly be humbled some time and will walk away in shame. Take care and model your lives on how I behaved through life, even though I had all knowledge."*

Later, at the Adoration Chapel, I saw people talking in a vision and I could physically hear many voices from the Rec Hall below. Jesus gave the message: *"Why do men grumble about each other? Many of My people rejoice at other people's misfortune or are quick to spread scandal about others. Some even spread rumors against those whom they are envious. It is hard for some to accept other's good fortune, but easy to berate other's faults. I tell you it cannot be this way for My disciples. Remember I taught you to say yes when you mean yes and no when you mean no— all else is from the evil one. So guard your tongue and say prayers for others instead of stories. In doing so you will be following My way for peace among you. Too much dissension is caused by ill will between people, so try to do things which are more positive and this will lead you to heaven. You must be constantly on guard over your spiritual life. Then you will reap your reward in eternity with Me."*

Saturday, February 19, 1994:

At the New York JFK airport to Betania while praying the Rosary I saw Our Lady coming and she said: *"My children, I am greeting you now to show you my love as you travel to my shrine. Many of my people have anxieties but fear not, I will be watching over you. I will be giving you my graces for this visit and I am asking you to share them with your friends when you return. Also, please give me your prayer petitions and I will give them to my Son. Keep praying throughout the trip for there is great need of prayer in your world to combat sin, and for peace to keep you from war. I am asking you to pray my consecration prayers for the Annunciation. Please continue to work during this Lent as my Son has directed, to continue to purify your life from habitual sins."*

Sunday, February 20, 1994:

At the Betania Shrine after Communion at the Mass of Fr. Moreta. I briefly saw Mary in white and then I saw a mountain and out toward the sky it was a little dark. Suddenly, the sky opened up with a bright red light and spread out and became brighter. Our Lady gave a message: *"These are my people. Listen to their lovely singing. They have a deep love for me here, as I do for them. I welcome all pilgrims to my shrine and I want you to reverence this area since it is holy ground. I will give you many blessings if you would just ask Me. Your prayers will be answered in my Son's time according to His will. The vision of red light is a picture of the beginning of the purification of the earth. After this time my triumph will occur in concert with my Son's plans. Thank you for your Rosary and continue in prayer often so you can save your souls and bring others back to my Son. Do not waste time but send a barrage of prayers to heaven. Thank you for responding to my call."*

Later, after the Rosary and supper Our Lady gave a visit. There was a vision of a lot of people in a room and I saw several children standing in the middle of the crowd and a bright white light shown down like a spotlight on the children. Our Lady said: *"My children I want you to take great care in the religious education of the young children. It is very important to me that these inno-*

cent be taught well in the faith. You, my faithful, have the responsibility to bring these souls to my Son and make them aware of coming to my Son in faith. It is important also that you give them good example by prayer and going to Confession often. In essence you too must continue to come to me and my Son as little children trusting in us completely with your consecration. Pray often to keep strong in your faith. Thank you for responding to my call."

Monday, February 21, 1994:

At the Betania Shrine after Communion I saw Our Lady greeting her Son and there was a beautiful shedding of light and a bright cloud around Our Lord. Our Lady offered her Son to give the message: *"This Gospel is so dear to My heart because it represents how all My people are joined to My one Body. You have seen some of the poverty in this land and I continue to ask your help to feed and clothe My people no matter where they live. Also, you now can more appreciate the blessings I have given you. Give thanks to God for all He has given you both physically and spiritually. Since you have been given much, more will be expected of you. Again I plead with you to continue to evangelize My people with your teaching and your prayers. Receive the sacraments often, especially Confession."*

Later, in Maria Esperanza's chapel I felt a radiating out of graces from the presence of the Blessed Sacrament. Carol fell slain in the Spirit. I saw a cross with much light emanating from it. I then saw a choir of ladies singing. It was about ten to fifteen rows high. Our Lord gave a message: *"I love you and your people so very much. My daughter here is very deep in My heart and My Mother's. It is hard to express in words to all of you how much I love you. You are indeed My chosen people and I will forever be watching over you. Please now take My love and the graces I have bestowed on you back to your friends at home. You must radiate My love to others like I radiate My love to you. You must be examples of My love in everything you do. You can teach by your words, your actions, and the love you express in your deeds. I ask all to keep close to Me in prayer. Never fall lax in loving and adoring Me. Then I will give you the strength to do My will in all you do on earth."*

Note: This was an extraordinary evening where we had four hours of time with Maria for all thirty-five of us at her house which is most unusual. She said my messages were true and from God. She said it had proper continuity. She greeted everyone, healed one lady of breast cancer and she had a vision of Our Lady and Jesus while we were there. When we left, she said she would come to me on Thursdays at Communion.

Maria's Prayer: *"Hearts of Jesus and Mary united in one heart have compassion and mercy on us and the whole world."* She said Fr. Moreta was the instrument of a banquet feast with us.

Tuesday, February 22, 1994: (Chair of Peter Feast)

At Our Lady of Coromoto Shrine, in the chapel, after Communion, I saw Our Lady in many icons and some with the Infant Jesus with Mary. Mary gave a message: *"My children I come to all the Americas-North, Central, and South America. You are all such beautiful people and I ask all of my faithful to continue my devotions, especially the Rosary. My shrine in Coromoto is especially close to me as I share my love with the Indians as in Guadalupe. I love you so much and I want to draw you to my Son as much as possible. Now is a special time since I am heralding my Son's Second Coming. Prepare your souls for Him as you would prepare for a King at a huge banquet. My love goes out very much to my shepherd John Paul II who is my delight—please follow him in all his admonitions to the faithful. He has a very important and difficult mission for my people during this evil age. I want to thank you for the many Rosaries and prayers. I am already sending you my blessings in answer to your petitions. Continue to pray and stay close to me and my Son, especially with the Holy Eucharist."*

Wednesday, February 23, 1994: (Los Frailles, Old Monastery)

I saw a glimpse of Mary and she was dressed in a wedding dress. I then saw a huge flame start and grow and it came close to me but it did not burn me because I was protected. Our Lady gave a message: *"I am coming as a bride because you my children of my Son's Church are joined to my Son who is your spouse. He loves you so intimately that He wants you all to be one with Him forever. He and I are joined so close that our hearts and minds*

already are one. This experience you have seen shows you why I appear often with my Son as an Infant. My Son is always reaching out to you to pull you closer to Himself. He loves you so much and I lead you to Him always in what I do. You must be rich in prayer and receive my Son in the Eucharist to strengthen your faith for you will have much to suffer to help sinners. Offer up all your troubles and trials as a daily prayer and put your trust in me and my Son that we will lead you to say what you need to save souls."

Note: On the way to Los Frailles the bus almost crashed into a big truck in the Andes Mountains. The driver said it was a miracle we stopped as fast as we did since he said he usually requires his emergency brake as well to stop fast. But he only had time to use his one brake. This was a sign of Our Lady protecting us on our trip as represented by the fire which did not burn me.

Later, (Reading on Nineveh) in Merida at the Museum Church after Communion, I saw Jesus on the cross and He was bleeding profusely from His wounds. Jesus gave a message: *"This day is an evil age as in the past. The devil is being allowed a time to test My people. But do not fear him since I will protect you. Man has worshiped himself more in this era than any other. He has become so perverted that the earth calls on My justice to be purified. There is no turning back My hand now. Only prayer can diminish the punishment but not stop it. My faithful must suffer their Good Friday as I did before they can be allowed their Easter Resurrection. I have died for your sins to allow you eternal heaven but you must show you are faithful to Me by obeying My will and becoming one with Me. Continue to send your prayers and follow My commandments so you can lead the rest of My people to Me."*

Thursday, February 24, 1994: (Reading on asking Prayer)

In the Hilton Hotel Room 107 (Paul and Al's room) after Communion, I saw a vision of Christ on the cross at a little distance. I then saw a picture of a monk. (I did ask a question about Muriel's experience.) Jesus gave a message: *"Peace be with you. I bring you My love and My peace. I have said many times only to ask for any graces that you desire of Me. I will answer your prayers in My way but ask in faith and sincere prayer. I love My people and*

My heart envelopes you with My love. I will continue to listen for your requests in whatever you do. In answer to your question on the little girl, her healing has started and with continued prayer she will be healed. Keep faith and you will see many cures. But this is an evil age and you will be asking My help and grace constantly to protect your soul from the demons. You must prepare yourself for battle with the demons with the Rosary, the cross with the corpus that you have, holy water and My Mother's scapular. Maria, My daughter, will continue to do My great work. All of My faithful will be united in one body through My Eucharist. Continue to keep yourself clean of soul with Confession to receive My graces."

Friday, February 25, 1994:

In the convent of the Miracle of the Eucharist in Los Teques after Communion, I saw Jesus suffering much from the scourging and a very bloody agony on the cross. Jesus said: *"I am showing you graphically how much I suffer for you to forgive your sins. I have been scourged with the whips tearing My flesh. I have suffered the crown of thorns which dug into My skull. I suffer still the nails in My hands and My feet. The sword pierces My heart. My heart is still broken since many of My people fail to appreciate My love for them. I am pouring out My blood still to amend for the many sins of man. As you sin you are making Me relive My crucifixion. But I love you so much that I continue to forgive you. You must return My love if you are to be accepted into heaven. You must adore Me as your Creator. You must give thanks to Me for your gift of faith. You must praise Me for the glory and graces I bequeath on you. For I treasure most lovingly every sinner who repents of their sin. It is a delight to all who are in heaven. You must continue your prayer and good deeds to guard your soul from the evil one. Everyday you must give witness in public that you will continue to follow My will."*

Saturday, February 26, 1994: (It rained, then the sun shined.)

At the Betania Shrine after Communion, I saw Our Lady come in a crown with her Infant Son also in a crown. They both appeared as in the woods behind the shrine. Our Lady gave a message: *"I am sending you my sign of rain in the sky to help purify your sins. I am bringing my Son to forgive your sins. I am also shining my graces of love on you with the sun's rays. We (Jesus and Mary) both are in one heart and one spirit. We are sending you (plural) on a mission back to your people to bring souls back to God. Right now it is important to bring knowledge of my Son and His love to those in most need of His help. You must prepare them before the evil age reaches such a state that the people will no longer listen. Ask for my graces and my Son's help to let them know how they must accept Him into their hearts and souls to be saved. Without my Son in their lives, they will be led to the eternal fires of hell. But if they accept Him, He will grant them eternal peace in heaven. It is His will you must follow, for this is what He created us to do—adore, love and give praise to Him."*

Later, at the Hilton Hotel's dining room after Communion, I saw a woman I did not recognize and then I saw a series of mountains. Jesus gave a message: *"I am greeting you on My mountain of love. Your pilgrimage has seen an outpouring of graces, especially through My servant Maria. You are spiritually on My mountain of grace where you have been basking in the light of My truth. Now shortly you will be returning to your homes. You will be coming down the mountain from this experience. I ask you to treasure this grace and opportunity to grow deeper in My love. You must work everyday now to keep pure and holy so you can do My work. In order to spread My word, you must continue to guard your interior life. You must make time for your daily prayer and frequent Confession. By preserving your soul from falling into temptation, you will be strong to tell others of your experience. I will be using your witness to give testimony to My faithful of the love and grace I freely give to My people. Show others how easy it is with Me to come to Me and receive forgiveness and give them purpose in their lives."*

Sunday, February 27, 1994:

At the Adoration Chapel, I saw Our Lady's face bright and warm. It would disappear then I would see Jesus with a crown in her place. I then saw hills from an airplane looking over the earth. Mary gave a message: *"I want to thank my chosen children for completing your pilgrimage to my beloved Betania as I requested. I have sent you many graces for your faith in me and my Son. We knew that you had trust that I would watch over you and protect you. But it is good for you to witness this protection and tell your friends of my faithfulness in helping you. You have been blessed with many spiritual uplifting experiences. Now is the time to let people see by your increased enthusiasm in the spirit that my love and that of my Son must be spread to all the faithful. Both my Son and I hate to see any soul lost to the evil one, so I am asking you to be our instruments in spreading the Gospel so the lost souls will have one last chance. Your mission of being apostles is important to my Son's Kingdom and will help in the fulfillment of my triumph. With faith and acceptance of my Son all who do so will enjoy my Son's peace. And I will feel fulfilled to help you bring these souls to God."*

Monday, February 28, 1994:

After Communion, I saw Our Lady in the shape of statues wanting to talk to me. She said: *"My son, I am happy with you and my faithful children to see you all at Mass today. It would be most beautiful if my children held their fervor for Lent throughout the whole year. This is a good time for reflection but also it should continue as well. For my children need to be recollected always and constantly on guard to fight the evil one even with the everyday adversities. My children you must continue to radiate the graces I have shared with you to all those around you. In that way, you will give witness and love to all. By your example, others can be on fire with my Son's love and see the futility of desiring the things of this world. It is only heaven and being with my Son and me that matters in this world. Pray for strength and my Son will help you to achieve your goal to be with Him always."*

Later, I saw a woman from Venezuela and I was greeting her on a very sunny day. Jesus gave a message: *"I am here in the Blessed Sacrament always waiting for you. I long to love each of My people with a close enduring love that will bind us together for eternity. I want to give you My peace and understanding of My deep love for you. With these gifts I have given you, it is now your turn to go out to all the people of the world and greet them with My love and peace. In sharing Me with others through friendship they will be joined to My one body through all of you acting as My instruments. By your baptism you are commissioned to spread My word. Those who have come back from Betania are even more in My debt. For you have given of yourselves to Me and My Mother. You too shall go out to My people and prepare them for My final victory over sin and death. I am coming for you soon. Prepare and be on guard that you are ready to receive My glory and that your soul is pure. In this way you can come into My presence and be absorbed in My oneness."*

Tuesday, March 1, 1994:

After Communion, I at first saw Our Lady and then some glimpses of Jesus and His many faces. Jesus gave a message: *"All of My faithful have been blessed with many gifts and graces. None of you are worthy by yourselves, but it is My freely giving them to you. As I have mentioned many times, to those who have been given much, more will be expected. You have been asked to evangelize My people. But I warn you, you have an added responsibility. You are teaching My love and peace. As such you must be close to Me and follow your teaching in your example. Because you will be teaching in My name, you must guard your souls more strongly since the evil one will try to prevent you from your mission. Your temptations and sufferings may increase but know that through My graces you will carry out My will. Continue to watch over your individual prayer lives and prepare yourselves well for My work. Then your reward will await you in heaven as My love draws you closer to Me in everything you do."*

Later, at the Adoration Chapel, I saw some Arabs and Yasser Arafat. Jesus gave the message: *"There are many war clouds hanging over the earth. For there is great hatred and greed for power which abounds. The evil one has a hand in wanting war so to cause great chaos. This will enable the Anti-Christ to come on the scene as a great peacemaker. But he will create a false peace and invoke an evil tyranny over the people. His reign will not last long and his kingdom will be conquered. This is the testing time I am allowing, to see how My faithful will come to Me for help. I am in total control and My plan is beyond your understanding. So do not question My will. It is enough to know that My plan is an instrument to purify the earth of its evil. You must prepare and go underground to avoid this evil time. You must pray and ask for My guidance as to what to do. Do not fear, I will allow you to endure this test with My graces. So continue your prayers to understand that My ways are not your ways."*

Wednesday, March 2, 1994:

After Communion, I saw a dawn only it was more of a vertical direction with the sun coming from the side instead of the bottom horizon. I then had a picture of the South American Continent. Jesus gave a message: *"A new dawn is coming on an era of peace. This will be a supernatural experience and it is why you are seeing a vertical dawn. It will be a time when the purified earth will be free of its present corruption. It will be as I originally intended before the fall of Adam. It will occur within your lifetime. It will be a joy for those faithful to live during this time. But it will come at a high price of endurance. The earth must go through the pain of My persecution and suffering in order for those faithful to persevere. With prayer and allegiance to My will, you will win the prize of salvation for your souls."*

Later, at the prayer group, I saw a scene of older women praying the Rosary. Jesus said: *"These are My faithful who pray to Me daily to keep strong in their faith. I love My people and My heart goes out to all of you so to envelop you into My protection from evil."* I then saw a dove above a priest dressed in a chasuble with a cross on it. The Holy Spirit said: *"I am the Spirit of Love and I bestow My special graces now on all My priest sons. They are in great need of help in these times when Satan is especially increasing his fight against My priests."* I then kept seeing many different faces of Mary from the various shrines around the world. Mary said: *"I am the Virgin of Betania. I come to bestow my blessing and graces on all present tonight with your people. Thank you for your Rosary and many will be helped by my graces tonight."* I then had a vision of Christ on the cross and the words *"Suffering servant"* came. Jesus said: *"I am your Suffering Servant because I continue to suffer for the sins of man. Many of you suffer with Me as victim souls. Offer up all your trials and pain to help sinners. Never waste your pain. They are given at times for you to offer up to Me in reparation for sin."* I then saw an angel blowing a trumpet. Jesus said: *"My angel sounds the trumpet of the end times. Many events will befall you but know now that this is the sign of My Second Coming. It is indeed at hand.*" A very emotional vision came of Our Lord in a crown of thorns. Jesus said: *"My love continues to go out to My people. Some have received Me, still others fail to understand My love. I am not forcing myself on everyone but I will give everyone an opportunity to see themselves as I see them."* I then saw a vision of God the Father in gold and He had a stern face. He said: *"My judgment will fall heavily on those who instigate and perpetuate wars which kill My people. They will pay dearly. Pray much that wars will be overcome by your prayers for peace. There is a great need for peace in your world amidst all the hatred and contempt people have for each other."*

Thursday, March 3, 1994:

After Communion, I was apprehensive of Maria Esperanza not knowing what to expect. A vision came to me of a burning torch of good size. The background was a picture of Maria's tabernacle in her private chapel. Jesus then gave a message on the Gospel of Divies and the beggar Lazarus: *"This Gospel became personal to all on the trip where beggars were abound. Some gave donations but many of you were either not open or fearful to throw some scraps from the table. Be open to My poor always in helping them or you will not be open to Me in their bodies. This theme of money and the importance of worldly things is one I talk of constantly. The things of this earth are passing away very quickly and soon will have no consequence. So set your heart and soul on things of heaven which are eternal and you will see their real value. It is only prayer and the grace of My presence that are of importance. Treasure My gifts and blessings for the gifts of the spirit far outweigh My material blessings."*

Friday, March 4, 1994:

After Communion, I saw a priest giving out Communion on the tongue. Jesus gave a message: *"It is reverence I seek more than sacrifice. It is love for Me I am seeking more than just going through the saying of many prayers. No matter what you do, if it is not out of love and in keeping with My will, it will count for nothing. For I am the vine, you are the branches. Apart from Me you can do nothing. You must pray from the heart and love Me with your whole being as I love you. The Scribes and Pharisees followed My old covenant to the letter publicly, but inside they rejected My new covenant of love. You must love one another and follow My ways if you are to gain eternal life with Me."*

Later, at the Adoration Chapel, I saw Jesus and He was bleeding very much on the cross. Jesus gave a message: *"Why do My people continue to make Me suffer on the cross with their sins? On Fridays do Me extra homage at 3:00 pm with My Divine Mercy Chaplet. By honoring Me in this way, you can offer up your prayers for the sin going on at that time. As man's continued indifference proceeds, will there be many faithful ready when I return? I am depending on you, My faithful remnant, to provide Me with your love and your intercessory prayers. In doing so you will afford Me an oasis of love in the desert of humanity which has rejected Me or has forgotten Me altogether. There continues a great need for prayers for peace in these times. Please ask more to pray for peace, if they want to stem the tide of continuous wars."*

Saturday, March 5, 1994:

At church, I saw Jesus very large and He was in the sky. Jesus said: *"It is mercy I desire and mercy which I pour out on sinners. I continue to make you aware of how much I love you and I am asking you to ask anything of Me within My will and I will grant it to you. Graces are abound but few request them. I am always present to you to give any help to you. I watch over you with love as a loving parent and I am also inviting those who are far from Me in sin to come and repent. I wish to give you little previews of the glory in My Kingdom which awaits those who are faithful. My Transfiguration before My Apostles showed you some of My glory in the radiance of My glorified body which you will share. Also, tell the people of your vision of heaven, how it is so peaceful and full of love. How when you saw it, that it convinced you the things of this earth are nothing and My love and pleasing Me are all that is required. My people need explanations so they can appreciate how My love is always awaiting them if they would just receive Me."*

Later, I at first saw Jesus carrying His cross, then displayed over this image Our Lady came down from the sky to greet the people. She said: *"This is my beloved Son whom I am one in spirit and mind. This time of life during Lent should bring you closer to my Son. It is a time to recollect how much you have offended Him. His love goes out to everyone equally for He died to forgive the sins of all no matter what walk of life or how serious the sinner. I want to thank my pilgrims to Betania for sharing my loving messages with you. They indeed have received many blessings. My messages from Betania are the same as from all my apparition places—pray much to bring you all closer to my Son. A life of prayer and a protected interior life will keep you on your pilgrimage to heaven no matter what trials will befall you in this life. Ask my Son to help you through each day by walking with you each step you take in all you do. By living my Son's will you will inherit His Kingdom in heaven."*

Sunday, March 6, 1994: (Woman Homilist on Aids)
After Communion, I at first saw some strange shapes then I saw a loving picture of Jesus coming forward. Jesus gave a message: *"I have many victim souls who suffer My passion with Me. Many of My people are sick or in pain but not all realize how they could offer up their suffering in reparation for sin. I have said before not to waste your opportunities for graces in offering up your pains. Again you must be careful not to judge others' behavior, for they are responsible to Me. You must love everyone equally for My Holy Spirit is in each of them. Each one of you is a sinner so be careful, lest you judge yourself in return. As My love goes out to all My people, you should follow My example. You may give witness to encourage My loving behavior. But do not turn people away by your righteousness. In a word you must love your enemies and be perfect as your heavenly Father is perfect."*

Later, after Communion, I saw a Jewish ceremony with rabbis dressed in gold vestments. Jesus gave a message: *"I came to My chosen people as the Messiah in their midst, but many have rejected Me. I have changed the old covenant to a new covenant of love. To have My people's sins forgiven I have freely given My life for you. This Lent is a time of preparation for the day I will receive you at the gates of heaven. Direct your lives to prayer and fasting to keep your soul on the narrow road so that you will not desire the things of this world. You are called to a higher life in faith to live in My will. By doing so you will join Me in My triumph with My Mother as Satan will be silenced. In My Second*

Coming you will truly enjoy the peace and love in heaven for which I have created all men to receive."

Monday, March 7, 1994:

After Communion, in a vision I saw many empty seats at daily Mass. Jesus said: *"Many good intentions are made at the start of Lent with a resolve to improve spiritually. But nearly half way through Lent and many of those intentions are no longer being kept. Man must realize his earthly resolve is weak by his nature in spiritual things. You must ask My help in prayer to keep your resolve, then you will be able to sustain any effort you desire. It is in union with My grace and love that all things are possible. On your own you will fail miserably. Once man learns he must work in harmony with Me, then all life takes shape and succeeds for this is the plan of My will and it is beautiful to behold."*

Later, I saw a galaxy of stars then I saw Our Lady and the words came *"Queen of the Universe."* Mary gave a message: *"This Lent I come to prepare you to receive my Son. In that first sorrowful time of my Son, I suffered much to see my Lord mocked, abused and finally crucified. We both suffered the pains in each of our bodies and spirits as we are joined as one. My Son's death on the cross was man's ransom for his sins. My Son's triumph on the cross gave man the opportunity to enter heaven. Even now my Son will soon share the triumph of His glory with His faithful. Through your prayer, fasting and Confession give glory to God that He has saved you. Through your suffering you come closer to Him. Prepare your hearts to receive Him as often as possible in the Eucharist. His love flows out to you even as He suffers on His cross today. My children continue to guard your spiritual lives this Lent. Then you can rejoice as my Son comes forth on Easter with His Resurrection."*

Tuesday, March 8, 1994:

After Communion, I saw in the distance a figure of a person but their eyes and face looked like a skeleton. Their eyes seemed hollow. Jesus gave the message: *"Many people put on airs or outwardly give one impression but inwardly they are plotting evil thoughts. I look into the heart to see a person's real intent in what they think. Out of the heart comes the true intentions of what people are considering. You cannot be hollow inside when it comes to abiding in My love and following My laws. Whatever you do on the outside must have equal meaning in your heart. Be true to yourself and true to Me. Pray that you may be consistent in your love and praise for Me in all you do. If you follow My will always, you will not care what others think. Nor will you have to hide your feelings, if they are not proper. Love is truth. You must live your life as an example of My love."*

Later, at the Adoration Chapel, I saw at first a sphere in the middle and a cloud ringed around it. Then there were flashes of white fire against some people. Jesus gave a message: *"You come tonight with many concerns but they are not important. Many of My people are at risk of war in several places in your world. Without enough prayer, the evil one will continue to stir up people against each other. Many confrontations are creating a situation for a serious war. But these things will happen. When My warning comes, it will signal the beginning of the last stages of the battle of good and evil. This is how you should view your earthly situation as good vs. evil. You must guard your spiritual lives now because your severe testing time is almost upon you. But once I have conquered the evil one, My peace will reign. Have hope that in the end My triumph will be all that matters."*

Wednesday, March 9, 1994:

After Communion, I saw a huge mushroom cloud and then a picture of the earth. It was white all around and on the ground a little dark as a nuclear winter. Jesus gave the message: *"Man at this point in time is being offered a choice. He can continue on his earthly plan of greed for money and possessions or he can ask for My mercy and live according to My will. If he chooses doing it his way, his greed for power and the things of this world could eventually lead to a world nuclear war. On the other hand, if he has a change of heart and sees the foolishness of leading his life without Me, surely I will forgive him and return My peace and love in your prosperity. It is a choice between My will and man's will. Much prayer is needed now because man is at a critical junction in his history. Whatever man ultimately chooses, he will reap what he sows."*

Later, at the prayer group, I saw several planes diving to attack some targets in Bosnia—also a sense of the planes we heard last April there. Jesus said: *"War will continue to break out in various places of Bosnia unless more prayers are forthcoming. More planes will be drawn into the conflict and possibly a larger NATO involvement will cause problems."* I then saw a time machine with a reference to seeing our past life before God. Jesus said: *"You will have a time when your lives and your sins will be very vivid to you. You will go back in time and see how you have progressed to the present. You will be given a chance to realize that you are in fact a sinner and should ask My forgiveness."* I then saw like a macaw bird with a big yellow beak. Jesus said: *"Many men spend long hours at peace talks but nothing seems to come of them. In order to be successful at peace, men must be ready to talk with their hearts of love. You cannot have peace with hate in your heart. Also, you must ask for My help. Peace without Me does not last."* I then saw many faces of Christ and finally a picture of the Divine Mercy: *"Peace starts with rest in the family. Once a family prays and is at ease and has love for each other, it soon spreads outside to others at the workplace. It is only man who controls how he will demonstrate his love from his heart. If it is cold, only unrest and wars will result."* Our Lady came in a shimmering image because she was weeping. She said: *"I am crying for man because he is not listening to my call for prayers for peace. Many have good intentions but their hearts are far from God. Prayer is needed to show your sorrow and request God's forgiveness."* I then saw a huge snake with great fangs and many other smaller snakes. Jesus said: *"Satan is preparing for his last push to destroy man. Through his one-world cohorts and the Masons he is readying the day to receive the Anti-Christ and prepare for his reign. When the thirteen countries join Maastricht, his time will soon approach."* I then saw some fetuses and Jesus said: *"In your own country many are deaf to an ongoing major war against the unborn. The casualties are higher than many of the world wars before. How blind can you be to not see this carnage and stem this tide against life? How can peace occur when you war on your own infants?"*

Thursday, March 10, 1994:

After Communion, I saw Maria with her eyes closed and she was raising her head to heaven. I then saw a man in handcuffs. Jesus said: *"This age asks for a sign but I give you none except that of Jonah. You must open your hearts to Me this Lent so I can empower you with My graces. If you continue to be a prisoner inside yourself, how can I help you. You must be open to My will and let Me run your daily affairs. Without Me you will not succeed. Depend on Me for help, not just on yourself. You start opening your heart with prayer. By staying in communication with Me, I will help you through life and it will be a joy. Without Me, life will seem like so much drudgery."*

Friday, March 11, 1994:

After Communion, I saw several priests and finally I saw a priest holding up the Host at Consecration. Jesus gave a message: *"Many of My people have made Lenten intentions to better their spiritual lives. There are various levels of success in carrying them out. But I look to your hearts at least to the extent My people are sincere and trying to do better. I love you all and I am always waiting to help you and grant My graces to you. It is you who comes to Me for Communion and Confession. I am with you always but you must receive Me into your hearts. Each day I offer you a bonus of graces if you would just ask for them. To improve your life you must walk with Me each day and do My will. It is only when you are in harmony with Me that I can perform great works through you. So keep close to Me and let Me lead you always."*

Saturday, March 12, 1994:

At St. Patrick's Church, in Maryland, after Communion, I saw some people in church then I saw an altar with Jesus in the distance. Then a web grew and clouded the scene. Jesus gave a message: *"I love My people but many times it is not returned with regularity. The faith I give you is a gem which should not be forgotten. You must guard it from the evil one. Do not let the cares of this world create a web and hide it from anyone. You should always revere My word and act it out in your daily trials and opportunities. Be a light to others and shine forth My love to all you meet. Faith is also likened to a garden. You must weed it and nurture it so it can grow and be fruitful. So with your spiritual life, you must enrich it with prayer and fasting. In Confession you must root out all your past sins and strive to be more like Me in all you do. In that way, you will please Me and will be able to join Me in My everlasting banquet."*

Sunday, March 13, 1994:

At St. Patrick's, Harvre de Grace, Maryland, after Communion, I saw a big heart shape and a woman's face. Jesus gave a message: *"I love My people with a never-ending love. I treasure the love you give Me in return especially your tears of joy and pain. Today focus on your senses in respect to the faith which is given you. You must wake up and keep awake in the eyes of faith. Do not let the cares of this life blind your ultimate goal of heaven. Do not let the sirens of your flesh or riches deafen you to only selfish pursuits. Open your eyes and ears to My word to you and speak it to others. Since you have been baptized, you must evangelize your neighbors to the graces of faith. Tell them life will come more alive to them if they walk every step with Me. Tell them and remind yourselves to keep a sound prayer life to preserve your faith and keep it healthy."*

Later, at the Adoration Chapel, I saw an outline of the cross and a sheet of flame covered the picture. The Holy Spirit gave the message: *"I am the Spirit of Love and I come to enkindle My fire of love in each of you. You are blessed to receive My graces. Treasure them but most of all share these graces with others through your prayers. It is important to let the love of Jesus be known among My faithful. Through your messages you can share that love with others. Be discreet and follow your spiritual director, but it is also of great value to Jesus to share His word with your friends. Also, the pilgrims with you should also share their messages and graces. They were given to be shared and to strengthen the faithful by your witness. Pray and ask Me and Jesus for guidance in these matters. We will give the graces for what you and the others are to say."*

Monday, March 14, 1994:

After Communion, I saw a white narrow cloud in the shape of an arrow pointing to the left. It pointed to a very dense white fog. Jesus gave a message: *"My love for you is strong and always do I want to point the way for you. But you must be willing to give Me a blind trust that where I lead you will be the proper direction for your life. Believe that My will is what you should desire and you will not be disappointed. Your ways may appear right to you, but you cannot always see the big picture of life and what it will lead to. Have faith in Me with prayer and life will become a blessing to you in all you do."*

Later, I saw a lot of people sitting around a banquet table. Jesus gave a message: *"My people I wish to share My love equally with all of you. No person is greater or lesser in My presence. Each of you are loved equally well. I tell you each person I send to you is a gift of life which I share with you until I call them back to Me. I ask you to see Me in everyone in your daily travels. My beauty of life goes with each of you. It is My will which keeps each of you in being. So I tell you to love even those you dislike for all are made in My image. Treasure each life and show forth My love by your loving everyone. In doing this you will perfect your love and make it more like Mine in being unconditional. Pray to Me that through My graces your love for your neighbor will be perfected in My one body of humanity."*

Tuesday, March 15, 1994:

After Communion, I saw a wall with a hole in it and for a long time I saw a small flame burning in a red enclosure as a sanctuary light. Jesus gave a message: *"Today I bring you My living water which you shall drink and never thirst again. I give you My Body and Blood in the sacramental appearances of bread and wine. As I give of Myself to you, you now become My sanctuaries. Inside of each person I have a living presence which should always be honored. As you honor Me in My tabernacle so also honor My presence in every one you meet. Each person may have individual levels of holiness but I am with each nonetheless. Pray for your holiness and that of others that each will keep themselves worthy of My presence and fountains of My love which can be poured out on others."*

Later, at the Adoration Chapel, I first saw a picture of a triangle representing the Trinity. I then saw a picture of Jesus carrying a lamb. Jesus said: *"Come to Me all who are finding life burdensome and I will refresh you. For My yoke is easy and My burden light. Bear with the trials of this life for it lasts but a short while. Your victory over sin with My help will lead you to My glory in heaven. Do not worry about the things of this life but put your trust in Me and become a part of My peace. When you are resting in My peace, I will protect you. With constant prayer and following My will, life should be joyful for you even through adversities. My love is your strength and it is enough for you. If you have My love, you have everything worth possessing. The gifts of the Spirit should be sought out most, for therein lies your most precious blessings. Enjoy My love and live it daily in everything you do. Once you live in union with Me, life truly becomes a joy."*

Wednesday, March 16, 1994:

After Communion, I saw a door slightly ajar and a rush of light coming through the slight opening. Jesus gave the message: *"My message today is to open the door to your heart that I may come in and give you My rest. Too many people have shut Me out of their lives to their loss. But I knock as a gentleman since I do not force My love on you. You must accept Me as your Savior and as your companion to walk through life with you. When you live in My will and let Me lead you, life's troubles are always kept at a distance with My love and protection. You will still have to suffer at times but the outcome of your life will never be in doubt. To My faithful I ask those who have received Me to witness to the cold hearts who reject Me. Tell them of your joy with Me. On seeing your example, they too might explore to finally open up to Me and see the reason for your joy in loving Me."*

Later, at the prayer group, I first saw a woman holding a mirror to see her reflection. Jesus said: *"Many are worried about their outward appearance to people, but I tell you that you should reflect My love to others. Do not worry what others will think of you, only be concerned with following My will and giving good example by your actions to others."* I then saw a ship and noticed they were using a compass and the stars of night to chart their course. Jesus said: *"I am giving you My roadmap to follow in order to reach your eternal destination of heaven with Me. Pray and read My Scriptures. That will be enough to lead you and others to follow My will for you."* I then saw a dim lit candle and Jesus said: *"I am the Light of the World. I show forth My love and grace of understanding so each will have an opportunity to find Me and find eternal life."* I then saw someone breathing on others. The Holy Spirit said: *"Receive Me into your hearts as I breathe My love on all of you here tonight. Cherish My virtues I bestow on you and live your life with the flame of My love."* I then saw a triangle of the Trinity and God the Father was speaking from a cloud: *"I blessed My Son at His baptism in the Jordan. By your baptism you are blessed also and are given a command to evangelize My people. All the faithful are called to witness in public to Me and I will see and receive you into eternity."* I then received the word *"Money"* and Jesus said: *"Do not place your trust in money or any of the things on this earth. Put your trust in Me and I will give you the peace of mind you desire. Use your money to help the poor and others. Do not pile it up selfishly for just your own use. For when you die, where will this wealth go but into the dust bin?"* I finally saw Christ suffering on the cross and He said: *"The sins of man are many and I suffer much because of them. I am asking you for your Lenten penance to offer up your suffering to help in reparation for sinners. This will help in holding back some of My Father's justice when accounts must be settled."*

Thursday, March 17, 1994: (St. Patrick's Day)
After Communion, I could see Maria E. praying fervently and then I sensed she wanted me to be united with her in Jesus at Communion. I then received a message from St. Patrick: *"I am glad my people are so happy with me this day. I also want to share with you how the shamrock can be used as a teaching of the Blessed Trinity—Father, Son and Holy Ghost. I am happy to share your Irish heritage as well. If you could visit here, it would be wonderful. I love you all and give you my blessing. Keep strong in the faith as I have taught much when I was on earth."*

Friday, March 18, 1994:

After Communion, I saw an altar and on it was a book which symbolized the Word of God. God the Father gave the message: *"My people always are asking for answers and where I come from. I tell you your ways are not My ways. I am the Creator and whatever I have given you is good. Do not question My gifts for they have a broader design than your will. I tell you look to the Scriptures for your answers. You must live with Me as one and follow My will. That only is what you should strive for. In your daily activities look to my Son and His example of how to live and that will be enough for you. If you have a question in life, ask how Jesus would have handled it. He sees with the eyes of love and not your justice. Ask the Holy Spirit to discern the Gospel and this will give you any answer you desire. In all things live in My love and you will have My peace."*

Saturday, March 19, 1994: (Wanda Gurstner Memorial Service)

After Communion, I saw a congregation and a cross was being held up. Jesus gave a message: *"My Son I am showing you a symbol of My cross that I hold up as Moses held the seraph snake on a stick. I tell you look to Me for your salvation. Keep your eyes focused on Me at all times. I love you all very much and I want you to keep close to Me always in prayer. For when you are communicating with Me, I can talk to your heart and give you My peace. When you are fixed on Me you can forget all your little problems and adversities of the day. My love should be your goal and destination in everything you do. With My love constantly in your life you will not fear death but it will just be a change of address. Continue to share with others, especially in any grieving process."*

At the Nocturnal Hour I saw some people standing in a raging fire but they were not consumed. Jesus gave a message: *"I have shown a picture of souls being tortured in hell. I tell you more souls are going to hell for the sins of the flesh—more than any other sin. Those who abuse My plans for married life by sex before marriage will pay a heavy price for their earthly pleasures. If man continues to desire the pleasures of life before Me, he makes those things his god before Me. This again is why this sin is so serious because I cannot forgive the sinner who does not ask for forgiveness. The sinner must pray to have contrition or have someone pray for them. But in the end, they must confess their sin and come to Me in repentance or face eternal damnation. This is the choice every man must make. Sin can be forgiven, but a cold heart will not find heaven."*

Sunday, March 20, 1994:

After Communion, I saw Jesus holding out His hand to a little child. He gave a message: *"I put My little children before you. They are My precious little gifts of life. The beauty of their innocence and the full trust they give their parents—these are the qualities I am looking for most in all of you. When you grow out of your childhood, you become choked with the cares and pleasures of life. It cannot be this way for My faithful children. You must come to Me as children in your spiritual life. You should desire My love always and treat Me as your beloved. For I am jealous for your attention. So put away the thoughts of this world and your own selfishness and put on the gifts of the Spirit— love, patience and a longing to do My will. When you walk with Me in childlike faith, you will better understand why My love for you was shown most emphatically by My death on the cross for your sins."*

Later, at the Adoration Chapel, I saw a man—he had his hands tied up with chains. Jesus gave a message: *"Many people feel tied down by the worries and problems in their lives. I come to free you from the shackles of your sin. It is your selfishness at times which sometimes exaggerates your anxieties. If you would concentrate on loving Me and giving your life over to Me to lead you, you would have a new found freedom in My peace. Pleasing Me is all I ask of you and in doing so life will seem much less burdensome. To be free of the bondage of sin and all its consequences will enrich your ability to love Me and others as well. With your freedom you can grow in My love and bring others close to Me by your example. It is prayer, receiving the sacraments and following My commandments that will set you free. So greet Me each day with your consecration and I will lead you through this life and into the next with Me in heaven."*

Monday, March 21, 1994:

After Communion, I saw some pews in a church and gradually the light inside the church darkened. Then I saw some strange designs on the walls like Egyptian figures as in the pyramids. Jesus said: *"The age of apostasy is quickly approaching to your churches. The afflictions of modernism and apathy will slowly choke the churches which you have trusted through the centuries. My people are being lulled to sleep by increasing subtle changes over time. Soon the reverence given Me will be hard to find. This is why I have stressed to My faithful remnant to keep strong in the faith by constant prayer. You must continue to treasure My love and guard your interior spiritual life against the increasing evil that will come about you. You will need My graces most desperately to protect you through this evil testing of the demons."*

Later, I saw a beautiful white butterfly with a great white light around it. Jesus gave a message: *"I am showing you this butterfly as a life cycle for My faithful. The beginning of your life on earth is like a caterpillar. You go through life's struggles as on a pilgrimage. Your life is directed only towards its glorious end. On earth it is your testing time to see if by My grace you can learn to follow My will. This prepares you for when you will be one with Me in My will in heaven. Once you have proved yourself by your life's dedication to Me, you will be ready for Me to receive you into My glory and love. It is at this time that you will go through a metamorphosis like the butterfly. Your body will be changed anew into a radiant new creation fit for being with Me in heaven. It is this glory for which I made you in the beginning to praise and adore Me in the splendor of My peace in heaven. You are indeed most fortunate that I died on the cross for all to have a chance for you to be glorious butterflies who will live in eternal joy with Me."*

Tuesday, March 22, 1994: (The sun was shining in brightly in a.m.)

After Communion, there was a bright sun and I had trouble seeing the vision. Gradually, I could sense Our Lord standing as if on Mt. Tabor with His Transfiguration. Jesus said: *"I have been showing you many messages portraying My glory. Today's sun shining on you represents My graces falling on all My people.*

You (plural) are being blessed with many things but few give Me thanks for what they have received. I am asking all of My people to stop and count all I have done for you and give some offering of yourself back to Me in appreciation. Many of you are offended if you do not get thank you cards for your gifts. Imagine how I must feel when so many snub My gifts. Still I continue to love each of you unconditionally and constantly I am waiting to hear from you."

Later, at the Adoration Chapel, I at first saw some medals of Our Lady and then I saw her in a white mantle and a blue dress. Mary gave the message: *"I am ever so happy that many of my children are doing my consecration. I had mentioned it at the outset of your pilgrimage and now it is coming to fruition. It is beautiful to let your will and everything you have be consecrated because now my Son can help you more when you are in union with His will. Your prayer life and even your outlook on the world will improve as a result of your giving yourself up to me and my Son. We both love you very much and as a Mother I want to care for my children. When you understand how God's plan intended you to be, it is much easier to fulfill His plan for you. In recognizing authority over your life, your obedience can be a living blessing. Continue to follow My request for prayer and fasting as I asked at Medjugorje. There is still much need of prayer for peace in your world. Thank you for responding to my call."*

Wednesday, March 23, 1994:

After Communion, I saw Jesus in His crown of thorns looking up to heaven. Jesus gave the message: *"I am showing you the crown of thorns from which I still suffer for men's sins. This suffering is for the evil thoughts which men conjure up in their minds. The evil one places an idea in your mind, but it is you who fancies it or carries it out in reality. Once you accept this evil it becomes sin for you. So this is where you must fight off sin before it takes hold. Purify your mind and pray constantly to ward off these attempts by the devil. You will always have temptations but you do not have to give in to sin. Even if you do succumb, I am here for you if you would ask My forgiveness in Confession. So pray to Me for strength to ward off any evil intentions."*

Later, at the prayer group, I saw Our Lady come and was most impressed with the twelve stars around her head. Mary said: *"I am coming to prepare you for my feast of the Annunciation. At that time I gave my 'yes' to my Lord in accepting Him. Now with your consecration you are giving your 'yes' to both me and my Son. Treasure our relationship and may it be everlasting."* I then had a picture of Jesus preparing for a feast with some people dressed as in the Middle East. Jesus said: *"I am preparing you now for Holy Week. Take time this next week to understand a little how much I love you. If you could imagine yourself going to be crucified as painfully as I did, you could have a better appreciation of how much I suffered and am continuing to suffer for your sins."* I then had a vision of Mother Angelica. Jesus said: *"I ask you to pray and be thankful for those teaching My word in public, especially Mother Angelica, Pope John Paul II, the clergy, and all catechists."* I then saw St. Therese the Little Flower holding some roses. She said: *"I see your prayers being offered as roses being sent to heaven. Our Lady and Our Lord are both very pleased with all of you. Continue to keep your faith strong with daily prayer."* I then saw St. Joseph holding the Infant Jesus. He said: *"I have played a role of foster parent for Jesus and spouse to Mary. My parentage of Jesus was a grace to understand Mary's conception by the Holy Spirit. For all who have family problems look to me to help answer your prayers."* I then saw an angel spread its wings wide as St. Gabriel came: *"I stand before God and bring my tidings of good news that your Savior has come to Mary. Jesus, the Son of God, has come to give His life for you—listen to Him."* I then saw an image of God the Father and He said: *"Be joyful My people that I have bestowed my Son among you. Even though He is rejected by some, He is your gift of life through which all will have an opportunity for salvation."*

Thursday, March 24, 1994:

At church, I could see angels on either side of the altar. Then after Communion I could see an image of Maria E. talking and the words *"Pray with me."* came. I then saw a cross of Christ rise up and come forward to me and Jesus said: *"As in the Gospel I have made My covenant with My people at the Last Supper when I instituted the Holy Eucharist at the first Mass. My ensuing pas-*

sion and death on the cross you are about to commemorate again next week. This is My greatest outpouring of love I have given to any people. On your part those who long to be with Me have an equal commitment to keep My covenant of My commandments to love Me and your neighbor. When you keep My word, life becomes more vibrant and alive with My love."

Friday, March 25, 1994: (Feast of the Annunciation)

After Communion, I could see Our Lady standing somewhat above me in a blue mantle and white dress but I had trouble seeing her face. Mary said: *"My son I am happy to greet you on my feast day. You have been doing a good work with your prayers and dedication to my consecration. Continue to spread our messages for they are helpful to my faithful. You will play a role in the coming events. You could not see my face since as I told you before I will not be appearing like this for much longer. The time of my Son's purification of the earth draws near. Only a few know the dates of some of these events. My Jesus keeps secret some of these timings but we will warn you at the proper time. Continue to keep yourselves in constant prayer. Go to the sacraments often for your daily strength and Confession to keep you humble. In all of this keep a childlike faith and witness of my love and my Son's love to all those around you."*

Later, celebrating the Consecration of Our Lady after Communion, I saw Our Lady standing and holding out her hand toward me. Mary said: *"I am happy many of my children are here to celebrate their consecration to me. It is good my children continue to pray and make reparation for so much indifference to me and my Son. How many times do I ask for your prayers to make up and help those who are trying to live their lives without me or my Son? My repetition for prayers are as often as you say my Hail Mary for your petitions. I want to thank Fr. Shamon for his inspiring words for my faithful—they are indeed what I preach to all of you. I love my children so dearly and continue to ask you to be humble always and I bring you to adore my Son always. His coming next week in Passion Week is a special blessing to you. Take His life close to your heart for He died for your sins with an endless and unconditional love. Thank you for responding to my call."*

Saturday, March 26, 1994:

After Communion, I saw Jesus standing as in the Divine Mercy and a beam of light came right at my face from Him. Jesus gave a message: *"I am giving you My love of understanding of My mercy and grace. Today, I am bringing My new covenant of love to fulfill My Old Testament covenant. You are still My beloved people but now I am inviting you to taste and see My love shown you in the commemoration of My passion. For I have given My earthly life so that you might have eternal life. This is My invitation to be one with Me in My will. As you go through life ask Me to walk with you in every step. I will be with you through your good fortunes as well as any troublesome times. Know that I am with you always and thank Me for My many blessings. Continue this coming week to give these events your reverence. Also, continue in your prayers to follow through on your consecration."*

Later, at the chapel after Communion I saw Our Lady coming and then gradually I could see a stone statue. Mary gave a message: *"I am happy to greet my pilgrims in their reunion. I continue to ask my faithful to help in evangelizing the people with cold stony hearts who are still rejecting me and my Son. You have all been granted many blessings to help you go forward to share our love with all those around you. By your example and your graciousness you will be able with my Son's help to warm the most stony of hearts. It should be said about you as the earliest Christians, that people will know you because of the great love you have for everyone. Continue to keep strong in your prayer life and you will always be united with me and my Son. The beauty of your love we both are so happy to receive. My peace goes with you always to help you in all life's problems. Thank you for responding to my call."*

Sunday, March 27, 1994: (Palm Sunday-Passion Sunday)

After Communion, I saw Our Lord riding a colt and then later I could see a white horse. Jesus gave a message: *"Today you are commemorating My triumphant entry into Jerusalem with the palms. Yet I tell you, you will see even greater things than these when I come again in glory to judge the earth. In spring you see the signs of its coming in the new growth. I tell you, you will also see the signs of My coming in the sky. The reading today demon-*

strates how much the Son of God humbled Himself for His people's sins in that He allowed men to kill Him on the cross. *You also must be humbled for My sake in giving your life to Me so you can be one with My will. I have given My life once forever but I still suffer pain for the ongoing sins of man. So by restraining your sins as much as possible you can limit some of that pain I must suffer. Again if you offer up your troubles and agonies to Me for reparation for sin, I will twice be relieved of more suffering. I will gladly suffer for you in any event since your spiritual lives mean so much to Me.*"

Later, at the Adoration Chapel, I saw many horsemen riding down a big wide plain. Jesus gave the message: *"After I had risen from the dead and returned to My Father, the Apostles wondered how long it would be until I would come back. Even today many people are saying the end will be shortly. I am telling you to live for today and witness My love. Do not worry about the date of My return since you may even meet Me at death before the end events occur. I have told you to pray constantly and be on guard for you know not the day when you have to account for your life. I will tell you events are progressing to the end times. Many signs of its coming have occurred as foretold in the Scriptures. There will be an era of peace ushered in at My Mother's triumph. But there will be a fierce battle of good and evil before that time. You must prepare as I have warned you before for this battle. Many of My faithful will be tested to the limit. You must rely on My help to endure it. But do not worry over that day for I will give you the strength to endure the demons' attempts to destroy you. Live for the hope to see My day in peace and that should be enough to sustain you. Stay close to Me in prayer and the sacraments.*"

Monday, March 28, 1994:

In church, I saw what looked like a tomb in the side of a hill. Jesus gave a message: *"This is the time of Lent when you can see if you have made any spiritual progress from your initial resolutions. As you approach My passion and death this week it might also be a good time to recollect your spiritual assessment of your life at this time. Are you prepared to die? Are you ready to face Me at the judgment? If there are sins to forgive, I wait for you always in Confession. If there are ways in your life to correct, now is the acceptable time to move forward to make the appropriate changes. In all that you do live for My love and continue to walk with Me in those things you do."*

Later, at a mission on the family, the Blessed Sacrament was exposed and then I saw a vision of three priests walking abreast. After that, I saw what looked like a picture of the House of Loreto. Jesus gave a message: *"I could not pass up an opportunity to tell all of you about My feelings on the family. I could say I helped arrange that I was born into a loving family of a perfect mother and father. By My own life on earth I have witnessed to you how life should center around the family. Many times I have likened the husband and wife relationship to that between Me and My Church. The setting of love between man and wife is the most beautiful that I could institute for the creation of new life. Parents have a deep responsibility to care not only for their children's earthly life but most importantly for their spiritual training as well. And children also are responsible to take that training close to their hearts and follow Me. All members of each family should have an enduring love for each other as I have for Mary and Joseph. Make a special effort to accommodate each family member and tell them how much you love them."*

Tuesday, March 29, 1994:

After Communion, I could see an arch of palms and Our Lord on the colt coming to the feast at Jerusalem in honor. Jesus gave a message: *"Many people on first hearing My word receive it with joy as the people of Jerusalem. Then when they realize what I am asking of their life—for a commitment to Me, sometimes men shy away and reject Me. As Peter in the Gospel, many give Me quick lip service, but when tested in life some soon forget My help. It is My faithful I rely on to tell My people who I am—here to help everyone along life's path. If people would freely give themselves over to My will, they would see how life's trials could be beared easily. You have to understand the true priorities of life in order to fulfill the plan I have for each of you. Even if you continue to fall away from Me at times, you must pick yourself up and return to ask My forgiveness for I am always ready to receive you and forgive you. My love knows no bounds for all of you. It is you who limit My graces to you. Ask for My gifts and I would gladly help you in anything. Be resolute in your prayers and help others and then you will see life better through My eyes of faith."*

Later, at the Adoration Chapel, I had a vision of what looked like a lighted scene at night from the Lincoln Memorial to the Washington Monument. Jesus gave a message: *"Your country is at a major turning point in the battle of good and evil. Your president will face so many trying events over the next year that it could send the country into chaos. Many things will happen as a continuing punishment for your country's many abortions. Expect more problems with the weather, your finances, rumors of wars and assorted controversies. Many prayers are needed to make reparation for the sins of your country. Victim souls and many prayer warriors are needed for your cause. Ask for My assistance in showing all of you what you should be doing in preparation. Life as you know it will be going through a great transformation. Continue to keep close in your prayer groups for interior strength."*

Wednesday, March 30, 1994:

After Communion, at first I saw a man standing with a little child. Then I saw the inside of a flying saucer circulating underneath me. Jesus said: *"I tell you My warning draws near. This is My grace of understanding to all mankind that they will see their lives before them as I see them. This is a grace especially for those fallen away and for those who do not believe in Me. This supernatural visitation will be the last evidence for some to prepare their lives for the judgment. Once this happens, events will move quickly and the time of the demon's hour will make it hard to repent. So I tell you prepare for this event so you will not be scared or afraid of what it means. The earth has been calling for My justice and it will soon witness a testing of good and evil yet to be seen. Pray constantly so you will be ready with My grace to endure this test. You will once and for all be given a clear choice to choose the things of earth with Satan or the things of heaven in following My will."*

Later, at the prayer group, I saw Our Lord in a plain tunic next to the tomb and Jesus said: *"I am asking you to die to yourself so you can live in My will. This is the most perfect love for Me you can have when you give everything over to Me in faith."* I then saw a picture of Our Lady with a daffodil and a lily in front of her. Then she was beneath the cross weeping for her Son. Mary said: *"My Lord has given me as Mother to all of you to watch over your spiritual lives and bring you to my Son. I suffered much to see my Son's agonizing death on the cross. But now our hearts are joined more beautifully than on earth."* I then saw Jesus in His crown of thorns as He was condemned to die before Pilate. Jesus said: *"Many have rejected Me by following other people's ideas of grandeur. I am pure love always ready to receive you just as you are with all your imperfections. Come forward into My loving arms."* I then saw the women of Jerusalem and Jesus said: *"For those weeping I have said pray for your children for they indeed will need your prayers especially in this evil age. At the same time, I pray that you will take care of your children—meaning avoid abortions."* I then had a picture of Christ on the cross and I was drawn up to Him and I was absorbed into His body to have a small sense of His suffering and I could look down from the cross. This was quite an emotional feeling—hard to express in words. Jesus said: *"I am asking you to help understand the pain I go through for the sins of man. You can offer up your pain and prayers to help in reparation for sins. Pray my Divine Mercy Chaplet daily to remember how much I suffer for you."* I then saw Jesus raising up the bread when He instituted the Holy Eucharist for us and He said: *"My death I have offered for your sins. I give you My Body and Blood in the sacramental bread and wine as an eternal remembrance of Me to keep My presence with you."* Finally, I saw Jesus at the tomb again only this time His robes were dazzling white. Jesus said: *"I am the Resurrection and the Life. I offer you a new life, even on earth, if you would just walk with Me in faith. I give you hope also that one day after this life you will be resurrected as well into My glory and peace."*

Thursday, March 31, 1994: (Holy Thursday)

After Communion, I again saw Maria E. praying and she said: *"I love you. Please join me in our love for Jesus."* I then saw several people walk forward all wearing crosses and I did not see their faces. Jesus said: *"I love you all so very much from the bottom of My heart. Now I am asking each of you to bear your individual crosses of life as I bore My cross on Good Friday. Take My cross upon you for My yoke is easy and My burden light. Each person is appointed their own special cross that no one else can carry. Each has been specially crafted by Me to fit what is right for you. I have told you I will give you My grace to bear your cross, if you would but ask My help. Your cross is a blessing since through it you will gain your salvation. For each of you must suffer and struggle as I did to prove your worthiness of My love and the glory I will give My faithful in heaven. Pray and endure your trials now for your glorious goal of heaven is but a few moments of time away. Then you will enjoy My peace and see how life is like the time a woman bears her child."*

Friday, April 1, 1994: (Good Friday)

After Communion, I saw in the distance a cup with the Host above it and rays of light went out in the shape of a cross. Jesus gave a message: *"Today is a special commemoration for My greatest gift of love to all My people. Know that I love all of you with an infinite love which you cannot even fully comprehend. I do not want to lose even one of My children. My love for you is so deep that I treasure everyone of you who comes forward to Me. Your adoration of My cross today brings many tears of joy to My heart. I would ask you to receive Me into your heart this day in a special way. Think as if I had just died for only you on this day. How this would impact you with My love. Yet it is how I feel about you everyday you receive Me. So pray and fast for all sinners that they may come to know My love. This love is not to be kept secret but spread from the rooftops."*

Saturday, April 2, 1994: (Holy Saturday, Easter Vigil Mass)

After Communion, I was in a dungeon grey pit and Jesus had His eyes sunken in. This later was revealed as Christ with the dead and He was about to raise them up. Then I saw Jesus as in the Garden comforting Mary Magdalene. Jesus said: *"This is as I told you in Scripture—how I descended into the place of the dead first to free the just and bring them salvation. In this I have conquered sin and death and have brought you forgiveness of your sins—a ransom forever. I still suffer from man's sins but your eternal salvation has been won for all those who accept Me into their hearts. This beginning of new life in spring is the dawn of a new spiritual awareness for all My faithful. This light coming at dawn will bring all My people eventually into full view of heaven. It is now yours if you would only embrace Me."*

Sunday, April 3, 1994: (Easter Sunday)

After Communion, I first saw Jesus in white triumphant in glory coming from the tomb. Later, I saw Jesus rising into a dim lit starry sky with His arms outstretched to me. I then felt myself rising also up into the stars. This was a picture of Christ rising to His Father and it looked like an image of His infinite love. Jesus said: *"Amen, amen, I say to you man has but a glimpse of the glory I will show at the final resurrection. I bring you My gift of life which is love personified. All life I give you has its own inner beauty which man fails to fully appreciate. If you think about your very existence, you can come to recognize how lucky you are in My grace to be alive. Even more so when you understand My love for each of you, you will see how beautiful it is for new life to come to you out of love. It is this joy of love which I want to share with all My people. If My people could see the true value of life, they would love each other more and not be fighting and killing each other over this world's goods. Also, if you were less selfish, you would accept new infants instead of committing abortions. How can you reject life when it is My will to share it with all of you? Love one another and return your love to Me in appreciation of My gifts to you."*

Monday, April 4, 1994:

After Communion, I saw Our Lord risen in the distance in the sky. Then I could see only a shining light and He said: *"My people after all this Lenten Season have finally come to realize I am their risen Savior who has come to forgive their sins. Yet, if My message touched their hearts, where are the people at Mass and in their lives the following week after Easter. My people have short memories and need to pray more for the grace to persevere in their beliefs and not let the worldly distractions deter their purpose. Pray to be strong in the faith throughout the whole year."*

Later, I had a vision of Jesus' face and there was a fire all around His head. Jesus gave a message: *"My beloved little ones please come to Me with your troubles and your infirmities. Give them to Me and ask My help to ease your problems. Put Me first in your life, then you will see that to please Me by your prayers and good works is your true mission in life. Many of My faithful are suffering for the troubled lives of those close to them where a falling away from My love causes them grief. I am calling on you My faithful to persevere in prayer and fasting to save these souls who are so close to you. Each soul has a particular price for their salvation to be saved. Some require long suffering over even many years before My Father will accept them. In the end you must do what you can also to give them good example and sometimes some gentle reminders how I am always waiting for them. In all of this effort you must be joyful and loving them with My love despite what evil they have committed. Peace be with you and My love goes out to all who are trying to bring sinners back to Me."*

Tuesday, April 5, 1994:

After Communion, I saw a flashback to my previous visions of Jesus and He said: *"I have given you many messages which should not be taken lightly. They are indeed for the faithful's edification. It is beautiful to reminisce on My Easter appearances. They offer much hope to My people and they encourage the sinner. My love flows out to you and My graces are continually showered on you as the spring rain. Ask to receive Me and I will come to you to give you My warmth in your heart. As your faith grows like the spring flowers, you reach heavenward to give Me thanks and glory. Continue, My little ones, to remember how much I love you and share My risen joy with others."*

Later, at the Adoration Chapel, I saw a Host and there was a big arrow above it pointing upward. Jesus gave a message: *"You come again to see Me and I am happy to receive you. Many blessings have been given you and many more are available for all who come to Me in love. I have told you often to not let anxieties over daily events disturb you. Do not let financial concerns lead your lives, for money is not an end in itself. Instead you must be directed to heavenly things, for these are all that matter. Things of this life will fade away but My love and your prayers will live on forever. My arrow shown in the vision is your life's main concern. So live to please Me and follow My will for you. Then you will be blessed with a grace and peace where nothing will disturb you. When you live in My love every moment of each day, life will seem like it was resurrected at Easter. Enjoy My love as I enjoy loving you and this gift of mine will be all consuming."*

Wednesday, April 6, 1994:

After Communion, I saw Jesus meeting the Apostles on the road to Emmaus. Jesus gave a message: *"The Gospel speaks of how My Apostles' hearts were burning with love and desire when I recounted the Scriptures of the foretelling of My Messiahship. My faithful's hearts likewise should burn with desire to see how My life conforms with history and Scripture. Would I fulfill only half of Scripture—the foretelling of My triumph is now your hope of seeing Me in heaven. Know that I am with you always. Again in the Scriptures it is said how I had to suffer to forgive your sins. But also My disciples as well must suffer in this life to show your love for Me and your endurance when things are not always easy. You must persevere in faith as did the Apostles and endure your everyday trials. Then the glory of My coming again will hold a promise of salvation for all those who come to Me."*

Later, at the prayer group, I saw Our Lord coming and the word 'trouble' came. Jesus said: *"Many of My people are troubled at times with daily problems. I tell you these problems are little and sometimes large tests which are given to see how you will accept them. If you follow My peace, you will give these troubles to Me and allow Me to help you. On the otherhand, if you try to solve everything your way, you will eventually stumble. Finally through being humbled you will see coming to Me is why I tested you in the first place."* Our Lady came in blue and was joyful. She said: *"I call all my children to come and behold my resurrected Son. He is all love and eternally waits for each of you to give you His love. You must make the forward motion to accept that love and thank Him for your salvation."* At first I saw a Frenchman and then St. Catherine Laboure from Rue de Bac and the Miraculous Medal came and said: *"All of us incorrupt saints have a special place before the throne of God. We have been blessed by Jesus for honoring Him and doing His will on earth. We have given you the miracle of our bodies so the faithful will have hope and see Our Lord fulfills all His promises to bring us to Him in heaven."* I then saw some birds in the sky flying north. Jesus said: *"When you see the birds return, you know spring is coming and with a beautiful sunset good weather comes. I tell you to look to the sky for My warning and you will know the great testing-time is near. Know also when earthquakes and the stars move, that soon My judgment time will come. Be at peace and be watchful by protecting your soul with prayer and Confession."* Our Lady of Betania came as seen by the statue in the woods and she spoke: *"For those pilgrims who have received many graces and blessings, I ask you to give me and my Son thanks for all you have received including even your invitation to come. Be faithful to my requests in your everyday evangelization."* I then saw an owl and the Lord said: *"Be wise in the things of heaven and you will always be at peace in My love. I ask also that you remain humble and always united with Me throughout each day. Once you are led to be thinking that you are wise in the world, know that you are slipping back to old habits of pride. Do not try to be smart in the ways of the world since Satan is tempting you with these things. But follow My way to holiness in prayer and humility and you will receive your reward in heaven."* Finally, I saw Our Lady dressed in the sun and she said: *"I am the virgin dressed in the sun who comes to crush the head of Satan. This will usher in my triumph and the demons will be cast from earth to the pit. Know that when my messages cease, the testing-time will begin and my triumph is not far off."* A sixth message was substituted since I had forgotten it originally. Here is the one I had forgotten. I saw a painting at Fr. Morfessif's exuding oil. Jesus said: *"Many signs of hope are being given to My faithful to strengthen them and give them courage to face life's problems. This oil also has curative power and can be used to lessen some earthly pain. But it is the spiritual uplift and beauty of My love which is most recognized. Pray to understand My love and let My will be your will."*

Thursday, April 7, 1994:

After Communion, I saw as in one image a picture of Jesus and Maria E. and we were all together. Maria said: *"We recognize you in the breaking of your bread."* Jesus then gave a message: *"Today is special since this is My first witness in the Gospel to My Apostles in a live physical body. I was real to My Apostles then and I am real today for all of you. It is I really present in the Host of the Eucharist. This is the bread of your life that I have given you forever until I return. I am precious in your sight and all people will bend their knee at My name and give Me glory. I ask that you give Me reverence in the Host at all times and visit Me often at the tabernacle or in exposition. I the Lord am ready to give you My grace and help each day to keep you close to My heart. Receive Me as often as you can at Mass and My real presence will give you real peace even in this world of chaos and evil."*

Friday, April 8, 1994:

At the Adoration Chapel, I saw a live white baby as if in a garbage can. Jesus gave a message: *"I have given you many messages to stop abortion but still you do not listen. Your president now wants to spread abortion even throughout the world through the UN. I tell you he will suffer for his actions and the people around him as well. Your country will pay dearly for the snuffing out of innocent life. Do not be surprised that dire things will happen to you since My justice calls out for retribution for this sin. I have sent you many gifts of potential scientists and future discoveries which will not occur because you have aborted My plans for you. Because of all your abortions you will reap the whirlwind of My wrath. Satan desires to destroy man. So by your actions of killing you are helping his cause instead of Mine. Your sins are so many and still you continue the millions of killings. Do you think I do not see this injustice? These infants' angels are testimony to your misdeeds. I tell you to pray hard to stop this evil for it is the biggest offense to condemn your nation. You are destined to crumble under the weight of your own iniquity. Lead a good example to those around you and do what you can to discourage women from having abortions."*

Saturday, April 9, 1994:

After Communion, I saw Fr. Jack talking with the people and Jesus gave a message: *"Your priests need much prayer and encouragement at this time for Satan is attacking them on every side. Many priests are being disgraced by Satan's temptations. The priests, for their part, must stay close to Me in prayer to continue their intended ministry. I tell you a time of evil is coming where My priest-sons will be scattered much like My Apostles*

were in disarray at My Crucifixion. Some will be persecuted and they will have to go into seclusion to save the faith. But fear not, My strength will be with you. You must ask for My help in these coming times or your body and soul will not survive alone. I will give you the graces to withstand this spiritual battle but you must remain faithful to Me throughout and keep your trust that I will overpower Satan shortly."

Later, at the Adoration Chapel, I saw two helicopters from above them as I was looking down. They looked like they were large enough to carry troops. Jesus gave a message: *"Your country could become involved in several more police operations where the army would come in. You will continue to have wars and insurrections as long as most of the people continue to live for their own gain and not in harmony with My plan. Until man sees and understands his faulty reasoning on war, he will continue as throughout history to make the same mistakes. I seek to give you My peace since I love you with an infinite love. But man must concentrate his focus on God for help—you cannot have enduring peace without Me. Continue to pray for peace for there are no winners at war—only Satan. It is the civilians who must suffer most. So ask prayers to change the hearts of some of the ruthless military leaders. Also, you can help the peace process by spreading your love among those around you—especially in your own family."*

Sunday, April 10, 1994: (Mercy Sunday)

After Communion, I saw a fireman dressed in a long brimmed fire hat and Jesus gave a message: *"My little ones, I love you so much that My love is like an eternal flame perpetually burning for you no matter what you are or what you have done. My death on the cross for you is a witness of how much I love you. It is My wish that I can instill that same eternal flame of love in you by the Holy Spirit. Once you appreciate and accept My love, you will have a peace and trust that no one or no trouble can take from you. The beauty of life will be better understood and you can see My plan for you is indeed the best way to follow. If you give your life over to Me, I can also mold you and refine you with My fire of love to fit the perfection desired by My Father for you. So pray and keep your flame of love burning strong for Me and you will witness My glory even here on earth."*

Later, after Communion, I saw Jesus as the Divine Mercy with the rays of grace and mercy spreading out in all directions. Then gradually the scene darkened and a cross of light formed where Jesus was and rose high into the sky. Jesus said: *"I bring you My mercy and graces on this Mercy Sunday. There is an abundance of them waiting for each of you if you would but ask for them. My people need to believe in Me always that I am with you guiding your every step. Trust in My love and accept My Divine Will that it be your will as well. When you pray, offer up all your sufferings and everything you do each day for both the sinners in the world presently and for the poor souls in Purgatory. By My grace and your offering, this will lessen the load of punishment due to sin. My mercy is so encompassing that soon you will witness a display of supernatural mercy in My warning to mankind. This will be a grace of understanding each will receive to understand how the sins of their lives so offend Me. You will then see how things you think so innocent or trifling really have a deeper meaning and insult My trust that you should have in Me. This experience will offer all sinners a true meaning of seeing how their lives must be perfected as your heavenly Father is perfect."*

Monday, April 11, 1994:

After Communion, I had a very strange vision. At first it looked like I was in an elevator and things were rising but there was no compartment—all I could see were things moving by. Then I could see something spinning around almost like a fast roulette wheel or a merry-go-round. Jesus said: *"You will see a time where events will seem like they are happening almost simultaneously. Time will appear as if it was speeded up. A time of chaos throughout the world will occur. All these events will cause people to demand some stable leadership. These things will make way for the entrance of the Anti-Christ. He will appear as a man of peace with great powers but his reign will not last long. Fear not, I will be with you to protect you in those times. But know that if the events were not speeded up, even the endurance of the faithful would be tried. I am always in control and My Mother's triumph will soon be upon you after this time. Pray and ask My help during these coming battles against evil."*

I saw a vision of bare trees as I was looking through a window. Then I was drawn closer to see the trees without leaves. Later, I saw a beautiful summer day and the trees were resplendent in their green leaves. Jesus said: *"Today, I ask you to think of your spiritual lives as these trees in the vision. A Christian cannot be barren of good works. I have bestowed on each of you all kinds of talents as well as My blessing of faith on you. You in turn must bear good fruit in this life because it is your opportunity to share My love with My people. You should be going forward to help those in need without being asked but also be willing to do it for love of Me. In this way you will store up treasures in heaven which no one can steal. In Scripture I have cursed the barren fig tree but I will give you time now to prepare for your journey to heaven if you would just share My love with your neighbor. Also, in Scripture many thought it a curse not to be able to bear children but I have Blessed Elizabeth with John the Baptist in her old age. So do not be discouraged for with Me anything is possible. Pray for My help and you will witness how your life will reach its fulfillment by helping others."*

Tuesday, April 12, 1994:

After Communion, I saw branches of trees in the sky and Jesus was going up to heaven. Then the angels appeared saying: *"This Jesus will return to you as you have seen Him ascend."* Jesus gave a message: *"As I strengthened the Apostles with My Spirit of Love in the Holy Spirit, so now I offer to strengthen you in the faith. This will enable all My faithful to go out and evangelize those who do not believe or who have lost their faith. All of this is in preparation for the day of My return which is coming shortly. The Apostles believed because they saw Me rise from the dead. Blessed are you who receive Me even though you have not seen Me physically. Even though you cannot see Me, you can feel My grace and power as you feel the wind. Know that I continue to be with you even since I left the Apostles. Pray and continue to ask for graces in keeping your faith holy and close to Me."*

Later, at the Adoration Chapel, I saw a young boy with red hair and he was about eleven years old. I did not really understand the significance initially. Jesus said: *"Many of My younger faithful are having their spiritual education neglected. Most parents care for their children's secular education but fall lax when it comes to passing on the teachings of the faith. Work schedules and other activities are leaving less time for this important training. Without learning how to pray and having a strong prayer life, the children will find life troublesome to bear. It is the parent's responsibility for their children's spiritual welfare. You cannot afford to lose a generation to the evil one by inaction. So pray and teach your children by your example to lead upright Christian lives based on a proper conscience and prayer life. Each soul is very important to Me and your children's souls should be important to you. So be watchful and care for your children and your grandchildren."*

Wednesday, April 13, 1994:

After Communion, I saw a vision of an elderly lady. I looked away and came back to the same vision. Jesus gave a message: *"You can see My loving spirit is present in each human being. This is why you must love everyone you meet whether you like them or not, since it is My presence you must honor in that person. Each person is drawn to perfection by My Father and should strive to honor My presence in themselves and direct their lives to holiness. Each person may appear at varying levels of holiness not because of Me but it is to the extent each person receives Me into their hearts. The more you give yourself over to My will, the more fully My grace can be active in you everyday. So consecrate to Me each day all your actions and deeds and it will be a prayer for all you do each day. Walking with Me each day will make life a joy for you and you will be preparing yourself to meet Me in heaven one day."*

Later, at the prayer group, I saw a white skeleton-face covered with a black shroud. Jesus said: *"Many killings are occurring in the world from wars, street killings and abortions. Much of this is happening because of the hatred in men's hearts. My love can overshadow this hatred if men would turn their attention heavenward for help. Once you lose respect for the value of life, the thought of killing as ugly and unthinkable now becomes an option for some."* I then saw Our Lady coming and again her face started to be blotted-out. Mary said: *"You must take my Son's Easter message of love close to your heart. He has freed you from your sins and only asks that you make Him more a part of your life. In doing so you will come to know Him and want to do everything He asks of you."* I then received the word *"Homosexuality."* Jesus said: *"I am warning you not to condemn the sinner, I am the judge. This sin of homosexuality is indeed serious, much as sex before marriage. But in this case it is unnatural and perverted as well. Avoid this sin and pray for those with this problem."* I then saw a glitzy-looking new car. Jesus said: *"Many comforts in your world have become almost idols in themselves to some people. You do not live this life just to desire to accumulate the things of this world. Instead you are here to learn of My love and how to follow My plan for you. You must start and end this pilgrimage of life with daily prayer and communicate with your beloved—Me."* I then saw a vision of a woman and a clock was overlaid on her face. Jesus said: *"As in Scripture there is a time for everything but time and schedules should not be the sole direction of your life. Instead of fears and anxieties over getting more done than is humanly possible, listen to the message of My love and be at peace. Throughout your day it is important to make some quiet time for meditation. In this way you can be united with Me in prayer and you can ask Me to help you in your life's pursuits. Give your life to Me and you will see that many of the things you strive for are truly not necessary for your soul's salvation."* I then saw a slot machine and Jesus said: *"Do not gamble with your souls. Many times you are drawn to prayer, good works and going to Confession but then you let the evil one allow you to put them off and intending to do them later. But alas, that later moment sometimes never comes. Be careful to take time as a good thought comes to carry it out right away especially Confession after serious sin."* I then had the words *"Eyes of the soul"* and Jesus said: *"I see into your hearts and I understand the intentions you have always. It is important that you form your conscience properly based on Scripture and My commandments. For if you do not have good discernment of faith, your peers may lead you into sinful things without you recognizing them for what they are. Pray for help from the Holy Spirit to enlighten you and you will not be misled."*

Thursday, April 14, 1994:

After Communion, I saw Maria E. receiving Communion from a priest and she said: *"Jesus and I are one with each other. Join us in this banquet."* I then had a vision of some praying hands. Jesus gave a message: *"When you are in prayer, you are in full communication with Me. Your life becomes a prayer to Me with your consecration of the things you do. Either personal prayer or formal prayer is the beauty of your love that you are returning to Me. It is your love connection that I ask for always. For prayer is humbling and peaceful. It is a linking of your heart to mine. I encourage you to pray often for there is much need of reparation for sin which is always in demand from your world. I enjoy hearing from each of you even with just a short few words. When you acknowledge Me before men, My Father in heaven will remember your devotion."*

Friday, April 15,1994:

After Communion, I saw some dark stone structure and then realized it was the tomb I knew at the Holy Sepulcher Church where Jesus was buried. Jesus said: *"I give you this day a ray of light of knowledge into your souls. You should realize more why you are here on this earth and where you will be going after this life. For you are to learn about Me and give Me glory. I have given all a choice to love Me or not. I have also given you the faith to understand My purpose in showing you My peace and promise of heaven to those who do My will. This life is indeed a training experience for knowing and loving God. It is not just to dwell on the things of earth. Once you have made your commitment to Me, you are ready for the graduation at your death into a new life with Me beyond your comprehension of My reward for you."*

At the Adoration Chapel, I saw a great darkness. Then I saw a canopy like a phone booth with a red shroud on the top and it was going straight up like an elevator. Jesus gave a message: *"You will live always in the shadow of My protection. The evil trial will be upon you in a short time. Know that I am with you always. Even if the Mass is taken away, you can still receive Me in spiritual Communion. Also, you have My Mother's weapon—the Rosary— to help you in your prayer. This will be a difficult time and you should not question My ways. It is My way of purifying all the evil on earth in preparation for My Mother's triumph. Some may die of persecution but others will be lifted up in My protection so they can return to the new heaven on earth. These will be those in white washed robes and will lead My people in the reign of peace. This is a great message of hope to all those who must endure this trial. Pray for My help and I will see you through this time. It will not last long."*

Saturday, April 16, 1994:

After Communion, I at first saw a little crucifix. Then I saw Christ on a large cross and He and the cross rose gradually up into heaven. Jesus said: *"I am being lifted up before you as Moses lifted the snake. I have conquered sin and death—they no longer hold Me. My Father's justice has been satisfied for your redemption. This enables you to have a spiritual freedom in coming to heaven because Adam's sin is now vanquished. I pour out My love to you and My cup is overflowing with graces for you. I want to help all of you if you would but keep Me close to you in prayer. A love relationship needs love in two directions. So please listen to My call and you will receive My saving hand to lead you through this life to the next."*

Later, at our Nocturnal Hour, I could hear rain hitting on the glass in the ceiling. Jesus gave a message: *"The rain falls on the just and the unjust. Each has an equal opportunity to come to know Me. Each has access to read the Scriptures. Each has an opportunity to direct their prayer to Me in glory and petition. I choose some though to give more grace, that their example may be the way to lead others to come to know Me. My love I send you always every day. You can come to know Me more intimately through fervent prayer. I call all of you to a life of following My will. This plan for your salvation is very simple in faith for those who know Me. Those who love Me raise their hope and yearn for that blessed day to see Me face to face. Continue to witness your love to Me publicly so that this may inspire others to come to Me."*

Sunday, April 17, 1994:

After Communion, I saw a set of stairs and they were leading up into the clouds to heaven. Jesus gave a message: *"Every day of your life is as one step closer to your eternal reward in heaven. My Easter love message will reach its fulfillment when you enter heaven. Each day you can reach out to others by your example and show My love is everywhere. You are all called by the Gospel to teach others of My love and how I want all who are fallen away to return to My love. Tell them My love is all forgiving, it is never conditional. It is the sinner who refuses Me, I wait always for their return. It is now though that you should tell all that their time for decision will soon be enhanced by My warning. Their trials also will soon increase when evil will seem strong for a time. But take courage, My protection awaits you."*

Later, at the Adoration Chapel, I saw a beautiful sunny day with a blue sky. Then suddenly there was a huge dark smoke and everything was burning in the path of the smoke. Soon I could see many demon spirits with ugly faces in the smoke above. Jesus gave a message: *"During the evil time of darkness there will be many demonic spirits roaming the earth seeking souls to claim for their own. My faithful must huddle together in their homes with the windows covered and blessed candles burning. This time will be as the Passover was for the Jews. I will protect My faithful from the demon clutches with holy sacramentals such as crosses and the Rosary. The devil will claim those who deny Me by following their own lust for the things of this world. For those who have put other gods before Me, this will be their judgment to hell. They will indeed be tortured by the demons. But after this short time there will be a new earth. My Mother will crush the head of Satan and the demons will be locked away in hell. A peace and My Mother's triumph will reign for a millennium. My faithful will then enjoy peace on earth as intended for the Garden of Eden. This will be a taste of your reward for suffering on earth and doing My will. Be faithful and endure this trial time for your reward will be great."*

Monday, April 18, 1994:

After Communion, I saw a hill and on it were several altars as for animal sacrifices. There was a cloth drawn over each of them. Jesus said: *"I am the fulfillment of the Old Testament. I have died once for all that the sacrifice of the Body and Blood of the Son of God has ransomed sin for all mankind. No longer do you struggle in vain but I have come to forgive you and offer you a chance for new life in My conquest of death. The shroud over the altars means no longer must you suffer but give your life over to Me and I will take care of you. For those of faith, life now will have new meaning in being cared for by a merciful God who knows and loves you forever.*"

Later, I saw a beautiful gold aura coming from the center of the sky and I recognized that God the Father would give the message: *"I am seeing man now so wrapped up in himself rather than Me. Man is so taken up with power struggles that he fails to see how Satan is using man's most base passions to his advantage. Instead of being so concerned with "having a good time" in the worldly sense, man should wake up to where he is headed. I have put everyone here as a training place to learn how to love God and prepare to be absorbed in My oneness in heaven. Man should realize he was created as a spiritual being not to lower himself to the lust of earthly things but to seek those things which will lead him to his goal in heaven. Once man comes to his spiritual senses he will see how power and possessing things are only the lower base instincts and not deserving of his concern. Instead, seeking the Blessed Sacrament for spiritual growth and knowledge of My love—this is the "good time" a Christian should be seeking. This is the only meaning your life should have—how you can know, love and serve God. Keep close to Me and your peace will know no bounds."*

Tuesday, April 19, 1994:

After Communion, I saw a vision of an altar and the priest was raising the Host as at the Consecration of the Mass. Jesus gave a message: *"I am indeed the Bread of Life. Again, I am the fulfillment of the Old Testament. For I am the true manna which the Father has sent you from on high. My love for My people is so dear to Me that I wanted to leave My memorial sign of love with you till I come again. The Blessed Sacrament is My loving presence among you—give this bread praise and glory for it is truly Me. This outpouring of My love is but a taste of the glory and love that awaits you in My heavenly banquet. Pray and keep close to My heart of love and I will continuously watch over you."*

Later, at the Adoration Chapel, I saw a long stone box which looked like a burial place for someone. Jesus gave a message: *"I come to give you a lesson in the deeper meaning of life. All of you will face the judgment one day so you should be directed properly how to lead your life on earth. Whatever you do, ask Me to be your partner in life to help lead you. If you keep close to Me in prayer and ask for My grace of understanding, I will show you the way that follows My plan for you. For without My help you will wander aimlessly and will come upon your ruin. It is with Me that you will truly find life and live it to the fullest. I love you very much and I want to see My little ones come to Me to lead them. Once you are united with My will, I will give you a peace that nothing will disturb you. This peace is a freedom from fear and worry because it is faith in Me that all will work out for your best interest. You yourself have experienced My peace and you can witness to others how they must let go and let Me lead them. Then they too will experience My peace and life will seem more beautiful through the eyes of faith. In union with Me you will enjoy the challenges of life to please Me by offering all you do up to Me. This joy will continue until you see Me in even more splendor in heaven. Go in peace, My children and witness My peace to all you come in contact with. They will see the radiance of My love in you and they too will desire to be at peace with Me."*

Wednesday, April 20, 1994:

After Communion, I saw two airplanes loading refugees. Jesus gave a message: *"Many places around the world will intensify in their conflicts because of the evil one. But it is man's greed for power and his desire for things given him that this continues. Man's selfishness and his inhumanity to his fellow countrymen will be at odds between him and Me. He will reap the pain and injustice of his own acts. When men refuse My help and My ways, they are condemning their actions to despair, hatred and all the punishment due to their sins. This again is a time crying out for prayers for peace. My faithful again are needed to put out the fires of war and make reparation for those neglecting Me. My justice awaits those who continue the senseless killing. It is not far off when I shall intervene to take these warmakers to task.*

Then there will again be peace according to My will and evil will be put to rest. Pray that this day will be hastened for the sake of the oppressed."

Later, at the prayer group, I saw a picture of a roof of a house and Jesus said: *"Many people build shelters or homes to protect themselves from the weather. I am telling you to erect a spiritual house to protect yourself from evil. For I am your cornerstone upon which to build your house of faith. I am here to help you buffet the winds of evil."* I then saw a picture of our house as it was being sided and Jesus said: *"Many of My people build shells around themselves to insulate them from others and the problems of the world. But I tell you to be yourself and do not worry what others think of you. I want you to put your faith on a lampstand for all to see its beauty. Share with everyone My love and do not be isolated but one body in My love."* I then saw an image of my Uncle Jim and also a picture of a porch. He said: *"Tell my brothers and sister how much I love them. This place I am in is beautiful and full of peace."* I then saw as in a city with some tall buildings. Jesus said: *"Your cities are breeding grounds for much trouble as evidenced by the drugs and killings. Many are struggling for survival and have given up hope of trying to make a good life for themselves. It is this frustration and despair that causes their trouble. Pray for the poor especially so they will not lose heart. Help them to see that My love is always there for them. With Me all life in any form can be beautiful."* I then saw a picture of a large fan spinning vertically with a blur. Jesus said: *"Know that when you see events speed up in sequence that the evil time will soon be upon you. It will be a hard testing time but My love will protect My faithful from the harm of evil."* I then saw Our Lady come holding the Infant Jesus and it was somewhat dark with a red glow overshadowing the image. Mary said: *"Your world is full of much hatred and wars are abound. Much prayer is needed for peace for your world is on the brink of a world war unless men's hearts are softened from their coldness. You do not realize how desperate your situation is with the evil one preparing his entrance."* I then saw a little child with a smile and I also saw how tall the flames were on our candles. Jesus said: *"How beautiful is a child's love for his parents. It burns like a flame always exuberant and trusting in their love. This is how I wish you all would see Me with the same yearning to love Me. You also can place all your trust in Me because I am a fountain of graces for you. My love always burns for you and I am constantly seeking your attention to show you that love. Pray and keep My love connection ever flickering in your heart."*

Thursday, April 21, 1994:

After Communion, I saw Maria E. at first with her eyes closed in prayer and then looking up to heaven with her eyes open. She said: *"Look to God for your salvation."* I then saw some tribal people and some writings on the wall. Jesus said: *"Instead of being civilized and living in peace, man is reverting back to his old tribal customs of proving himself in combat. Choosing war as a means for settling things is not going to make friends. As conflicts spread they engender further hate which perpetuates itself. You must not allow the evil one to continue discord among you but seek peaceful means to settle arguments. A prayerful life and a spreading of love will always help harmony which your world should be striving for. Continue to build up your own communities with love instead of continued hate which only destroys lives."*

Friday, April 22, 1994:

After Communion, I saw a priest at the altar in a dimly lit room and he raised the Host as at the Consecration. Jesus gave a message: *"I am the Bread of Life. Without Me you are nothing. I give you My Body and Blood to nourish you with spiritual food everyday you wish to receive. I am here waiting to help you and ward off the evil one. Continue to build up your strength with prayer and My sacraments for many war clouds hang over your world. Men are resigned to continue being belligerent with each other on a war footing. No one considers the idea of peace, they are more determined to grab what they want despite their repercussions. Your world must grab hold of its senses or more serious problems will befall you."*

Later, at the Adoration Chapel, I could see a long beam of light up and down a path. It was then revealed to me that it represented a time continuum. Jesus said: *"You are seeing a person's life as one picture of time in a line. This is another version of the warning which will be coming. Each person will be outside of time and will be able to view their life from infancy to the present time. They will see all the good deeds and bad things they have done. Most of all you will recognize which things utilized your time on earth the best. You will see how effective your prayers were and what value came to all your actions. In this way you will realize that praying and doing good works with love are the best use of your time. It is these treasures that are of any value to you in the next life. So make an effort to follow My will and make the best use of what little time you have at your disposal."*

Saturday, April 23, 1994:

After Communion, I saw Our Lord standing in a synagogue. Jesus gave a message: *"Today, I am asking you all to arise from your sinfulness for you are called to be holy. Even in this time I am working miracles. I am still offering spiritual healing to all those who would come forward to receive it. You must indeed accept this in faith for I will not force myself on anyone. Once you have accepted My graces for curing your sick spirit, you must be like Peter's mother-in-law when she was healed. Go out and do likewise in helping others and comforting the sick. You, by your example and prayer, can also offer spiritual healing by bringing My word and love to others. Each person who receives Me— receives My peace. You should also give thanks to God for all healings and even for your gift of faith."*

Later, at the Adoration Chapel, I saw Jesus on His throne in heaven and the view came about Him from various sides. Jesus gave a message: *"I am the eternal loving one who reigns outside of time. I am changeless while you are prisoners of change in time. I have set My commandments before you and I have enhanced them with love on My coming to earth. Even so not one jot of the law have I ever struck down but I have added a spirit to the law. I give you My life with My death on the cross. I have died for your sins but this did not remove sin all together. Many times I have called you in love to come to Me and be holy. I am asking only one condition—that you follow My commandments to love Me and your neighbor. Out of love for Me you can follow My will for you. Yet if you persist in your pride and fail to recognize Me as Lord over your life, then I will deny I know you before My Father. It is giving over your life and will to Me that I ask. This*

means a life free from sin and in accordance with My command-
ments. Many dispute over what sin is but only ask if I would ap-
prove as a guideline. My love is infinite but My justice must be
served as well. Pray for discernment from the Holy Spirit on any
issue you are unsure of and live your life in My peace."

Sunday, April 24, 1994:
After Communion, I saw some beautiful flowers on an altar.
Jesus gave a message: *"I am giving you many gifts and talents. It*
is your responsibility to blossom forth like the joy of Easter. You
should shine forth with the fruits of your labor. For by your fruits
I will know how you are using your God-given talents. Many have
to labor under difficult conditions just to manage, but ask help
from Me through prayer and I will see to your needs. You should
be satisfied with what you receive. It is not your place to desire
things beyond your needs but be content with your lot. You will
encounter many difficulties through life but you should be thank-
ful for the many blessings you have received—both spiritual and
physical. For those who seek My Kingdom first, many things will
be given beyond their requests."

Later, at Holy Hour, I saw a vision of an old Gothic church
with a high arch and there was a procession with the priest holding
the monstrance with the Blessed Sacrament. Jesus said: *"I am call-*
ing My faithful remnant forward to help preserve My Church.
You are the ones to witness My holy presence to My people. It is
My divine presence in the Blessed Sacrament that you should
encourage to give reverence to and to visit often. For I give you
My presence to strengthen your spiritual lives. In Communion I
am your Bread of Life which feeds you spiritual bread that will
last forever. Continue, My dear ones, to give Me praise, honor,
glory, and thanks for all I have bestowed on you. I ask you to
especially treasure My presence for it may not be with you as
such much longer. It will increasingly be hidden for protection
as the evil one will seek it out to desecrate it and destroy it. But
you must protect My presence from harm. You must guard it dur-
ing these evil days. They will not last long and you will then see
Me clearly as I truly will be present in spirit before your very
eyes. Pray constantly to endure this test and keep Me close to you
always in everything you do."

Monday, April 25, 1994:

After Communion, I at first saw Jesus standing in front and then I could see from behind a gentle person with long hair but I could not see a face. It was the feast of St. Mark and I sensed it was my guardian angel Mark who would give the message: *"I am with you always to protect you. It is good that you have come to know Jesus better and to let Him lead your life. You are called to prayer and a life of holiness. Work to avoid occasions for sin and distractions. Do not allow the evil one to have sources where he could tempt you. I stand before God with your offerings and actions. I am His witness for you. You can communicate with the angels if you would but pray and make that effort. I will help you if you would let me."* Mark had a low quiet voice much different from the thought messages from Jesus.

Later, I at first saw the outline of Our Lady and the shadow was all red. This then changed to the outline of Our Lord and again the shadow was all red. Jesus gave a message: *"My people you do not know the magnitude of My suffering as it continues even now. For each person who is murdered in the streets, killed by war or killed in the womb, I go through the same pain as that person. For you are all a part of My body. So when one part dies or is in pain, it is equally felt by Me as well. Many times I have pleaded with you to pray for peace and stop abortions. On all these fronts the evil one is showing his presence. Man continues on his way without Me as a part of his life. You must understand how painful it is to see so much injustice taking place. As your people rise up against the carnage in Yugoslavia, I myself am enraged at all such events as well. My love wants you all to witness My peace. If man continues to refuse Me, he is only hastening My justice to purify the earth. If you fail to come to Me in My peace and stop the wars, it will be inevitable that My intervention will be required. Evil will appear to win for awhile but in the end My victory will bring evil to an end."*

Tuesday, April 26, 1994:

After Communion, I saw Jesus standing a little in the dark. Jesus gave a message: *"I am always here for you. I am like your guardian angel, always watching over your shoulder to take care of your every need. Many times I am helping you when you least expect it. Many of these things happen by My intervention and not just by chance. Because I love you very much, I am so concerned with each of you. I ask that everyday and during the day that you take concern about Me also with some prayers or a few words that you love Me as well. Lovers must always be in communication or soon love grows cold. So continually barrage Me with your needs, your prayers and your love messages. It is your tears of love I treasure the most. Peace be with you and keep Me in your thoughts always as I do for you."*

Later, at the Adoration Chapel, I saw what looked like an ugly horrible red demon that could have been Satan himself. He was racing forward to attack some souls. Jesus gave a message: *"Prepare! Prepare! Prepare! The time of evil days will soon be upon you. You must pray constantly and keep close to My power for you are seeing the beginnings of the great apostasy. My churches will either be closed by the government or slowly taken over by those teaching a humanistic religion devoid of Me. They strictly think helping man is only enough. Their love for Me will grow cold. My remnant Church will be forced in their houses to meet as My community. This is why your prayer groups are necessary to keep close together. Evil will begin to run rampant and it will call out for My justice. Once the appointed time has come, Satan, his angels and all who follow him will be cast out from earth into the great abyss of hell. The earth will be purified and renewed. This will be a glorious time for My faithful as My Mother will enter her triumph. Pray that your souls will be with Me during this time ahead."*

Wednesday, April 27, 1994:

After Communion, I saw a shrine and encased were two gold tablets as in the form of the Ten Commandment tablets. Jesus gave a message: *"I bring you My new covenant of love in the commandment that you must love God and your neighbor. This is the fulfillment of Scripture that you love one another. I have died for you that My blood has washed away the guilt of your sins. There is still punishment due to sin but I have paid the price for you that forgiveness will always be open to you if you would make the forward motion to ask. This is My covenant of love that you will be My people and I will be your loving God. I am warning you of those accursed false witnesses in this end times who will try to change My moral laws. I am the eternal and changeless friend. These laws I speak of cannot be defiled without being forgiven. For those who preach against them they will be thrown in the fire with the devil and his angels. Heed these words for many will come in My name trying to dissuade even the elect but do not listen to them. Pray to Me for discernment and I will interpret any false teaching."*

Later, at the prayer group, I saw a woman's face and she was smiling. Jesus said: *"Many times we greet people during the day. I ask you to be a fountain of joy and My love. Be enthusiastic about all life, be happy and show this with a loving smile to all you meet. By responding with joy and humor you will lift up other people's spirits. Even though you have problems, do not be despondent but continue to be cheerful. By spreading good will, there will be less sadness and despair."* I then saw a staircase looking down from the top and each step had like an Egyptian monument at the end of each step. Jesus said: *"You should treat each day as a special gift to you. It is another opportunity to give Me glory in all that you do. With each day you draw closer to Me and it offers you a chance to increase your spirituality as well."* I then saw a vision of Mary coming and she had a Rosary in her hand. Mary said: *"Thank you for offering me your Rosaries this night from all of you. Many blessings will be used for your intentions. Keep close to my Rosary daily, for it is your spiritual weapon against the evil one."* I then saw a picture of trees with their leaves coming out and birds and other life were teeming as in spring. Jesus said: *"Nature, if you look closely, is very much in harmony with all the plants and animals. It is continuing to follow My plan for each. You also should be in harmony with nature and other humans in following My will for you. When you follow My will and live according to My commandments, peace will reign. But if My people decide to follow their own selfish ways, this is where struggles and wars result."* I then saw a beautiful gold cross gleaming with light. Jesus said: *"I am reminding you that once you have given your life and come to Me in death, you will be resurrected with beautiful glowing bodies. You will be so radiant and your life so peaceful that you will praise Me for bestowing this beauty and peace on you. For those who follow My ways on earth, their reward will far surpass any dream they have had about heaven.*" I then had another vision of lush green fertile crops and grass after a new spring rain. Jesus said: "*See how My rain nourishes the grasses and crops and makes them bear much fruit. Also, observe those places without rain that are parched and dying. Know that My divine graces are like the rain. I shower both upon you. When you receive My grace, you also will flourish with the fruit of love and good deeds. And for those who refuse My grace, they will whither as the branch is cut off from My vine.*" I then was given signs of spring with budding trees, new flowers and green grass growing. Jesus said: "*Notice how you read the signs of spring coming. The days grow longer, the birds are singing and the trees bring forth their leaves. Know also that you should be always ready to recognize the signs of the end times as well. There will be great signs in the skies, evil will increase and many natural disturbances will occur. My Second Coming may come at any time, so be watchful and prepared to receive Me.*"

Thursday, April 28, 1994:

After Communion, I again saw Maria E. with her eyes lifted to heaven and she said: "*Love Him dearly, my children, love Him dearly.*" I then saw at a distance a bishop's miter. Jesus said: "*I am asking you to continue to pray for your bishops and priests. They are My servants on earth who I have entrusted to bring you My sacraments. They are the ones who hold My faith communities together. They are human as well and they need your prayers to encourage them and keep them faithful to their vocation. The evil one is forever tempting them. So pray for their leadership that they will not falter. They are My representatives here on earth. Listen to them.*"

Friday, April 29, 1994:

After Communion, I saw an old church in Rome with a statue of a woman—I could not tell who she was. But a young woman's voice came and I believe it was St. Catherine of Sienna (feast day). She said: "*You all must come to Jesus especially to receive Him in the Eucharist. For He is your strength and you are nothing with-*

THE LORD IS MY LIGHT AND MY SALVATION: WHOM SHOULD I FEAR?

out Him. He feeds you the bread of angels. He is your life bread which allows you through Him to do His will and give Him glory. Remain in trust of His love. I know you revere Him very much."

Later, at the Adoration Chapel, I saw a bright light on the altar shining out at me horizontally and then it was redirected upward. Jesus gave a message: *"I am the Light of the World and I have come to share with you My good news of salvation. I love you so much that I am revealing to you in Scripture what My Father wants revealed to you. You know of My love through the Eucharist and you now understand My Easter message that every one will be resurrected with Me who follows My way. Know also that you must carry My torch of love and knowledge. You must be a light of My love for your neighbors. For when My light shines, many evil doers avoid the light in fear of having their sins exposed. Some are afraid to accept forgiveness and do not want to be a part of My light. At death, you will see My light of peace again. It is the same light of grace that shines on you every day but it is not always visible to you. Pray that My light permeates everyone and warms all hearts to receive Me. I am always waiting for you, tenderly patient to share My infinite love with you. Carry My light of joy and love in your hearts and shine forth this love on your friends as well."*

Saturday, April 30, 1994:

After Communion, I saw a cross with corpus lying on the ground in the dark. Then a light shown upon it and it rose up by itself and came forward until it was standing before me. Jesus gave a message: *"I am asking you daily to pick up your cross and carry it for My glory. Give up all you do each day to Me and I will bless it and present it to My Father as your prayer. I have risen from the dead and suffered for your sins. You yourself are no less than Me, in that you too must suffer as I did. For I give you a hope of eternal life, if you would but live a holy life in My love and service. By following My plan for you, you will enjoy an everlasting joy with Me in heaven."*

Later, at the Adoration Chapel, I at first saw a pencil point. Then I saw people in a dark tunnel. Jesus gave a message: *"Prepare for your future religious persecution. Many people will be misled in their faith on beliefs which are heresy to Me. The reli-*

gious leaders will let their pride mislead them and their people. You will at first have to seek out underground Masses to avoid the heretical teachings. Then there will be confrontations, and they will try to ban you from your churches for believing in My true faith. The people in this evil time will allow the demons to cause them all perversions of sex and drugs. It will be much like Sodom and Gomorrah in Lot's time. This is why My judgment must come again with fire to purify the earth. It will be so perverted that it will require My intervention to bring peace once again to the earth. There will only be a small remnant left to preach My true Gospel. You will be honored to keep your faith through these trials. Pray for strength now that you can endure this test of evil."

Sunday, May 1, 1994:

After Communion, I saw some men standing in a choir. Later, there was some form in the darkness looking like a demon. Jesus gave a message: *"Greetings to My people—you are indeed My body. I love all of you as one big loving family. I call on all of you today to concentrate on peace in your daily lives amidst all your trials. You must live your life for Me every day. Be always positive in your outlook on life and be cheerful with all you meet. I ask that you work on even overcoming the little everyday things in your life. Do what you can to not complain and make a special effort to be nice to those close to you. Do not be snapping at each other over every little thing that is unnecessary to quarrel over. By working on the little things in your life, you will be prepared to handle the harder big things that will test you along the way. Continue to pray for spiritual strength on these problems and then you can enjoy My peace."*

Later, at the Adoration Chapel, I saw like some old cars and then one car was driving into a setting sun. Jesus gave a message: *"I have told you many times to prepare for the evil times to come. In your preparation you must study the tenets of your faith and read My Scriptures so you can discern My proper teaching. Know your prayers and sources of strength in the Eucharist and My Mother's Rosary. With these in hand you will be able to withstand the false witnesses who will come in My name as wolves in sheep's clothing to mislead My elect. With the knowledge of the faith, pray to the Holy Spirit to direct you what to say in defense against these evil witnesses. The most precious thing to remember is to pray often and keep close to Me. For these times will test your faith but with full trust in Me you will overcome this onslaught of the evil one. Many will say they cannot believe this will happen but I assure you this test will be upon you sooner than you thought it could happen. Pray My little ones and continue your preparation.*"

Monday, May 2, 1994:

After Communion, I saw a young nun in a black old habit and then an older nun in the same black habit. Jesus said: *"My daughters have given up their traditional ways for more ways of the world. Even My priest-sons have also changed their ways to those of the world. Now even the laity have become more lax in going to church and personal Confession. The evil one has succeeded in putting the clergy and the laity into a spiritual sleep. The need for fervent prayer in a lot of lives has fallen dormant. Why are My people so blind to Satan's tactic of letting worldly desires take your attention away from Me? I am asking all to wake up for this is one of the signs of the end times. You all should be inspired to increase your prayer life for love of Me. The less of the worldly cares you attend to the better. Refocus your life on Me—it is all that matters.*"

Later, I saw a bright light and then I saw a picture of several gemstones coming at me in succession in various shapes. Jesus gave a message: *"My little ones, you have been given many precious gifts from My bounty of gifts. They have all been given freely on My own without you earning any of them. My first gem I give you is your very gift of life itself. To My faithful I have also blessed you with your gift of faith to know and love Me. A most blessed gift I give you is Myself in the Blessed Sacrament of the Host. The most precious of all My gifts was purchased by My death on the cross. This is My gift of salvation to be with Me in heaven. This is spoken of even in Scripture as the pearl one would sell everything to buy. If I may go on, you have even been given more gifts—as your wife, your children and grandchildren. All of these are yours without even asking. I have graced you very much. There is one thing I only ask of My servants. That is that you would offer Me up the gift of your will over to My Divine Will. This gift I treasure very much because it also is freely given by you to Me as well. My little ones, pray often to stay in My grace and give thanks to God for the many gifts you have received."*

Tuesday, May 3, 1994: (Feast of St. James and St. Philip)
After Communion, I saw a brief vision of Jesus and then a picture of an open book. Jesus gave a message: *"When you celebrate My Apostles' feast days, you celebrate the mission I have given them. Go out to all the nations and preach My good news of salvation. This is in keeping with My Easter message as well. For the basis of your faith is the teaching how all of My people make up My one body. It is your responsibility by Baptism to continue to tell all of My people how I love them. By your witness you are renewing My presence over all the earth. As those are told of their salvation which waits to be claimed, it will then be each individual's duty to choose for Me or not. This ultimately is your life decision. Once made for Me, it will awaken in each a spirit of joy and fulfillment."*

Later, at the Adoration Chapel, I saw a steering wheel to a boat and Jesus gave a message: *"I have mentioned to you before about those who are not on the proper spiritual course for their souls. Many are in need of continuous prayer to soften their hearts and open their minds to My action in their lives. Once people can appreciate how I can help them in both their spiritual and physical lives, a love connection can be made. Until then they are blinding themselves to My love. My main message tonight though refers to the leadership of My Church. Presently, my son John Paul II is the one whom I have selected for this time. He will be afflicted with increasing internal strife in My Church. Some have evil intentions to either assassinate him or exile him. They do not prefer his traditional stands on the moral issues. He will be tested dearly and I ask your prayers to continue his leadership. Once he would be removed, beware of the coming Black Pope and the Anti-Christ to follow. This indeed will be a dark time for My Church. Pray daily to withstand the coming test which will stretch everyone's faith to the limit. Pray especially for My help during that time. Man has chosen this course because He desires more earthly-centered leadership."*

Wednesday, May 4, 1994:

After Communion, I saw a bunch of chairs and tables and people were serving food. Jesus said: *"You must be servants to the rest of My people. At My Last Supper I gave you My example by washing My Apostles' feet. The people should know you are Christians by the way you love one another. You must be as the early Christian communities. By working and praying together you can feed My people both physically and in spirit. But the sharing of the gifts of the spirit are most helpful to support My people in their quest for Me. This is the desire for Me that I wish all of you to instill in all those around you. With My love and your faith secure in the hearts around you, My peace will reign among you and your troubles will be little."*

Later, at the prayer group, I saw some tassels and Jesus said: *"As I have told My Apostles do not seek honors and glory from men. Do not strive for important seats of honor or great social status. For these are the things of this world and they will come to nothing. Do not let your pride try to lord it over others. You must instead seek My Kingdom and look to be humble in all your activities."* I then saw a rake and Jesus said: *"I want you all to do some spiritual spring cleaning and prune out your excess desires for the things of this world. Start with much prayer and frequent Confession to keep yourself holy and strive for heavenly perfection."* I then saw two frightening eyes of a demon which I could not dwell on long. Jesus said: *"There truly are demons among you tempting you to do wrong at every chance. You must be aware of their presence and know that their influence will increase as the evil times draw near. I am always at your side to protect you. Call on Me and your guardian angel to keep your soul holy through this time."* I then saw a yellow and white flag representing the papacy. Jesus said: *"You have been blessed with My son John Paul II. He is a great spiritual leader and listen to him especially on his writings of faith and morals. Pray for him that his leadership may continue for you as long as possible."* I then saw some toys and a baby playing with them. Jesus said: *"Protect My little children from abuse and from being perverted with sex and drugs. Do what you can to prevent child pornography and other abuses. Their innocence is too precious to be lost by some trying to gain this world's goods."* I then saw some electrical device in the ceiling with two little eyes like a mouse. Jesus said: *"Be watchful of all electrical devices that can be used to eavesdrop on you in your home. The government will be seeking information on you in their religious persecution. Be aware of even the abuse of your cable TV in the future."* I then saw a potted plant with many leaves. Jesus said: *"Your spiritual life is much like a plant which requires water, sun and nutrients. Your soul requires grace from My sacraments and prayers to communicate My love. Keep close to Me as the sun for the plant, so My radiance of love will fill your heart and give you hope against all adversity."*

Thursday, May 5, 1994:

After Communion, I saw Maria E. praying and she said: *"Love Him as I do."* I then saw some hands joined together. Jesus said: *"To those joined in marriage, I ask you to keep My love close to your hearts to make your love all the more perfect. For this is a blessed union which I want to see as the sole basis for forming your society. The family should be preserved and kept sacred in your eyes since the world is forever trying to tear it apart. Again this union I have likened to My Church as a spouse to Me. I ask also that you pray to keep your churches together and practice your faith without reservation of what others think of you. These are My two favorite institutions made for your welfare to lead you on life's journey of faith."*

Later, at FOCUS on the Eucharist, after Communion, I saw a Bible sitting in a drawer partially open with some letters and other clutter around it. Jesus gave a message: *"I am showing you that reading Scripture is very important for your interior spiritual strength. You must read My word often and put it into practice if you want to be My disciple. Once you hear My word and take it to heart, My will will be active in your life. The more you follow My life on earth and try to imitate My ways, the closer you will come to the perfection desired by My Father for you. In My word you will see My love and My justice as well. But in the end each per-*

son must make a decision for or against Me. Pray to discern the Scriptures properly and you will be in true love with Me—a love no one can take from you."

Friday, May 6, 1994:

After Communion, I saw a dark church with pews and only one person was present. Jesus gave a message: *"Your attendance at My churches continues to wane. My faithful remnant is still present no matter what may come their way. As evil increases those numbers attending will continue to diminish until Masses will have to be in hiding. Also, in the later days there will be division and strife even among the remaining churchgoers. Know that this division is from the evil one. Many will be confused by the coming schism in the Church and will not know which way to turn. But I am instructing you to stay with My traditional teachings and the Scriptures. Those who do so will never be misled. Continue to pray to discern these times and I will be with you to the end."*

Later, at the Adoration Chapel, I saw a little porcelain box in the shape of a heart. Jesus said: *"I ask all of you to come humbly to Me with all your weaknesses. You know that I love you even when you are the most pitiable of sinners. Once you admit you are sinners and in a weakened state, it is the first step in your conversion. Your next step is to ask My forgiveness which many who frequent Confession are willing to do. When you seek Me for My mercy, it is now easier for you to see how only giving your will to Me is the answer for all your problems. By offering yourself humbly, I can begin to work through you and help you carry out My plan for each of you. In this way I will lead you on a path which will take you to heaven. Now you can see that hidden in your weakness, it is your way to salvation. For I am so elated to receive the sinner back into My bosom. Once you make Me Lord over your life, you will see that My love will shine through all you do. You must see Me as your redeemer, your Savior and a lover who accepts you unconditionally. All I ask is that you come to Me for help and I will show you how to live. This life can be the beginning of your peace, if you would let go of your pride and your control."*

Saturday, May 7, 1994:

After Communion, I saw an award on some black velvet and then I saw a serviceman wearing an army hat with a brim. Jesus gave a message: *"I want you all to be My loyal soldiers in My army of love. You should strive to receive heavenly awards and honors and do not seek any glory on earth. For those good deeds your Father sees in secret, He will repay you many fold over. If you are to be My disciples, you must follow My ways and have true allegiance to Me. As in the army, you will lovingly follow My wishes for you without any question because you will have trust that what I do for you will be in your best interest. Pray much to keep on the narrow road which leads to Me in heaven."*

Later, I saw a cross with a dark veil over it. Then the veil was seen as Our Lord's clothing as He was above the cross in glory. Jesus gave a message: *"I am pleased, My people, to see you praise and adore Me here tonight. For when you are with Me, it delights Me with your fervor. I ask you to always keep Me close to your heart. My presence is before you in My Blessed Sacrament but I am also with you in your soul at all times. When you have your attention fixed on Me, My peace will be with you and the evil one cannot tempt you. Oh, if you could keep Me focused as the center of your life, you would not have to worry about the evil one for he would be powerless. Once you let the earthly distractions take your focus off of Me, this is when you are susceptible to sin. So pray My sons and daughters to be ever strong in your prayer and keep your gaze fixed on Me. For if you live My will, you will see peace in all you do and your salvation will be assured. Do not let your will or the cares of the world disturb you. It is My way which will bring you to heaven. Continue to praise and honor Me in your heart and that will suffice to lead you into everlasting glory with Me in heaven."*

Sunday, May 8, 1994: (Mother's Day)

After Communion, I saw a small heart shape and then Our Lady's face came inside the heart. The vision then changed to a complete picture of her standing wearing a crown. Our Lady said: *"I am the ultimate Mother in being blessed as the Mother of My Savior and my Son. This is a wonderful celebration for me in one of my favorite months. All mothers should especially be joyous today for they too are celebrating in partnership with the ongo-ing creation with God of the human race. Life is such a beautiful gift which many people treat lightly. It is such a grace to see new life come forth. Each life is a new Christ because they are part of His body. Pray that more people will come to a more spiritual appreciation for life and as a result will treasure it dearly as my Son intended."*

At the Adoration Chapel, I saw a man in black clothing with a cape and then when he stepped into the light he had a suit on in the place of the black. Jesus gave a message: *"There is an evil band of men influenced by the devil who are disguised and preparing for the Anti-Christ takeover at the proper time. They are tracking your leaders and those in authority especially those controlling food and buying. Once given the signal, they will attempt a take-over and throw your country into confusion. Once they have es-tablished control, they will seek out those who threaten to lead the people against their ideas. They will try to rid any political activists or religious leaders who would stand in their way. This will be the time when they will try to force the mark of the beast on all for his total control. This will also be a time of religious persecution. Men's faith will be at such a low ebb that many will give in to these fanatics. My faithful remnant will be forced into hiding at this time for their own protection. Call on Me in prayer during these times to protect your souls from these demonic men. Do not take the mark of the beast, for you will surely die in your sins. You will see My mark on the foreheads of the faithful to recognize My people. You must take care in these times to fight temptation and keep close to Me."*

Monday, May 9, 1994:

After Communion, I at first saw a football and then in the dark sky there was a little light on a circular object. Jesus gave a mes-sage: *"Pray much and do not lose hope through the coming days for there will be ominous portents for your future. Events are leading up to the evil times which I have talked of often. It is important that your spiritual house be in order. Prepare your-selves with frequent Confession and My Eucharist because My sacraments may not be as available in the future. My warning will announce the beginnings of these evil times. Be watchful and prepared. Ask for My help and I will protect you during these times.*"

Later, I saw a Roman soldier riding a horse and he appeared to be riding down one of our expressways with the cars all around him. Jesus gave a message: *"You have understood, My son, with My grace that this vision represents how your country is now falling into decay much as the Roman Empire did. Your morality is now at a low ebb as witnessed by your regard for sin. Your entertainment in movies and TV has degraded to the point where sex and violence is all that is seen. Your laws have embraced those with a right to commit murder in the womb. Even now laws are being framed to make homosexual activity an accepted way of life. Death is becoming acceptable for the sick and the elderly via euthanasia and killings in your cities run rampant. A wave of materialism has swept through your country to the point where things now have become idols for some. This pervading evil will soon bring your country to ruin since it is drifting away from the foundation it once had on God and His commandments. You must pray to strengthen what little faith you have left. Know this, that when you are visited with My justice, it is you who have chosen to abandon Me. I will protect My faithful but those who deny Me will not taste any of My heavenly banquet."*

Tuesday, May 10, 1994:

After Communion, I saw some faithful people gathered together. Then in another scene I saw a group of men dressed in black capes. Jesus gave a message: *"Today, I want to bring you a loving message of hope in face of all these later day happenings. It is true there will be a great testing time. But do not dwell on this since it is My Mother's triumph that should be looked forward to. Mankind will be shown an era of peace he has yet to see since the Garden of Eden. You must look on this time as a mother about to give birth. She endures her suffering to bring the joy of a new life into the world. Or again view it as I did My Good Friday. I loathed having to go through the pain of My scourging and death on the cross. But I had a world to redeem and I did it freely for the forgiveness of your sins. You must now endure the evil days much the same way thinking beyond this short time to the joy of a purified earth and a constant heaven on earth in My presence."*

Later, at the Adoration Chapel, I could see a long bunch of barbed wire along a road at night with cars going by. Jesus gave a message: *"During the coming days you will see the UN become a global police as national boundaries will run together. Soon your laws will become subject to the laws of the one world order. This will set up the conditions for the Anti-Christ to command the whole world with his influence. This evil time will be stressful but your hope is that it will not last long. When I come in glory to put aside the evil one and his evil men, the earth will be free from his clutches for a millennium. Once you witness this peace, you will see that your suffering was short and that it was well-worth waiting for this new era of Mine to dawn on you. Keep My love in your heart and remain faithful. Then you will witness your reward and see how much I have protected you."*

Wednesday, May 11, 1994:

After Communion, I saw a man praying alone and kneeling in a church. Then I saw what looked like his guardian angel with wings standing beside him. My guardian angel, Mark, gave the message: *"You must pray constantly to prepare yourselves spiritually for what lies ahead. During the coming evil days you must stay in close communication with Jesus for He will be your only source of strength and protection. This time will be a true test of faith and your trust in His help. It will test each person's humility since you will not be able to stand the demon attacks by yourself alone. By accepting Jesus' help through prayer and asking help also from your own guardian angel, you will save your soul. It is this trust Jesus is looking for in each person that will mark you as one of His faithful. Continue to pray to Him for guidance and start becoming acquainted with your angel to help you through this ordeal."*

At the prayer group, I first had an image of a triangle representing the Trinity and God the Father said: *"My Son has promised that when He would leave the earth, He would then send the Holy Spirit on all of you. You now have the blessing of the Holy Spirit among you. Call on Him to help you through life's trials."*

I then saw a picture of Abraham Lincoln with his black top hat and Jesus said: *"This president of yesterday struggled for the freedom of the slaves that they would have citizenship. Today, who is struggling for the freedom of the unborn? If they were recognized as citizens, maybe the killing could be lessened. I solemnly tell you the punishment for these sins of abortion will not go unanswered."* I then saw a picture of a computer display of *"Virtual reality"* and Jesus said: *"Do not be enticed by this virtual reality display. It can be a form of mind control and may allow the demons a vehicle to control your minds."* I then saw Our Lord ascending into the sky and Jesus said: *"As I have told My Apostles long ago, you also are to go out to all the nations and spread My good news of salvation. If possible, teach all you can of My Gospel. If you are not a teacher, at least spread My word by your good example of My love to all those around you."* I then saw Our Lady coming in a veil with her Rosary and she said: *"Pray, pray, pray constantly with My Rosary. You will need much spiritual strength to endure the coming days. Thank you for your prayers and encourage others to pray more as well."* I then saw my Uncle Jim several times and realized he wanted to speak with me again. He said: *"I am pleased to see the good work you are doing for the Lord. I want to tell you Jesus is calling many of His people home to Himself to spare some the suffering about to come. Please pray for all those you know who died. Those who have reached heaven already will pass those prayers to Purgatory. But those in Purgatory still can use your prayers desperately for their release."* I then saw the darkness again with several spotlights as I have seen before. I also had a vision of Moses when he was in a house and the angel of death passed over them. Jesus said: *"During the three days of darkness My faithful ones huddled in prayer will be protected from all evil influences during that time much like in the Passover. This will be the last test of evil before I will greet you with My Mother's triumph. Then My peace and glory I will share with you on earth."*

Thursday, May 12, 1994: (Ascension Thursday)
After Communion, I saw Jesus standing at a distance and then I had a picture of the one in my Bible which has a special significance. Jesus said: *"At My Ascension I did leave My Apostles in*

*My physical presence. But I ask you to reflect on the words—'I
will be with you to the end of the world'. In this sense I sent My
Holy Spirit to empower My Apostles for their spreading My message. I have also bestowed a new presence among you by means
of My Eucharist. In commissioning My first priests at the Last
Supper, I gave them the power to maintain My presence in the
Mass. This new gift of My manna to My faithful is My presence
among you that I promised. It is this presence which you must
treasure where you can still praise and give thanks to Me. Through
this Bread of Life I can nourish you everyday and give you
strength to carry My word to My people. This feast is just a foretaste of My glory which will be shown to you here present in the
not too distant future. So take hope from the initial promise to be
with you always."*

Friday, May 13, 1994:

After Communion, I saw Maria E.'s face and it was strong that
she still wanted to speak. She said: *"Trust in the Lord."* I then had
a vision of a tombstone with many people around it. Jesus said:
*"You are witnessing a vision of the death of your freedoms in
your nation. Little by little your government will strip you of your
rights guaranteed by your original constitution. There will be
increasing religious persecution under the guise of fairness. This
will truly mark the beginning of the end times as you know them.
You must stay close to Me in prayer for protection of your souls.
For there will be a great testing time all will have to endure."*

Later, at the Adoration Chapel, I saw a crucifix and it turned
into a sphinx-like Egyptian and then into an Arab with the white
headpiece. Jesus gave a message: *"Those who are students of history realize there never will be peace in the Mid-East since each
claim it to be their own. There will continue to be unrest in that
area of the world. It will all culminate in the battle of battles at
Armageddon between the good forces and the evil forces. Just as
the Anti-Christ and his legions seemed poised to win, I will intervene and start his downfall. I have told you he will rise to power
for a time, but it will not last long. The evil testing must be shortened to save My elect. This is a message of hope in the end but a
trial for a period of time. Continue to pray constantly and keep*

close to Me. Being a part of My will and My body is indeed My calling to you always."

Saturday, May 14, 1994: (Jim Leary's funeral service, my uncle)
    After Communion, I saw Jim's image and then it was like I saw his many faces from his youth until his later life. He gave a message: *"I am happy to see my brothers and sister with their friends and relatives. My heart goes out to all of you. Thank you for honoring me today and I will be praying for all of you. Keep your eyes fixed on Jesus. This peace is well-worth following His way."*
    Later, at the Adoration Chapel, I saw a man with an evil dark face crowned with a crown like a king. Jesus gave a message: *"What you are witnessing is the coming to power of the Anti-Christ. I have warned you often of his coming. It is very much in Scripture but I tell you his reign will shortly occur. All those means of world control will lead to his coming into power. He will thrive on control of the trade, food and finances. The horrible scenes as in Africa will continue to get out of hand prompted by the evil one. As chaos drags on, people will call for a leader to stop the killings. This is how he will come to reign—by claiming to bring peace to the world. Once in power though, he will use his tyranny to persecute My faithful elect. This religious persecution will seem hopeless but I tell you it will not last but an inkling of time. For I will bring My swift justice to this evil lot and they will all be cast into the fiery abyss of hell never to threaten My elect again. Then My era of peace and grace will be with you. I have given you this message in many forms but it is true as sure as I fulfilled My promise to die for you on the cross. Continue to have trust in Me and My words of Scripture. I will not let you down for anything you ask for in My name."*

Sunday, May 15, 1994:
    After Communion, I could see everyone joyful in what looked like a parade of celebration. Jesus gave a message: *"Eye has not seen nor ear heard of the glory and peace I will bring to My people. After a brief tribulation, My elect who have been faithful in following the narrow road, will celebrate with Me My mother's triumph. It is impossible for you to fully understand such a dra-*

matic facelift of your earth but believe it is coming. This era will resemble My Garden of Eden. The earth will be restored to its former beauty. All evil will be removed. There will be no anger, no death, no sickness, no killing—nothing but a sharing of My love with My people. You will have the opportunity to see Me again face to face and My glory will know no bounds. Pray that you live for this moment. It will indeed be a grace to experience this glory— but you must choose Me now over the world to graduate to My happiness for you. Pray and bring all you can into the hope of sharing My day."

Later, at the Adoration Chapel, I saw some water and the sun reflecting off of it and some people were enjoying themselves on the beach. The next scene I saw the waters parting and huge waves of water were now going toward the beach. I then saw a machine harvesting the wheat. Jesus said: *"The time of judgment draws near. Many times I have told My people to prepare and be watchful since you do not know the time of My visitation. I have given you many messages and, My son, one of your appointed missions is to warn My faithful of their impending fate. It is wise to listen and see to your spiritual preparation. Do not tarry with the time I give you since you might not have this opportunity much longer. Instead of making merry in this world, you should be preparing to receive Me after the judgment. By getting your spiritual life in order you will be ready for these end times. They may be fearful to some but you can be assured My hand will protect your soul. My elect are too precious to lose. Have faith and trust in Me and I will give you all you want and more."*

Monday, May 16, 1994:

After Communion, I saw a long line of people mostly older and one nun. They were all headed for a large cave along the road. Jesus gave a message: *"I come with love to caress My people. I have been telling you many times to keep constantly in prayer to withstand the evil of the coming days. But the end times talked about are almost upon you. It is My love that wants to envelop a shield around you to protect you. But you must go into hiding for a while to avoid those who are looking for the mark of the beast. I have told you often not to accept this sign of the evil one but it will not come without a price of persecution. Pray that you may be strong through these trials but know it will not be long until you will enjoy My glory."*

Later, I saw the Blessed Sacrament exposed on a very ornate altar. Another scene later I saw a picture of a dove. Jesus gave a message: *"The Blessed Trinity is a mystery to My faithful to fully understand. My Father's love comes forth and He generates the Son. The love between Myself and My Father personifies that love in the Holy Spirit. Whenever you see Me exposed in My Blessed Sacrament, remember what I told My Apostles. Wherever I am, the Father is also, for the Father and I are one. So also when I breathed the Holy Spirit upon them I was blessing them with the love of the Father and the Son. This Holy Spirit is dwelling in all of you as you learned from your catechism. Without My presence in you through the Holy Spirit, your being would not even exist. For it is the will of God which perpetuates your very life. So when you give thanks to Me or ask anything of Me you are also asking help from My Father and the Holy Spirit. I have come to earth so that you would have a model, an example to follow in your life. I came to show you how to live and be holy thus pleasing the Father. I ask you also to pray to the Holy Spirit for spiritual strength to carry you through each day and all your special trials."*

Tuesday, May 17, 1994:

After Communion, I saw standing in front of me an angel with the wings spread out in glory to God. Jesus said: *"To each person I have appointed a guardian angel to watch over them while on earth. You may not all fully appreciate what these heavenly beings can do for you. You can approach them for advice to help you through life. They can also communicate to other angels as well. Pray to your angel to learn more from them. They are always ready to help you as I am. In the future years of evil, they will be playing an important role for you in your protection. So call on them whenever you are being tempted or tried by evil spirits."*

At the Adoration Chapel, I saw in space a huge collision of objects and a comet then was directed toward the earth. It was soon captured by the earth's gravity and then landed in the ocean as I have seen before to cause huge tidal waves and block out the sun causing the darkness. Jesus gave a message: *"You are seeing the vehicle of My judgment of the earth. You will experience a cataclysmic event which will shorten the reign of the Anti-Christ and his persecution of My faithful. Even though the earth will shudder and great events will be terrifying to the inhabitants of earth, know that My ending of evil is near with this event. You will almost welcome this intervention when you see how terribly evil things will get on earth. Those against Me will perform all kinds of perversions and the demons will torment them. I and your guardian angels will show you how to hide and avoid these evil people. You must pray constantly to withstand this time. Do not lose hope, I will be watching over you. It will be unnerving with these events but with your trust in Me you will live to see My splendor even on earth in a short time away. Again pray and be faithful to My will."*

Wednesday, May 18, 1994:

After Communion, I at first saw a picture of a car and it came closer. Then I saw a picture several times of a boat on the water at sunset. Jesus said: *"In the future times you may be forced to move to a safe haven away from your persecutors. In that time your travel will be restricted for your own safety. I will instruct you in the future where you are to go. Have hope and trust in Me that I will protect you and lead you to safety during this evil trial. I will provide for your needs. It is your responsibility to remain faithful and concentrate on My Mother's triumph over Satan. It is this joy which should give you hope. Pray and keep My faithful close to My heart."*

Later, at the prayer group, I saw the top of a stained-glass window of a large church. Jesus said: *"I tell you they will desecrate My churches even as has happened before. They will be made into museums and the like but My presence will be profaned as the religious persecution begins."* I then saw a goat with horns of a ram. Jesus said: *"This is the time when I shall separate the goats to My left and My sheep to the right. To those on the left I will say go you accursed into the place set aside for Satan and his angels. But to those on My right I will welcome them into My glory."* I then saw a flying saucer object coming towards me. Jesus said: *"I have told you often that My warning will be soon upon you. Even now it draws closer as I am preparing you, My children, for these end times and I ask you to be in constant prayer."* I then saw a dove representing the Holy Spirit and a group of people were present with tongues of fire over their heads. God the Holy Spirit said: *"I am the Spirit of Love and I am bestowing My grace of understanding on all of you. I am giving you the grace to speak what will be required of you as you enter these end times. Be faithful and pray for My help in your need."* I then saw a huge red sanctuary light before me and then it turned into a picture of Jesus with a suffering face and a crown of thorns. Jesus said: *"I am calling My suffering servants to bear with this short trial of evil. You will suffer much for My glory but your goal and hope in Me will not be in vain. For I will shower you with My love as the triumph of My Mother will soon dawn on a new era of mankind."* I then saw Our Lady kneeling with a tongue of fire over her head and I heard *"Blessed are you My highly favored daughter."* Mary said: *"My messages will soon diminish to my faithful. I have many times shown you my face fading. I have come to announce my Son's coming again and have encouraged you to pray much to prepare for His coming. Now you will see that when I no longer come to you it will be a sign to you of the beginning of the end times. Pray my Rosary as you prepare to meet my Son."* I finally saw a building from above and around this building emanated a green light. In the middle there was a smaller square which seemed like a depression into the ground. Jesus said: *"There will be another disaster with a nuclear plant much like at Chernobyl. Much radiation will emanate causing death and sickness around it. It will poison the air and water around it as well."*

Thursday, May 19. 1994:

After Communion, I saw Maria E. kneeling in her chapel and she said: *"Love Him forever."* I then saw a large white door closing in a room. Jesus gave a message: *"In just a little while I will be closing the latest chapter on man's concupiscence. Since the fall of Adam, the consequences of sin have left man in a weakened state. But now I will make all things new after the tribulation. On that day I will open a new chapter in men's lives—especially those faithful to Me and living at this time. With My grace man will then experience his full potential as I created him. All this to show you My glory and that your joy may be complete in My presence. This new heaven on earth will be a revelation to man that he did not think possible—but all things are possible with Me. You will see My love poured out as never before. So keep hope and pray for guidance through this present hour for your faith will win you your salvation and an unimaginable joy in My Mother's triumph."*

Friday, May 20, 1994:

After Communion, I saw a large planet which appeared to have the colors of Jupiter and there was a large white flash off the surface of the planet. Jesus gave a message: *"Many times I have told you to look to the skies for the signs of the times. As these happenings occur, more will be made aware of this announcement of the end times. I love My people and I am always with you drawing you to Myself. I tell you, you will see greater signs than these when I come in glory with My Mother's triumph. As you see these signs occur know that you are drawing ever-closer to the time of My visitation with more gifts for you than you can imagine for My faithful."*

Later, at the Adoration Chapel, I saw bars in front of me and inside the cell I saw someone in chains. Jesus said: *"I have shown you a taste of the religious persecution to come. Many will be imprisoned for the faith and some will be tortured or martyred. That is why during the evil times I have warned you to go into hiding from the authorities. Know that after My warning it will not be long before the Anti-Christ comes to power. You will see the present structure of My Church dismantled and the evil termites will take over. But My faithful remnant will preserve My one true faith, for I will be with them for protection. You must pray much during this time for you will have much to suffer. But fear not, I will give you the grace to endure it if you keep close to My heart. Put your trust and faith in Me and I will save your souls. There will be a fair number I will bring through this trial alive. They will live to see My Mother's triumph and enjoy My glory. Those who do die for My name, rejoice, for My reward for you in heaven will be great."*

Saturday, May 21, 1994:

After Communion, I saw a large trapezoid shaped flat object and it pushed into the earth making a huge cave. Jesus said: *"I go to prepare a place for you. I love My people so much that I will not leave you orphans among the devils and wolves in sheep's clothing. Do not worry about the evil of the end times but remain faithful to Me in prayer. I will protect you and provide for you. Remember I will never test you beyond your endurance. This test will not be without suffering. But I will intervene to keep the devils at bay from My faithful. You will be safe in your hiding because I will confound the evil men in their plans. They will be so drunk with their power and lust that they will not think properly and you will be able to avoid them. But with your endurance you will live to see My glory in the end. As at Sodom and Gomorrah do not watch My justice when I dispatch the devils and evil people to hell. Continue praying in private and give thanks to Me for your deliverance. For who can stand the might of your God. This has been My plan for My people since I created man that you should see My glory."*

Later, at Nocturnal Adoration, I saw an image of the Statue of Liberty representing our country. Jesus said: *"My people of your land, what am I to do with you? Your actions and sins cry out for justice and many do not even realize how perverse your generation has become. The evil one has so seduced you over the years that evil has been made to look good and good made to look undesirable. Your greed for self-gratification and lust for the flesh has blinded your senses and reduced your spiritual life to that of an animal following only earthly pursuits. You must raise your hearts and souls to God and give Him praise. Already My justice waits to be meted out to you for your abominations. The evil is so bad that I will be forced to purify the earth. It is the sins of abortion and now increasing homosexuality that will weigh heavy on the scales of justice against you. Prepare and pray, for shortly those perverse people will be found guilty and removed from the earth, while My faithful will rejoice to see My day. Pray that this time of tribulation may be shortened."*

Sunday, May 22,1994: (Pentecost Sunday)

After Communion, I saw faces of the faithful and overlaid as in a double exposure was a picture of a dove representing the Holy Spirit. The Holy Spirit said: *"I am the Spirit of Love and today I shower My graces and gifts upon all of you as I did to the Apostles years ago. I am spreading My love upon all of you and uniting you under the one true God. Many times you have been told you are all members of the Body of Christ. So when one person is hurting, all share in response to that need. Also, when there is a joy of new life, this lifts everyone up in their own joy. It is by sharing your gifts with each other that everyone is helped in their needs. For this is how each life has been planned from the beginning and why each has been given a certain talent. This is why it is important that each person brings to fruition whatever talent you have been given by God since it ultimately contributes to the overall good of God's community. Pray that you will use My gifts for the glory of God and not just your own gain. I am asking you each day to offer up all the trials and good things you do as your daily prayer to the Father. He will see your deeds and bless your efforts with success."*

Later, at the Adoration Chapel, I saw that I was on a stage and there were many lights over me shining down. Jesus gave a message: *"Many do not think of themselves as acting out their lives on the stage of life. All in heaven can look down and see all of you playing out your roles—both the good and the bad. Each soul is given the same opportunity in My love to see their purpose in life. You struggle for survival everyday. But those who see that My plan is for each to give their life over to Me, then a light of faith goes on. Life seems like you are swimming downstream when you are in concert with My will. When you drink in My love and see pleasing Me is My desire for you, everything becomes easier. It is so beautiful when you appreciate My love and visit Me in My Blessed Sacrament to give Me thanks. Many feel life is too hard. But if they only listened for My words to them, then they would see the joy and glory that lies ahead. Continue to pray and give Me glory and every good thing will be given you. For those who love Me I cannot but help in showering you with My gifts. It is a pleasure in heaven to see each soul which craves the Lord for their daily sustenance. It is this trust I wish each of My faithful would understand and come to My joy.*"

Monday, May 23, 1994:

After Communion, I saw a big dollar sign and then a big plain concrete building which may have represented a bank. Jesus said: *"Pride and avarice are the two big stumbling blocks which stand in the way of perfection in many of My people. If you see anything in the world which takes you away from My attention, you might better avoid it than face the fires of Gehenna. If something in your life leads to an habitual sin, it is better to root it out than allow it to be an occasion of sin for you. For I call on you to be perfect as My heavenly Father is perfect. You must be willing to look at your life and see that you are struggling to make it better. If there are things or money which draw more of your attention from Me, try to blot them out and ask for My grace to desire heavenly things instead. Unless you are willing to give up the things of this world for Me, you are not ready to enter the Kingdom of heaven. You must be willing to give your will to Me and follow My ways, if you are to have eternal peace with Me."*

Later, I saw what looked like an Arab dressed in a purple robe and kneeling in a tent. Jesus said: *"I am showing you that the Arabs will play a prominent role in the end times. While many are devoted to following their religion, there are some leaders who have taken advantage of their power to mislead their people. The time is coming and is indeed upon you when the trials of men will be tested by a battle between good and evil. While the evil elements may appear to be in power for a time, know that I am allowing it to test you. For I with My Father are always in control of all events. This test is meant to humble all who think they are in control, even including Satan. For when My Mother humbles him completely by crushing his head with her foot, it will be the ultimate in humiliation of him to be treated so by a human. You must be earnest in your resolve to be with Me always in prayer for I will be protecting you always."*

Tuesday, May 24, 1994:

After Communion, I saw a distant picture of Jesus as like an icon on the wall and then it turned into a picture of Lenin followed by some evil spirits. Jesus said: *"Do not think the evil one is on a vacation with your so-called peace from the cold war era. Satan is effecting his evil ways even stronger but more subtly. Whether you want to believe it or not, you are always locked in a battle of good and evil for the souls of men. If you consider it, you will see it is the fight for souls that should most concern you. My people continue to be persecuted in those countries touched by Communism—it is not totally defeated. In its wake of godlessness there is still a void lacking of Me in the hearts of these people. The persecution they have experienced will soon be your own and worse. Pray much to preserve what is left of Christianity, since the evil one intends to try and devour My faithful. He is very much active. Continue to ask My help in warding off the evil spirits."* (An angels program was on TV this evening from 8:00-10:00)

Later, at the Adoration Chapel, I asked Jesus if I could receive a message from my guardian angel, Mark. I then asked Mark if he would give me a message and he said I needed to ask Jesus' permission. Jesus permitted this opportunity and I saw in a vision an angel in the distance. Mark said: *"We are heavenly beings at a much higher level of being than you who are human. For we see God as He is constantly. One favor Jesus has granted you which we do not experience, is your receiving Him into your soul in Communion. You do not realize fully what an honor this opportunity is for all of you. This is why, if you receive Him often, you are taking advantage of the many graces He offers through this sacrament. You must also understand how I am helping you often in your life's work and watching over you for your protection. I help you in discerning evil in its various forms. You have been very fortunate that the Lord has chosen you as an instrument to inform His people of the present and coming times. You will indeed need my help most sincerely in your future testing. The Lord has ways of rewarding you with His graces for doing good works. We angels also receive little love embraces from Jesus as we help those we guard come to a closer union with Him. But as Jesus said, you do nothing more than your duty by following Him—it is a joy to please Him just the same. If you desire, I can give you more messages if you would just ask Jesus' permission for me."* (I had a very ethereal, peaceful feeling during the message.)

Wednesday, May 25, 1994:

After Communion, I at first saw the shapes of tombstones standing in a field. The next scene of the vision showed rows of crops and an abundance of food at a large grocery store. Jesus said: *"I have told you there will be many famines at the end times. This is the reason for the tombstones. What I am now telling you, as in the past, some of these famines and shortages will be contrived and manipulated by those controlling prices for their own gain. Still further as the time of the Anti-Christ comes upon you, food and money will be controlled by the mark of the beast. Again, I have told you many times not to accept this mark for buying and selling. Since I have asked you so, I know this will work hardships and persecution on you all for My name's sake. But do not fear, I will provide for your shelter and food even if I have to provide manna to you as I did for My people through My Father to those in the desert. I will take care of you in My love for you, even though there will be some suffering. I ask you to trust and have faith that what I do for you will be the best for you as you will soon approach My time of glory."*

Later, at the prayer group, I saw some disaster scenes and men were dressed in yellow. Jesus said: *"Increasing numbers of disasters and diseases will occur. These are the new suffering servants needed to make up to the Father for so much sin in the world. Pray to diminish the sins of men and these things will diminish also."* I saw an arm sticking up at an angle and it was shaped in black plastic with a metal thin thumb sticking out at the end. Jesus said: *"This is a representation of how all your financial dealing will occur soon. This beginning of the cashless society will be preparation for the Anti-Christ's control over people."* I then saw a big heart outline and inside was Christ on the cross. Jesus said: *"I am the Hound of heaven eternally knocking on the door of your heart. I love all of you so much that I seek each of you out to know and love Me. If you would but open your heart to Me, I would empty it of all your self-love and fill it with My Divine Love—a love which desires to consume you and make you one with Me."* I then had an image like the angel last night with eyes piercing right into your soul. Jesus said: *"I have been asking many of My faithful to come in closer communication with your guardian angels. Ask My permission and I will grant you requests through them. For they are ready now more than ever to help you through these evil times to come. Each angel could use tremendous power over you but I hold all angels in check to My will so that your free will, will not be violated."* I then saw an old city of stone and the letter *"J"* came. This represented the city of Jerusalem as I understood the meaning. Jesus said: *"The time of My Second Coming is at hand. I ask you to guard your spiritual lives with prayer and be always ready to receive Me. I love My old Jerusalem even though I was so mistreated by My people. I will be coming through the golden gate with all My glory and angels."* I then could see images of pyramids and a sphinx as on a computer screen and it was being made new once again. Jesus said: *"Much as My Mother's apparition places are holy, there will come in the future evil times a renewal of all those places in the world where demons were invoked. These spirits will return to their old haunts to torment mankind. Pray for My protection during those days."* Finally, I saw in the clouds in the sky a picture representing a new heaven made out of jasper and other gems. It was gleaming with beautiful gold colors befitting a king. Jesus said: *"My picture of heaven's glory is a joy to your eyes and a hope for your future to enjoy. This is the goal of your most heavenly dreams to be united forever in My love. The beauty of where you will be is beyond your comprehension for it is not of earth. Pray that you may be delivered here and bring as many souls with you as will listen and follow."*

Thursday, May 26, 1994:

After Communion, I saw a room with an open door and light shined in reflecting off the floor. Then a man with a grey beard in robes walked in and I shied away from him. Jesus said: *"Beware of the false witnesses who will claim to be Me or those who mislead you about the faith. They will be most prevalent in the later days. They will try to lead you astray. But I tell you pray to Me and the Holy Spirit for discernment so that you will hold fast to the one true faith in Me. The devil and his followers will have convincing arguments but they will all have only horizontal meaning—meaning no reference to a deity. They will even appear to perform miracles but in actuality they will only be illusions. The worldly will be drawn into this mentality because they have itch-*

ing ears of pride and greed. Do not be misled by this lot and avoid their gatherings."

Friday, May 27, 1994:

After Communion, I saw a huge fissure in a road from an earthquake. Jesus said: *"I tell you, you will see many earthquakes increasing towards and during the end times. The increase in such calamities will continue as signs of the time of tribulation to come. You must understand this test of faith is needed to determine My faithful's trust in Me and mostly to purify the earth of the evil which has heightened in this century. Know that I love My people but justice will be served as well. Much as I threw the money changers in the temple out, so will I throw these evildoers into the eternal fires of My wrath. Pray constantly and prepare for My coming again."*

Later, at the Adoration Chapel, I was looking from a car as I was driving along some narrow roads on the sides of some steep mountains. I knew I was up high because I could see no trees and it may be out West since I saw no guardrails. Jesus said: *"You are seeing one of the safe havens high in the mountains where few will seek you out. Know that My end times grow closer as time diminishes and My judgment looms in front of you. It is an exciting time to live but it will also take great courage and trust to follow Me blindly in the face of great odds. Remember I can make things possible which are not by just your hands. Believe that I will take care of you and you will have no fear. My words are the words of eternal life. Keep close to Me in prayer and protect your souls with frequent Confession."*

Saturday, May 28, 1994:

I was backing my car out of the driveway and I looked to my right and initially I could not see a car coming. Then at the last moment, I caught sight of a flashing car in my peripheral vision and I slammed on my brakes to narrowly avoid an accident.

Later, after Communion I saw a vision of an angel moving about to the right. I received a thought message from Jesus that it was my guardian angel who helped me see the car and apply the brakes in time. I then received a second thought message which said Our Lady's mantle again had protected my wife and myself from being hit by the other car. It was interesting later that our priest offered a votive Mass to Our Lady and discussed his devotion to her in the homily. I could detect also a little humbling of my pride in this incident. It was a message to me to put more trust and follow the Lord more blindly than following my own intentions. This was a bit of a flashback to our Betania visit where Our Lady protected us from a serious accident as well.

Later, at the Adoration Chapel, I saw a huge white object which I at first thought was the sun. Then in the next scene the sky was full of smoke and fire. (Vision of the comet) Jesus said: *"You again are seeing the signs of My judgment on the earth. Many times I have told you how the people of the earth have gone to sleep spiritually. You concentrate much more on worldly things to survive and not enough on heavenly things. If you could only see the connection in doing things for Me and not just for yourselves. When you lead your life to please Me, you will concentrate more on heavenly things as a result. This is the way of life I call you to. Then you will have little concern of financial gain in this world or how you may please your senses. It is understanding the big picture of where you are headed that will direct you to heavenly things. So work hard at prayer to direct your quest for heavenly things, then you will not even desire your earthly allurements."*

Sunday, May 29, 1994: (Trinity Sunday)

After Communion, I saw a triangle and it was moving from one side to another going around. Then I had a picture of Jesus on the cross, a dove and a voice from above saying: *"This is My Divine Son in whom I am well-pleased."* Then Jesus said: *"We are Three Persons in one. We are the personification of life and love. It is a mystery to know of Us perfectly but it is enough to know We represent unity and oneness. Many times I have told you all people make up My One Body—both the good and the bad. This is true also of all creatures that creation is made up of one reality with good and bad angels as well. Everything brought into existence is good in and of itself—it is the choices which creatures make for themselves that decides their fate. We want all to come, to know and to love Us but We do not force it on your free will. It must be freely chosen. Pray for understanding to know how to follow your faith to the goal of being one with Us."*

Later, at the Adoration Chapel, I saw a bicycle with two wheels moving; a car from the side-looking at the wheels; cars racing by and then airplanes in a row ready for take off. Jesus said: *"You again are seeing various modes of transportation as I have shown you previously. As the end times approach nothing will be of importance to you but Me. For I will lead you and protect you. It is true that it will be safer for you if you move to one of My safe havens. For the Anti-Christ's men will be looking for you to torture you and even put some to death as an example to the others. He would want to keep you alive to try and bring your soul into his camp. If you die fighting his temptations, he will lose the battle for you. So if you stay away from them finding you, you will have less temptation and distress to bear. Pray that My faithful will listen to My word when this time comes. For following Me is your best path to your salvation. You must continue in your prayer efforts. Do not let the worldly concerns take you away from what I am asking you to do. Be vigilant and stay close to Me for this is all that matters for the eternal life of your soul."*

Monday, May 30, 1994:

After Communion, I saw a squared-off opening to a thatched hut. Jesus said: *"My people are too affluent. You have built your lives around things so much that you have little time for Me, your Creator and Redeemer. You have become so accustomed to acquiring and using things of this life, to some they have become a god in themselves. You were made a spiritual being and directed to a spiritual life adoring Me. This should be the direction of your life and not love of the world and the things in it. Lift yourself to a higher life in the spirit with prayer and private meditation. It is through renouncing the things of this world that you will come to know Me better. Keep Me constantly at the center of your life and I will grant you My peace."*

Later, at the Adoration Chapel, I saw a theme park with some kind of a ride which was rotating in a circle from top to bottom like a clock. Then I saw in space faces flashing in front of me—Hitler, Stalin, Mao and the like. Jesus said: "You *are seeing the representation of time speeding up as the events of the end times are about to begin. You also are seeing pictures of some of the earlier Anti-Christs. But now not long after My warning you will see the last*

Anti-Christ. Since Satan's time is short, he will help this last Anti-Christ so that he will almost be the devil incarnate. Also, be watchful of the imposter who will take over My Pope John Paul II's place in Rome. Together these two will lead men against God in the last battle of good and evil. Read the last book of the Bible to understand their roles. Despite Satan's help, they will not reign long for I have power over the evil one by virtue of My death on the cross. Fear not therefore, My Mother's triumph will bring you to My glory as long as you remain faithful to Me. I will give you the strength to overcome evil if you would just will to be one with Me."

Tuesday, May 31, 1994: (Visitation)

After Communion, I saw a picture of Our Lady in an icon and her face was obscured. She said: *"I greet you, my son, and all the faithful with a joy of salvation which you will be experiencing more fully in the near future. I have been sent to announce my own Son's visitation upon the earth. At the same time it will soon be my own triumph I will celebrate with all of you. In order to be ready to greet my Son—'do whatever He tells you.' Listen to His word in the Scriptures and His gentle stirring in your hearts to be with Him. Jesus' heart and my heart are joined as one. He invites all His faithful to be also united with Him."*

Later, at the Adoration Chapel, I saw a horse with various spokes of metal fanning out in all directions. Jesus said: *"The New-Age movement will be applauding the false peace that the Anti-Christ will portray. There will be increasing controls put on your money system with international ties. The electronic cards called 'debit cards' as you heard today will gain increasing acceptance for handling all financial transactions. It is through these means that the Anti-Christ will control or attempt to control your lives. Each stage will be pushed under the guise for your protection from theft. In reality, it is their means to gain control of the money of the world. Once you are forced to accept a mark on your hand or forehead for doing transactions, do not accept it. This will be the mark of the beast which I have told you to shun. For those who accept this, accept the devil's world and not Me. You must seek Me first no matter at what cost in order to save your soul. The world will try to entice you with pleasures and things not meant to save your soul—refuse to be a part of the worldly. What I am asking you will be against your nature but rely on your spiritual foundations and not your carnal desires."*

Wednesday, June 1, 1994:

After Communion, I had a vision of some faithful and then I kept seeing more pictures of caves. Jesus said: *"I love My people. You are all so beautiful—each in your own special way. You do indeed reflect My image which I have placed in you. Look for My presence in everyone you meet and respect Me in them. You all mean so much to Me such that I am always reaching out to protect you. The image of the caves again brings up that feeling of protection. I will be with you always at your side leading you to find the safe havens in these coming evil days. Be faithful and trust in Me and you will not be disappointed."*

Later, at the prayer group, I saw Our Lady standing outside of a glass door and she was showered in a gold yellow light. She said: *"I give you an example with my Visitation that you may help your neighbor in their need as well. I am also showing you that my triumph is near. This will be my glorious visitation which you will welcome with joy that it is my time to be with you as my Son completes the purification of the earth."* I then saw a huge circling platter which again represented the warning. Jesus said: *"Prepare for My warning. It will come when you least expect it. Be watchful and have your soul ready by frequent Confession. Those in mortal sin will experience great grief at the time of the warning."* I then saw several mouths talking and then I saw a lot of rich foods. Jesus said: *"You have not been properly thankful for the many blessings of food I have given you. You have many times wasted food for controlling prices. I tell you there will soon be a time of food shortage. Food will be limited by either crop damage or contrived food shortages."* I then saw a black threshing machine and it was grinding up all kinds of weapons. Jesus said: *"I will destroy all your weapons of war in preparation for My era of peace. At that time there will be no anger, no armies, and no wars."* I then saw someone blowing a trumpet and then it seemed like angels were present. Jesus said: *"These are My angels preparing to launch the trumpets mentioned in the last book of the Bible. The end times draw near and men will witness their domi-*

nation of the earth." I then saw a black horse which represents *"The Famine"* in Revelation. Jesus said: *"This will be the time of the great famine over all the earth. It will be a plague to torment men and show them My judgment time is at hand. Prices of food will be very high because of the food shortage."* Finally, I saw sweeping white concentric circles moving around a huge galaxy. Jesus said: *"You are seeing a representation of My oneness which every creature is a part of. It also represents My infinite love and shows you the size of the universe which is endless and beyond your comprehension. So fear not, I am controlling events. Have trust and faith in Me and I will deliver all My faithful to your eternal salvation."*

Thursday, June 2, 1994:
After Communion, I saw Maria E. with her eyes closed and raising her head to heaven. She said: *"Praise Him and be one with Him."* I then saw a bare cross in the distance and it came forward to me. Jesus said: *"You all will be asked to carry your cross and suffer as well with Me into the coming tribulation. You have been sheltered from persecution physically in this country but soon it will change. Your religious freedoms will slowly slip away as your courts make laws to suit those who want no authority over them. Atheism will abound and soon you will see more persecution. Know that I have warned you beforehand but be stouthearted and stand by your faith. Then you will be able to say you have fought your enemies and have finished the course. With Me at your right hand you will not be denied."*

Friday, June 3, 1994:
After Communion, I saw some fringe decoration on a couch. Then I saw a priest at Mass. Jesus said: *"In the Scriptures is found My true word written by the inspiration of the Holy Spirit. These are My words of revelation to My people. Yet it is the Church you must listen to for the proper interpretation. It is the Magisterium of the Church which has preserved My teachings as you should know them and hold dear to your heart. I say this because you are entering the age of the great apostasy which is heralded at the end times. People and even clergy will proclaim in My name those things that have been heresy throughout the ages. Do not*

believe what these false theologians are professing for they are spewing the evils of the devil from their mouths. Beware of those who attempt to mislead My elect in faith and morals. Their punishment will be severe if even they endanger the loss of one soul to Satan. Follow My Pope John Paul II in his teachings and you will not be far from the Kingdom of God."

Later, at the Adoration Chapel, I saw an hour glass with the sands slowly sifting downward. Jesus said: *"My people do you not realize how fragile life is? You can be alive one moment and then with some circumstance, you may be called home with Me. Many people when they die, cannot believe it happened and as a result are not prepared for heaven. Many souls go to hell because they think they have plenty of time to get spiritual later and continue on the road to worldliness. It cannot be this way for My faithful. I must be first in your lives at all times such that you are always prepared if your death should come quickly. When you are one in spirit with My heart as I ask in constant prayer, you will be ready for that great transition from your earthly life to a totally spiritual life. It is important that you keep your focus on Me and love Me always as I love you. This all-consuming love of mine awaits you in a most beautiful way when you enter heaven. Here you will taste of My peace and join My many creatures who ceaselessly give Me praise, glory and thanksgiving. You do not know or understand eternity outside of time. Your life decision to choose Me will determine if you want Me or the devil's world of selfishness. Love must be shared. When you reach out to Me, you reach out for love forever. When you desire the world, you seek yourself and will find eternal despair without Me. Think of the gravity of your eternal life and you will be drawn to Me every minute of every day."*

Saturday, June 4, 1994: (Votive Mass of Our Lady)

After Communion, I saw a statue much like the one in the woods behind the shrine altar in Betania. Only I could not see Our Lady's face on the statue. Our Lady gave a message: *"You will be experiencing my disappearance at many of my shrines as I have told you would happen. I have been enabled to prepare you, my children, for my Sons's Second Coming. I have asked many times through various visionaries to pray much, especially my fifteen decade Rosary for peace in the world. Not just the peace of no war, but pray for the peace my Son brings. In a short time, the last days foretold will be upon you. I urge even more that your prayers will be your only salvation. Keep close to my Son and He will protect you. Soon after this tribulation, my Son will allow my triumph over Satan. At that time, you will see all things new again in the Spirit. This will be your hope to see my triumph for it will be a glorious day in the Lord. Be thankful you are living in these times and persevere in faith constantly. Thank you for responding to my call."*

Later, the International Image of Our Lady of Guadalupe was on the right side of the altar during exposition and right under a yellow flag representing the papacy. I later saw a vision of a cross on the sides of some closet doors in a sacristy and I also saw a picture of Pope John Paul II. Mary gave a message: *"You are blessed to have my Pope son, John Paul II, as your reigning pontiff. He is a holy man and very close to my heart. You must be watchful as the end times approach. He will suffer much for my Jesus. He is steadfast in preserving the Church's teachings. But he will encounter much persecution. I have interceded with my Son to protect him from harm. Do not be surprised if he is exiled and that it may occur on the thirteenth of some month in the future. There will be a political upheaval at that time in Italy which will precipitate his exile. In his place a false prophet will be installed through the agents of the evil one. These and many events will occur before my triumph will be ushered in by my Son. Pray, my children, and keep close to my Son."* I asked for a confirmation of this at Our Lady's Image of Guadalupe and I received an odor of roses.

Sunday, June 5, 1994: (Feast of Corpus Christi)

After Communion, (Fr. Jack's 40th Anniversary Mass) I saw a triangular mirror and in front was a cup with the Host on top. Jesus gave a message: *"My people, I love you so much that you cannot begin to understand how much. My love for you is most demonstrated in My death on the cross for you. A man has no greater love than he give up his life for his fellowmen. My love for you knows no bounds. I would have done so even if it was just for one of you. But I love and watch over each of you individually since I knew you from your mother's womb. I have given you Myself to be shared in My Holy Eucharist as long as time exists. Through the Eucharist I am joined with you more intimately so you can feel My love and I can feel your love in return. I am always asking for your committment to be one with Me so you can yield your fruit a hundredfold. It is sharing My love which draws Me to search for each of you. I offer you My heart to come home to Me and embrace Me in the Spirit. When you follow Me, I will bless you with eternal life and love. You will be in constant peace when your will is joined with Me."*

At the Adoration Chapel, I saw a monstrance and then a picture of a bright sun. Jesus said: *"My love for you, My people can be likened to the sun as it shines down on you providing light and warmth. So with My love I shower you with graces and envelop you with My embrace as I warm your heart. I even warm cold hearts and melt them into My own. The light of love I give you also is a light of understanding My word in the Scriptures. I am constantly showing you how I want you to lead your lives by loving Me and your neighbor. Many times I have answered your prayers or have bequeathed you with My gifts, both spiritual and temporal. But where are My faithful to come back and thank Me? It is as when I healed the ten lepers and only one came back to give Me praise and thanksgiving. I asked then and I still ask now. Where are the other nine? Were they not healed also and shouldn't they want to return thanks to Me? When you come to Me and visit Me in exposition or the tabernacle, you are doing this out of love and are not forced to do so. I enjoy your visits of love very much because you see how important My love and support are in your life. I wish and pray that all My souls would see My light in this way and come to give Me thanks for My loving kindnesses. You must see and understand how just as you see rain at times, you would not fully appreciate sunny days without this contrast. So also with your spiritual lives. If you were not tested at times, you could not appreciate the beautiful moments of love I give you in peaceful mountaintop experiences. So live and pray for guidance until that day you will have eternal bliss in My love in heaven."*

Monday, June 6, 1994: (50th Anniversary of D-Day)
After Communion, I saw a large cloud much like a mushroom cloud of an atomic weapon representing times gone by. Then more clouds could be seen on the horizon representing the current day. Jesus said: *"My people you give Me so much frustration in your earthly attitudes. Instead of listening to My message of love which would truly bring My peace to your world, you insist on bickering with your neighbors. Man has lived by the sword in yesterdays, but he still is committing the same mistakes even today. You need to sit down and realize why wars are still prevalent. If there was not so much envy, greed and anger in men's hearts over even the most petty of reasons, men would understand how peaceful life could be if given a chance. But since men refuse to change their position and are stubborn in their thoughts, he will continue to make the same problems for himself. This is why there are still war clouds in your future. Men will continue to reap the agonies of death and destruction because he will not come to grips with the fact that he is his own worst enemy. Men's minds have listened too long to the sirens of the evil one. It is up to Me now to intervene in order to purify My earth. Evil has reigned too long and it will soon come to an end. So prepare My people to see how life must really be lived in My love."*

Later, I saw a large face of Jesus with criss cross blocks representing "The many faces of Christ." Jesus said: *"Many times I have spoken to you about loving Me and loving your neighbor. I want to emphasize loving those who do not love you back. In each human face lies a soul with Myself a part of them. You must begin more to see My presence in everyone and have love for everyone equally. It is a grace to live this message but if you are to know Me as true love you must be like Me in loving all of My people. If you love those who love you, what merit is there in that? Even sinners do as much. But to be perfect and more like Me you must reach out to even those you dislike or who persecute you. You, by loving them, will give them My example and will heap coals of love on your enemies. They will not know how to understand this and their hearts may be softened to Me with prayer. Live for today as I have asked, since your time grows short."*

Tuesday, June 7, 1994:

After Communion, I saw at first a white object and gradually as it came forward it was a bride with a white veil over her face. This represented the Church as the bride of Christ—as I was given. Jesus said: *"My Church that I have established on earth through My disciples, directs My teachings to all My faithful. It is My representative in the Pope to lead all mankind to a knowledge of Me and a devotion to following My example. I will not leave My Church unprotected. You are always loved deeply in My heart and I will keep the evil one in check over My faithful remnant. Believe and have trust that I will be with My Church to the end of time. Know though in these end times that the devil will try to scatter My sheep through the venom of his hate for you. There will be many attempts to divide My Church against its members. But have hope and keep faithful to My commandments. If you are loyal to your promises at Baptism, I will be loyal to My promise in protecting you. Be joyful for your eternal reward is close at hand."*

Later, at the Adoration Chapel, I saw a man and a woman dancing for joy separately. Jesus said: *"I long to be with My faithful especially when they can visit Me in My Blessed Sacrament. I pour My love out on those who come. You saw the dancing and these people full of My joy. If you would receive Me into your hearts, I could bring you a peace and trust in Me you could never find in the world. When you come to visit Me, cast aside all your earthly distractions. For I wish to feed you with My love so you can drink it in and I can be absorbed into your spirit. All things that keep you away from Me, except for the necessities of the body, could be deemed distractions. For I am a jealous God and I wish to share your precious time as often as possible. Your time on earth is so short compared to My eternity. So please try to spend as much time as you can in contemplation of Me or in prayer. I enjoy your company and long to be with you for any time you can be with Me. It is true there are only a handful of souls drawn to this deep a devotion to My Blessed Sacrament. I assure you those who love enough to spend time with Me, will even receive earthly and spiritual gifts I only reserve for My special daughters and sons. So continue to visit Me often. You will not be disappointed and I will see to your every need even in the evil times to come."*

Wednesday, June 8, 1994:

After Communion, I saw cliffs on the seashore and big waves were breaking in against the cliffs. A message of explanation was *"Cleanse your sins."* Jesus said: *"My people, how can I receive you when I find in your soul all kinds of abomination and where it is overgrown with the debris of the world? You must first be cleansed of your sins. Go to the priest in Confession and be reconciled with Me so that you can be purified and receive My grace of life in your soul. You must be dead to sin and not dead to Me as your soul is in mortal sin. Most important is that you have contrition for your sins. It is this willingness for forgiveness that you must keep focused on. I will forgive you, but you must be sincere to please Me by giving up your will to Me. Then your soul will be clean and tidy and I would be pleased to be with you. If you would prepare yourself to meet your King, you would not come to Me in tattered clothes. So put on your wedding garment and have your sins forgiven. Then when you enter My banquet, all will be ready. It is important that you be watchful and ready for you do not know the hour I will call you home to Me."*

At the prayer group, I first saw a telephone and Jesus said: *"I have asked you many times to be watchful and ready for the day when I will call each one of My faithful home to Me. This is not to be feared but I am only asking you to be prepared always—be vigilant in prayer. I want you to be close to Me so you will appreciate My splendor when you can see My glory."* I then saw some people getting food on their plates at a picnic. Jesus said: *"You are always invited to My banquet at My Mass. It is in the breaking of the bread that you see My real presence before you. I share My graces and blessings on all of you here tonight."* I then saw a pink balloon with helium and a string attached. Jesus said: *"You must be willing to let go of your earthly life if you expect to rise up to Me on a higher spiritual plane. Do not become tied down to your earthly distractions but receive Me as Lord over your life."* I then had a vision of the Holy Spirit coming down on a row of about ten crosses. The Holy Spirit said: *"I am the Spirit of Love and I come to protect the souls and console those who will be martyred for the name of Jesus. Some will be asked to give their lives but in doing so they will be an inspiration in faith for those who will carry on the faith."* I then saw an icon of Our Lady and she said: *"I come as your Mother to calm your earthly fears. Do not be concerned that this life should continue as it is—it is not to be like this for long. You were made to be a spiritual being and you should be anxious to greet your Lord when He comes. But do not worry about what date these things will happen. My Son told this to His Apostles—not to be concerned when He shall come. Continue to pray, my children, and my Son will be very pleased with you."* I then saw some police handcuffing some people. Jesus said: *"Many faithful will be persecuted for My sake but know I have suffered much before you. It is necessary that My purification should come. But there will be a great conflict between good and evil before you see My Mother's triumph."* Finally, I saw a runway and a jet taking off. Then I had a picture from above and could see an aircraft carrier. Jesus said: *"You will hear of wars and rumors of wars and you will understand that these will be signs of the end times. You will see many on-going conflicts as wars will continue until the evil one is conquered in the great battle. But fear not, these things will happen to fulfill My prophecies concerning these days."*

Thursday, June 9, 1994:

After Communion, I could see Maria E. and she said: *"Love Jesus before the Blessed Sacrament."* I then saw some faces of the faithful in the center of some darkness. Jesus said: *"I am repeating My previous message that you should love one another. Many divisions creep into your everyday lives which are based on petty differences or misunderstandings. You must be most aware of this in your own personal families. Satan is trying to divide and split the family. Do not allow him any success. Love each other in your family as I did in the Holy Family. Patch up your differences and struggle to preserve family unity instead of building up animosities. In a word, again love one another both in your family and outside as well."*

Friday, June 10, 1994: (Feast of the Sacred Heart)

After Communion, I saw a big numeral ONE with an arrow on the top. Jesus said: *"I am emphasizing with this vision that I should be your only concern in this world. It is your task on earth to know My love in making you was to adore Me constantly. I have given everyone a free will and you are foremost a spiritual being* made in My image. You are attracted to Me since I am your object in life to follow by your spiritual orientation. My love for you is poured out on the cross for you. This day commemorates My love and shows My loving heart is constantly reaching out to touch your heart. I follow you always and am right beside you encouraging you to know and understand My love for you. My glory and joy are always at your disposal if you would accept Me into your heart. I will give you a peace and desire for Me such that all else in your life is nothing. Pray constantly to be with Me, for I enjoy your presence and want to consume you in My love."

Later, at Holy Rosary after Communion, I saw Our Lady as a young girl and there was a small flame coming from her heart area. She said: "You see, my little one, how my heart burns with love for my Son for we are one in spirit. As your Mother my heart also burns with love for my faithful children. It is important to keep your heart uncluttered with any worldly love for things. Instead I am asking you to keep a pure heart in prayer and fasting. In this way you too will have time to give my Son praise and your heart will burn with love for Him also. He is the one to focus your attention on and this will lead you to do everything possible to please Him. By loving my Son and keeping close to His heart you will enjoy being in one spirit with God."

Saturday, June 11, 1994:

After Communion, I saw Our Lady come radiant with joy in her face and light coming from her and she put her hand on a little boy. Mary said: "I greet you with my heavenly love for my faithful. I am your Mother and I come to teach you how to glorify and honor my Son. You are constantly beset by problems and adversities on this earth, but it is a training to control yourself and direct your attention to my Son's plan for you. Do not let your pride and greed for things or envy of other people's good fortune lead you astray. Do not allow Satan to keep your mind tied up so much with worldly things. You must find more time for prayer and see what my Jesus desires you to do for Him. Offer your day up to Him from the morning till it is over. It is His will He calls you to follow. Do not be taken up so much with your own agenda, but leave room for Him to operate in your life. Once you follow Him closely and close out your worldly aspirations, He will grant you

His graces and peace which will prepare you to meet Him in heaven. By giving everything over to Him you will lose your worldly life but gain an eternal life with your Savior."

Later, at the Adoration Chapel, I saw a very bright white light shining down over some buildings. It was a feeling that this was either a visit from outer space or a supernatural visitation. It was definitely not earthly in its origin and maybe even angelic. Jesus said: *"You are seeing the beginning of My glory in this heavenly encounter. I have told you often that I am the light of life for you. This will be a sign of hope for you in the many places of appearances of My Mother and Myself. It will be a sign in the skies— one of the many that will signify the end times. Do not be overjoyous, since this time will see great trials and sufferings for My people. If you fail to understand the extent of My love for you in this display, you will miss the whole purpose of My purification of the earth. Continue in your prayers and strive to be one with Me in your will to follow My commands."*

Sunday, June 12, 1994:

After Communion, I saw in the center of a vision a cup that was overflowing. Jesus gave a message: *"How My people continue to drift along in their sinful ways without realizing I will come like a thief in the night. I tell you, My people, wake up to the reality of your actions and deeds. Do you think I am pleased with what you are doing? This is a question for all My people but only My faithful remnant are listening. Woe to those who are content only with the things of this earth and do not even think of Me. For soon I will come with My swift justice. You have seen the cup overflowing with the sins of man. My justice is calling out since there is not enough reparation of prayer and sacrifice to offset this tide of sin. It is beyond turning back My wrath. So I warn you, take care of your spiritual lives for I intend to purify this earth of its evil. It is now the time of the great harvest which you will soon see manifested before you. Be watchful and prepared with constant prayer. For those found still adoring Me will receive a prophet's reward."*

Later, at the Adoration Chapel, I saw a spider at a distance. I could then see the spider descending into a deep well and there was a spider web as well. Jesus said: *"My dear people, I am show-*

ing this web because it represents how evil men are planning for the day of Anti-Christ. For many years these same men have controlled political power in one form or another. The deep well indicates that these men are serving the devil's needs instead of those of God. Satan's agents are planning one last thrust to control men's souls through money and people's craving for only an earthly survival. Be forewarned of their evil intentions. For what you are witnessing is a preparation for the last battle of good and evil. There will be those who also will fight for Me who I will empower with My graces to fight also for men's souls. It is this struggle for souls which is the real prize sought by each side. You must therefore prepare yourself for the devil's attempts for he will be strong for a while. Keep constantly close to Me in prayer and receive the sacraments while you can. This will build up your spiritual strength so you can stand up to the demons in the coming tribulation. Listen to Me and follow My instructions and you will be protected."

Monday, June 13, 1994:

After Communion, I had a very vivid vision of a map of Korea and its surrounding areas. Jesus gave a message: *"You are seeing one of the areas where I speak of rumors of wars. I am not telling you the outcome but know there will be several of these problems and smaller wars as now. These things will always be with you because of men's cold hearts. Do not worry over them but instead pray for peace. It is only by trying to warm men's hearts that peace will have a chance. Men's greed for fame and power bring him only ruin. He must strive for the higher goals of God to bring peace and harmony. When love of God is the center of man's life, then life will conform to love of neighbor as well. See to it that you start with harmony and love in your own families. Then world peace will have more of a chance for a reality."*

Later, I saw a Host being raised up. Then I saw a large metal candle rack with many small candle offerings. Jesus said: *"My people, how many times have I asked you to give up your whole being to Me for this is your start on the road to your perfection? As you see this candle offering many people put only coins in as an offering. This also is how many of My people treat Me. They only are willing to share a short time with Me. This is truly a tokenism mentality. When I love you, I love you completely. I died on the cross to give My all, My life for you. When lovers are committed to each other, they share everything they have. It is this commitment of your whole life to Me that I am asking for. When you let Me lead your life, you can trust your salvation is assured. Walk with Me each day in all you do. Then all your actions will be as a prayer. You will not have to depend only on yourself. With My help you will reach your full potential on earth for the tasks I have planned for you. Go and encourage all men to follow Me in this way and there will be true peace for everyone."*

Tuesday, June 14, 1994:

After Communion, I saw what looked like some priestly vestments in the distance. Jesus said: *"I am asking you to be perfect and serve God and your neighbor. In this world of yours it is all caught up in serving oneself only. The world and the demons are tempting you to follow the idols of self-gratification and love of material things. I tell you, you must change your life and concentrate on pleasing Me instead of yourself. When you fall in love with Me, you will have the desire to serve the rest of humanity. I directed My Apostles to serve as when I washed their feet. This follows the commandment I have given you to love God and your neighbor. You will see as you are perfected that you will lovingly want to help others out of love for Me. So continue on each day with prayer and service to your God and those who need your help."*

Later, at the Adoration Chapel, I saw what looked a little like a casket but it had very modern looking bubbles all along it. Jesus said: *"You must bury your modern toys and distractions, for your time is too precious to waste on such foolishness. People waste too much time watching TV and pleasing their curiosity for things. Time is short and you must put it to work to help in the nearing battle of good and evil. When you have spare time, spend it on Me in prayer where I can use them to help souls that may otherwise be lost. Keep close to Me and follow My plan for you. To help My faithful you must prepare yourself for the spiritual battle at hand by putting on your breastplate of faith and nourishing your soul with My sacraments. Many do not understand the importance of helping Me in this time of evil. I will need many footsoldiers for*

God in fighting those deeds of the evil forces. If you follow My will, you will be rewarded for fighting the good fight for souls. This is an important time which I cannot stress enough to you. Protect yourself from evil and do not fritter your time away on useless activities. Concentrate on helping the good forces to succeed in any way you can help. I am calling all My forces to be ready for the big battle with Satan."

Wednesday, June 15, 1994:

After Communion, I saw some pews in a different church. Then I saw some black curtains as at a funeral parlor. Jesus said: *"My people in a short time your churches will no longer be My place of Mass. Yea, it will soon be a time of persecution instead. Relish the joy of My service and receiving Me freely now since not long and you will be at an underground service. You will be in hiding from the authorities as I have advised you previously. In My time of persecution My faithful ones will be tried as never before in history. The evil one and his agents will seek you out to torture and kill you. Do not be afraid, I will protect you from the evil one's attempts. Keep faith in Me and you will soon see My glory as you cannot comprehend. Pray for strength and help those faithful around you to endure this test of purification."*

Later, at the prayer group, I saw a budding flower and then it came into full bloom. Jesus said: *"I see each of you with all your imperfections. Yet I see a beauty in all of you which is the reflection of My image in you. You all have an inner beauty of spirit when you are in union with My will. Shine forth your love and beauty to all those around you and you will warm their hearts."* I then saw an insignificant little bug on the water. Jesus said: *"All of My creation shows forth My glory even to the least noticed organisms. All of My creatures are important and serve a purpose in My plan. I love all of My people equally for there are no insignificant souls which I have forgotten. You too should look for My presence in everyone and not just glorify those of importance."* I then saw a picture of a young girl about eight years old. Jesus said: *"I want you to bring the children to Me much as I asked My Apostles to do. These are My most precious and innocent of souls. It is your responsibility to bring them to the faith, so that they can know and love Me as you do."* I then saw an old nun dressed in a black habit and then I saw a priest as well. Jesus said: *"I want you to pray for My priests and nuns. They are in most need of your prayers to keep them faithful to their vocations. They are always needed to help your spiritual life with the giving of My sacraments. They too will be severely tested by the coming tribulation."* I then saw a picture of a modern city in the future with flying vehicles and all the latest scientific inventions. Jesus said: *"You have made many advances in worldly knowledge. You have taken many courses in your training for your job. But I am asking you to give even more effort to learning those things of the spiritual order which will bring you closer to Me. For is not the spirit more important than the body? Work toward this goal of learning more about the faith."* I then saw Our Lady and she came forth with her Son who was wearing a crown. Mary said: *"I am always bringing you closer to my Son in any way possible for you to be enlightened. For He will soon be coming to show you His Kingdom which you will indeed experience in due time. Prepare yourselves with prayer and fasting so you can greet Him and show your love for Him."* Finally, I saw a desk with some paper and writing implements on it. Jesus said: *"In these coming trials, I will not leave you orphans and alone. But I will enlighten many of My faithful with messages to prepare My people for what they need to do in that time. With these directions from many visionaries and locutionists, you will see how I truly will give you My protection from the evil one."*

Thursday, June 16, 1994:

After Communion, I saw Maria E. and she said: *"He is the only one to adore."* I then saw some ugly demons as if coming up with orange flames below them and with smoke around them. Jesus said: *"During the tribulation, where I will purify the earth, the demons will be loosed from hell to roam the earth. They will be allowed to claim as their own those souls who have rejected Me and failed to repent of their sin. At the same time I will protect My faithful in their safe havens from the demons. Just as I have told you, the demons will return to their old haunts. Some of the safe havens will be the holy ground where apparitions have occurred. Many angels from heaven and your guardian angels will be abound also to protect you. There may be suffering and even* some martyrs, but the souls of My faithful should never fear that I will abandon them. After a short time, you will witness My love in the splendor of My glory and My Mother's triumph."

Friday, June 17, 1994:

After Communion, I at first saw a lamplight alone. Then later I saw what looked like a long big pyramid being carried by thousands of people. Jesus gave a message: *"My message today is one of warning. As you have seen the lampstand, be watchful and vigilant not only of My coming but also when the evil days of the Anti-Christ come. I tell you many people will be drawn to him as he may deceive even some of My faithful. They will carry him off to be their ruler. But his kingdom will be of short duration. Do not be taken in by his cunning and seeming miracles. His real intent is to destroy and consume as many souls as will accept him. But you are to remain faithful to the one true God. For in time I will break the evil one's fetters and he will be thrown into hell. You will need faith and trust in Me and I will protect you. After this time you will enter My glory and know My infinite love more intimately."*

Saturday, June 18, 1994:

At St. Bernard's in Easton, Pa. after Communion, I saw Jesus at first standing in a boat. Then He was standing in the darkness with light radiating out from Him. Jesus said: *"Many times you have faced the storm of unknown events. As you come upon the end times, you will see My love manifested in the protection of My faithful. You will be buffeted with the tests of the demons. But you must know you can trust Me to help you, if you would but call on Me in faith. For I am at your side always ready to embrace you and help you in your need. Pray and invite Me into your heart and I will come forward to your defense through all the storms of life you will encounter. Be at peace always for I love you with an all-consuming love and will protect you from the demons."*

Sunday, June 19, 1994:

At St. Joseph's Church in Easton, Pa. after Communion, I saw a cup of wine representing Christ's presence and overlaying it I saw a stained-glass window representing the traditional Church. Jesus said: *"You are seeing My real presence which is with you in the Eucharist—in My Body and Blood under the appearances of bread and wine. I want you to fully believe in this by faith because I am truly with you always. During Communion I am the most intimately close to you so I can share your love and the things you are suffering. Now I am again showing you that the traditional faith that you have come to know and love will be under attack in the evil days as the tribulation draws near. I am telling you not to be afraid of these attacks for the evil one will try to draw you away from Me. You must repent of your sins and love Me as I love you with nothing else interfering. In other words I must be first in your life to all your comforts and material things. If you cling to Me in faith, I will protect you from all evil."*

(At this time a red circle came around the moon.) Later, at the Adoration Chapel, I saw what looked like a mushroom cloud. Then the scene changed to a flower. Jesus said: *"O, what foolish men you are. You continue your bickering over power and weapons. You fail many times to realize the results of your actions even those made in haste. I tell you, if there continues to be fighting, it could lead to a nuclear war. My people, you must pray vigorously for peace and even that nuclear weapons are not used. If the parties involved are threatened with losing, they may use these arms as a last resort. Pray that men will see the error in their ways and that they will come to the peace table. More men must acknowledge Me as master of the universe or they will call down My wrath on them for their sin. This is why the earth will eventually need purification of the evil extent to which it will come."*

Monday, June 20, 1994:
After Communion, I saw a little light bending around a corner. Then I saw a blur of activity almost in a stream as in a time-lapsed photograph. Jesus said: *"My people take life at too fast a pace. You are so intent on doing so many things in such a short space of time. Because of that, you either do things poorly or do not have time to understand what you are doing. Doing things just to get them done is not your only concern. You must start your day by offering up everything you do to please Me and follow My will for you. With Me as the center of your life, let Me lead you so that*

you will always know what and why you do things. If you let Me, I will give order and direction to your life. When you do things in conformance with My laws, time will not be your concern but only a measure of how you can please Me each day."

Later, I saw a strange tubular object being pointed at me. It seemed rather ominous as it was some kind of detection device. I then saw several tunnels where cars were going through. Jesus gave a message: *"This is indeed another warning concerning the evil times I have told you about many times. As people take the mark of the beast, it will contain something that can be detected by some electrical device or scanner. This is the object which you have correctly seen in the vision. It is a warning that Satan and his agents will seek you out and test you with this device. They will only tell you are one of the faithful by virtue of a non-reading. They will need to see you to test you. This is why you again are seeing the hiding places. For underground, they will not be able to detect you. I am protecting you My people since I wish to preserve My faithful remnant. I will be giving you such messages for your protection but even more it is a sign of how much I love you and will guard you through this purification. Keep close to Me in prayer and you will please Me greatly. With a little endurance, you will come to see and enjoy the glory I have waiting for you in My Kingdom."*

Tuesday, June 21, 1994:

After Communion, I saw a sparkling crystal and a pyramid. Jesus gave a message: *"Do not be deceived about those in the New-Age movement who use pyramid power, crystals and other charms. You are not to even be concerned with such things since they do not deal with power from God. Instead they invoke the powers from evil sources. Sacramentals such as crucifixes, Rosaries, and statues or pictures of the saints or of God—these are your weapons to fight evil. All the rest is from the evil one. Warn your friends and relatives not to be taken up with the evil powers of the New-Age. This is important that you should discern where miraculous powers come from. All good is from God and all evil from the devil and his agents."*

Later, at the Adoration Chapel, I saw some Indian paintings and drawings of figures on the walls. Jesus said: *"I have many faithful people who believe in Me in many ways. My Mother has appeared at various places of apparition for the American Indians. They have received her well in Guadalupe and other places in South America. Many times messages were given then to bring the people closer to God and away from child sacrifices. Even today, the people are still worshiping material things and are killing their babies for convenience. I tell you these sins will not go unforgiven. If men do not repent of their sin of abortion, they will face My wrath and I will take away their material things and destroy them because these things disgust Me. Some value life so low they think more of their possessions. When their own lives are threatened, then they may take notice how much a gift that life is for them. Pray My people that abortion will be overturned and men will see the true value of life, especially as I see and love it."*

Wednesday, June 22, 1994: (Sts. John Fisher & Thomas More)
After Communion, I saw a small enclosure of a little altar and there was a nun there with the old habit. Jesus said: *"As in the past many of My faithful have been persecuted and martyred. So in the coming evil times, this will continue because of My name. You will be drawn to protected areas I have prepared for you to avoid the demons and their agents. Many in your country have yet to see religious persecution. But this time will be most trying and will require courage and trust in Me. Pray constantly and witness to the faith for those who are struggling to know what to do. Your shining example should keep the faithful strong and give them hope for when I shall come in glory. This test will last but a moment of time, but you shall reap an eternity with Me in the splendor of My love for you."*

Later, at the prayer group, I saw a picture of ornate objects and some peacocks. Jesus said: *"I have given you individually many gifts of material things, the very talents special to you, and your very life itself. In all these blessings I ask you to have humility and not be a braggart. Instead praise God and thank Him for these special gifts to each of you."* I then saw a picture of our grandchildren. Jesus said: *"I have graced many parents with My gift of life in their children and grandchildren. These lives are very precious and should be easily seen and appreciated. Also, you are gifted with the many lives with whom you come in con-*

tact each day. Please thank the Lord for such beauty in seeing Me in everyone around you." I then saw some bags of groceries with a long loaf of bread sticking out. Jesus said: *"I give you My gift of plenty in the very food you eat for your sustenance. Your country has very much been blessed with an abundance of food because of your very foundations. Keep faithful to Me by following My commands and you will continue to be provided for."* I then saw a bee going from flower to flower. Jesus said: *"You have been given the gift of faith but you cannot keep it to yourself. You must go and share it with those willing to receive you. As each person has their own faith conversion, you can witness to others how I have given meaning to your life."* I then saw a pride of lions. Jesus said: *"I have blessed each of you with your own family and relatives. This gives you a personal sense of belonging and a support for each of you to help each other's needs. You witnessed the Holy Family as the model for all of you to follow."* I then saw Our Lady bring her Son forward. She said: *"This is your most precious gift from God the Father—His own Divine Son. He has given His life so that each may have salvation. He gifts Himself also to you in Holy Communion. It is this beautiful union by which He loves all of us in the Body of Christ—His Church."* I then saw a beautiful outpouring of creation brought forth by God the Father. He said: *"I present all of you with the gift of creation that you may understand the beauty and love of your God. You are all beautiful in My sight and I bring you close to Myself in seeing My reflection in all the creatures and things I have made. Give praise and glory to God for all the many gifts you have beheld this night."*

Thursday, June 23, 1994:

After Communion, I saw Maria E. and she said: *"Love Him as Christ would love in the Trinity."* I then did not have a vision but heard the words *"In Jesus' name."* Jesus said: *"You all believe even though you do not see Me physically. Blessed are you for such faith. It is for My name's sake that I continue to do My work. For many will taunt and persecute you for belief in My name. Every knee will bend at My name and My glory will soon be upon you. Live in My name as I live in you and My remem-*

brance will be present in all you do. Pray for strength in these days and give witness to others so they may believe as well."

Friday, June 24, 1994: (St. John the Baptist's Birth)
After Communion, I saw an image of Christ as the Infant of Prague with glorious light radiating out from Him. He was wearing a crown. Jesus said: *"I give honor to men to announce My coming to earth for their salvation. St. John's stirring in St. Elizabeth's womb was the second annunciation of My coming after St. Gabriel's announcement to My Mother. St. John was My herald in the desert mirroring the angels who greeted Me at Christmas. Many do not realize how much of a gift it was from My Father for me to come to earth to die for your sins. This personal sacrifice of Mine is the most dramatic outpouring of love and grace to you that you can imagine. This gift should be ever so precious to all My faithful. For in it, all of you are forgiven and now are allowed into My Kingdom forever in eternity. When you finally experience My presence face-to-face, you will be eternally grateful and give praise and glory to Me. You will in truth be giving thanks to Me for the rest of your life. So be joyous for this beginning of your salvation."*

Later, at the Adoration Chapel, I saw a vision of sound waves reaching to someone's ears. Jesus said: *"Take some time each day to be quiet and listen for My message to you. If you are always busy and talking instead of listening, you will not know what I am asking of each of you. Each person is special and unique such that they have a different plan molded to that person's talents. If you would listen, I can enter your heart to show you which way is best for you. My gentle love and requests are easy to follow if you would make room for Me to operate in your life. I love you so much to follow each of you throughout your life waiting to inspire you with what to do and say. Reach out to Me as often as you can and I will be there ready to embrace you and show you the way to your salvation."*

Saturday, June 25, 1994:
After Communion I saw a picture of Jesus and there was a shroud or dark object covering His face. Jesus said: *"I find My*

people in disarray spiritually. Many of My people have forgotten Me. They go about their lives trusting only in themselves to do things. I am given lip service at best one hour on Sundays and begrudging at that. Why have you fallen asleep to My messages of My word and My prophets? Have you no fear of God? Because you depend on yourselves, there is a lost sense of sin. If you fail to need My redeeming power, how can I forgive you? If all you care about is how you run your lives, how am I to respond to you? In a word, you must wake up and repent. See that indeed you are sinners in need of repentance. I will send you a warning to give you one last chance to see the errors in your life. If you still fail to come to Me in faith and trust, you call on Me to visit your land with My justice. For soon I will purify the earth of those who fail to repent and refuse My love. If you do not let Me lead you and become My loving children, you will be cast out of the earth to the place in hell reserved for those angels who also refused Me. Pray, My people, for you will be severely tested by this coming purification. Remain in faith and full trust in Me and you will receive My eternal reward."

Later, after Communion, I saw a picture of a dark black person maybe from Haiti or Africa. Jesus said: *"Be careful of prejudging people. Do not criticize those that you do not know—all their circumstances and hardships. Most of you here are fairly affluent compared to the rest of the world. Have compassion on others who are less well off. I love all peoples—both the rich and the poor. So do not worry if you have to help others. You are helping from your excess while they may be asking for help out of their want. Do not begrudge the poor of any donations for they always need your help. Remember My Spirit is present in everyone so treat each person with equal value. Pray to understand My loving and gracious justice instead of your demanding worldly justice."*

Sunday, June 26, 1994: (p.m. late - Davenport, Iowa Motel)

I saw a clock at 12:00 o'clock. Jesus said: *"My dear people, how am I to help you? You are not saying enough prayers to counter the evil in your world. I am asking My prayer warriors especially to redouble their efforts to pray to make up for all those who are not praying and could. All My Marian people must lis-*

ten to My Mother's messages on praying the Rosary often. If My faithful become lazy in helping Me, how can I get the rest of humanity on their knees? When My warning does come, many will have a renewed desire to come back to Me. At that time, you are to help and direct these penitents to Confession and show them how to pray. My faithful remnant must bring back to Me as many souls as possible. Go and teach My people My message of salvation to all that will receive you."

Monday, June 27, 1994: (7:00 a.m. Mass) At St. Anthony's in Davenport, Iowa after Communion I saw a cross turned upside down. Jesus said: *"Yes, your Church will be turned upside down— such that you will no longer recognize it. A schism will occur where this new Church will follow the ways of men and not the ways of God. They will implement all manner of abomination. My faithful remnant, do not follow this Church—it is a ploy of the evil one to create division. Follow only My Pope John Paul II. He will lead you on the proper path to Me. Stay with the traditional priests for My sacraments for as long as they are available. Even My Pope will be in exile not much longer for the evil days will be a dark day in My Church. Pray often for the strength to endure these coming trials."*

Later, at Winterset, Iowa (Refuge of the Sacred Heart) in chapel after night prayers (7:00 p.m.) I saw a priest at the altar and then overlaid was a lighted candle. Then I saw a picture of a cross and it faded into darkness. Jesus said: *"You are seeing the coming of the end times where My presence will not always be available to you. My fading away will be the absence of myself in Holy Communion, when the priest will not be available. You will be in a spiritual darkness with My Mother's Rosary and your sacramentals left for strength. This will be a testing time for man. He will be left to his own devices because he refuses to accept Me. You will see how men who do not repent will be tortured by the demons. For some it will be too late to realize how I protected them and begged them to repent. To those who refuse Me I will say 'depart from Me you accursed sinners.' Pray My people, for spiritual strength in these days and show others by your example how important it is to know, love and serve their God."*

Tuesday, June 28, 1994: (Mass at night in Chapel) At Winterset, Iowa on the Refuge after Communion I saw an empty pew at a church and then I saw some faithful. Jesus said: *"Why are you My brothers and sisters failing to even attend My Mass? Some are falling away from My worship on Sundays. How will you maintain your spiritual strength without My strength and My Eucharist? My faithful, I am calling on you to arouse your fellow Christians back to a practice of their faith. Make them see, by your example, how important I am to be in their daily lives. They must live for Me and not themselves. Come to Me in prayer and Mass to receive My graces so we can be united as one. You are called to be evangelists. This is your mission now more than ever since you must all prepare for the coming battle with evil. Your duty is to struggle to save souls by bringing them to Me as My Mother has been doing. The battle for souls is your most important work. Pray for strength to keep strong in your faith and witness it to all who meet you."*

Wednesday, June 29, 1994: (a.m. Mass of Sts. Peter & Paul)

At St. Thomas More in Denver, Co. after Communion, I saw three crosses laying down along a hill. Then Jesus appeared with a great light and said: *"My people time is growing short to help all My faithful. There is a deep need to evangelize as many souls as possible that are now in the faith. You remember how you were brought the faith by teachers and how gradually you came to make a decision for Me in your heart as your conversion. Even cradle Christians must be nurtured in the faith. Faith is a gift I bequeath on My faithful. But at one spot in their lives they must choose Me freely as the Master of their lives. You must direct all you do to please Me and help win souls to God. Since time grows short, I am calling on My faithful to teach as many as possible the love I have for you. Also, encourage them to choose Me over the world and praise and adore Me. Winning souls I have told you is the most important mission. Soon the persecution will be great and it is then you will have to protect yourselves among your prayer groups. I will help you if you would call on Me. It will be very hard to find conversion at that time."*

Later, at St. Thomas More Adoration, I saw some monks dressed in the brown robes of St. Francis. Jesus said: *"I am calling all My people to a life of prayer. A monastic life would be ideal, but not always fully possible. Instead you can try to put the worldly concerns out of your mind and focus on heavenly objectives. When you choose Me as the focus of your life, you will see pleasing Me by giving your will over to My Divine Will is necessary if you are to prepare for heaven. When you follow My will, you will look forward with My peace to the time you can spend with Me in prayer and listening for My word for you. Be at peace in My love and you will have everything your soul strives for and was meant to exist for. For you are a spiritual being and seeking Me and My will should be your only desire. I love you from the bottom of My heart always. Nothing you will do will ever stop Me from loving you. But if you are to be with Me in eternity, you must choose to be one with Me in My will. Then I can fill you with My graces and your heavenly salvation will await you.*"

Thursday, June 30, 1994: (Rita there, Mass at 9:00 a.m.)

At St. Thomas More after Communion, I saw a crucifix with the body in a rustic appearance with logs for the wood of the cross. Later, I saw the cross and a shadow came across it. Jesus said: *"My people I love you so much. I am constantly seeking you out to show you My love. I have an eternal unconditional love which desires to hold you close to Me in My bosom. I know there is sin in your world since the first sin in the Garden of Eden. But in My plan I have come to earth to forgive you your sins and bring you close to Me again in faith. I have loved you so much that I died for you on the cross for everyone's sins. This was meant for those in the past, the present and the future. This is why I am still suffering for the sins of man. You can lessen that suffering if you reform your lives and make a concerted effort to avoid sin as much as possible. But alas, My people, you do not realize how sin offends Me and even some do not realize they are sinners. Your priest is right to encourage the faithful to visit Me in Confession as often as possible, for My grace of forgiveness awaits you. Go, My people, to encourage others back to Confession for the dark days of My Church are upon you.*"

Later, at the top of the hill of the Mother Cabrini Shrine I saw a vision of a large burning bush covering the top of the hill. God the Father spoke the message: *"I love you, My children, more than you know. You are seeing how My love burns for you in the burning bush. I have given you my Son so I can be present among you and so you can relish My love. You must recognize Me as your Creator who has given you life both physically and spiritually. Seeing My glory in creation it should draw praise and honor to Me from every one of My creatures. But woe unto you, My children, for you have not harkened to the messages given by Jesus or His Mother. My justice will soon be upon you for the many sins of men and especially those who refuse to honor Me and give their life back to Me. You have very little time left for My people to choose Me over the world. In this remaining time, you must fall on your knees in prayer and ask for My forgiveness. If you do not repent, then prepare for My judgment."* I saw one last vision with Maria E. and there was a small flame and then it grew to cover the earth. She said: *"Prepare to meet the judgment."*

Index

choose life 121
Christ 11
Christ the King 20, 21, 28
Christian communities 185
Christmas 67, 74, 77
Church 9, 16, 23, 25, 32, 35, 52, 84, 89,
  119, 199, 216, 233
churches 111, 146, 186, 187, 197, 224
circling saucer 35
city of God 28
clergy 183
clock 10
clothed in the sun 7
comet 9, 49, 196, 207
commandments 149
commitment 152, 167, 223
communication 177
Communism 95, 97, 203
compassion 64, 232
Confession 26, 70, 95, 140, 185, 187, 210,
  218
Confusion 120
conjunction of stars 36
conscience 112, 166
consecrate 14, 24, 60, 84, 147, 149
conversion 119
couch potato 83
country 55, 106
covenant 148
creation 207, 224, 230
creatures 83
cross 3, 4, 8, 10, 16, 26, 30, 46, 58, 97,
  128, 136, 154, 181
cross on your forehead 63
crosses 9, 15, 18, 19
crucified 61
crystals 228

D

daily lives 182
damage 3
dark 6
dark shadows 34

darkness 1, 73
death 1, 70, 144, 212, 218
debit cards 209
demons 2, 5, 14, 16, 22, 31, 38, 43, 47, 69,
  169, 185, 192, 205, 225
Denver 52
destruction 3
devil 10
direction 71
disaster 1, 33, 35, 37, 48, 204
discernment 205
disciples 61, 188
diseases 204
distractions 96
disunity 9
Divine Mercy 121, 150
Divine Mercy Chaplet 134, 154
Divine Will 10, 23, 92, 184, 220, 235
doorway to heaven 50, 113

E

earth 5
earthquake 2, 206
Easter Sunday 156
eavesdrop 186
education 123
empty cross 9
encyclical 32
end of time 23, 108
end times 82, 118, 151, 178, 179, 183,
  198, 202, 206, 233
entertainment 47, 190
era of peace 15, 132, 190, 194, 210
Esperanza,Maria 106, 124, 133
Eucharist 4, 57, 68, 80, 109, 113, 159,
  179, 193, 227
euthanasia 98, 190
evangelize 81, 114, 124, 131, 140, 150,
  164, 184, 234
events 118
evil 38, 172
evil age 63, 127, 128, 154, 162
evil days 175, 177, 191